THE
COSMOGRAPHICAL
GLASS

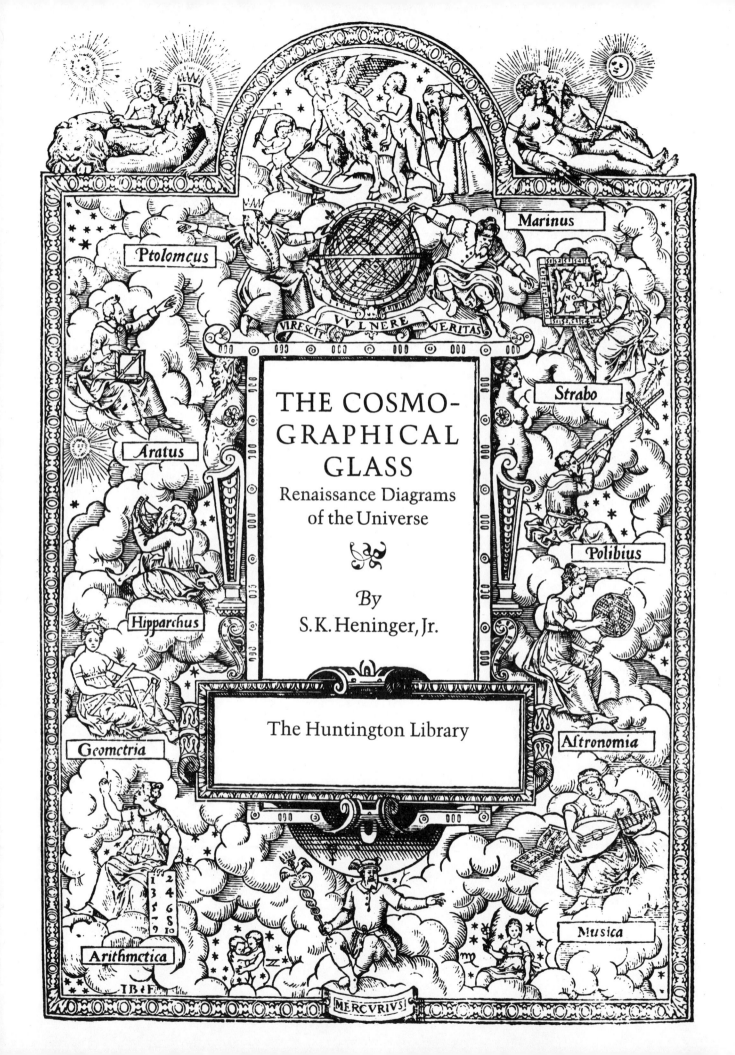

THE COSMO-
GRAPHICAL
GLASS

Renaissance Diagrams
of the Universe

By

S. K. Heninger, Jr.

The Huntington Library

First paperback printing, 2004
Printed in the United States of America

Published by Huntington Library Press
1151 Oxford Road, San Marino, CA 91108
http://www.huntington.org

Original book design by Grant Dahlstrom
Paperback cover design by Doug Davis
Cover illustration: Detail of Atlas bearing the heavens on his shoulders, from Gregor
Reisch's "Margarita philosophica" (Freiburg, 1503)

Library of Congress Catalog Card No. 76-62637

The cosmographical glass : Renaissance diagrams of the universe / by S. K. Heninger, Jr.
        xx, 209 p. : ill. ; 29 cm
Includes bibliographical references and index.
ISBN: 0-87328-208-6 (pbk.)
1. Astronomy—Europe—History. 2. Renaissance.
QB33.E85 H46
520/.94

TO DOROTHY LANGSTON HENINGER

TABLE
OF
CONTENTS

Foreword

The National Aeronautics and Space Administration has a Web site for the Hubble telescope (http://hubble.nasa.gov), which opens with a salute to the cosmologists collected in this book:

> Not since Galileo turned his telescope towards the heavens in 1610 has any event so changed our understanding of the universe as the deployment of the Hubble Space Telescope.

To be sure, we have pictures—in their initial beauty—of cosmic phenomena that occurred millions of light-years ago. And now with the Cassini-Huygens mission, we see images of Saturn's rings and moons in almost real time. But have we come any closer to answering the motivating questions of Renaissance cosmology? What entity or force created the universe? Where is its center? Does it have a limit, or is it infinite? What is our position in the universal scheme of things? Indeed, is there a universal scheme, either theological or physical?

Are we any clearer about the ultimate purpose of cosmological inquiry? N.A.S.A. speaks of "missions" in the plural, not an underlying "mission." In the time of Galileo there was widespread agreement that, despite the great diversity of proposed world-systems, cosmological study had at least a common aim. As I summarized this objective in 1977:

> Turning one's eyes to heaven provides a means of knowing the divine will and parallels the introspective quest for personal perfection. Study of the macrocosm reveals the attributes of God, and also reveals the patterns for the microcosm so that we can know ourselves. (*The Cosmographical Glass*, p. 10)

For cosmologists of the Renaissance, study of the heavens involved parallel inquiries, both theological and introspective, and led to recognition of a providential plan. While I wish in no way to denigrate or deride the accomplishments of my own generation of cosmologists, I still must ask, where are they leading us?

S. K. H.

Chapel Hill, N.C.
August, 2004

Illustrations

xiii

Preface

THE RENAISSANCE was a period of rich variety. The world teemed with the old and the new, the handsome and the grotesque, the sacred and the profane, the simple and the complex. And man was the center of this world. He was the heir of Adam, ruling over creation by virtue of his God-given reason. By exercise of this same reason, he also became father of the modern pragmatist, who built great cities and subjugated nature to his will. The renaissance was a period of rapid change, and man grew increasingly uncertain about the forces that affect the human condition. He asked insistent questions about his environment and about his place in it. At no time in our intellectual history have world-systems proliferated and metamorphosed more busily.

This volume surveys the wide range of those world-systems. In essence, it is a portfolio of diagrams which in one way or another depict the world as someone in the renaissance viewed it. All of the figures are illustrations taken from books printed before 1700, and what holds them together in a single cover is a common concern to describe our universe. Except for those in the introductory essay, each figure purports to reveal the world as a total construct, usually articulating its component parts and delineating their interrelationships.

The intent of this book is to display and explain rather than to argue, so my task has been straightforward. First, I selected the diagrams that best exemplify the vast range of cosmological thought in the period, including those that are difficult as well as those that are obvious. Next, I arranged them in a convenient way, grouping together diagrams that share a subject matter, though not proposing any inexorable sequence. Finally, I unfolded the meaning of each diagram down to the least detail. Recognizing that much of our cultural past has blurred, I sought to focus the background sufficiently to make the diagrams clear to a modern reader without cluttering the text with irrelevancies. And wherever pertinent, I have indicated cross-references between diagrams that comment upon one another.

Whatever else, the figures themselves are the raison d'être of the book. They represent the sweeping assumptions, not always otherwise formulated, that set the course of renaissance culture. And it is my conviction that we shall have a myopic view of the renaissance, seeing it in our own image, unless we make the effort of comprehending that most fundamental of their sciences, cosmography. Therefore I offer these diagrams to anyone interested in the period, with the hope that he will find them helpful in pursuing whatever particular concern he might have. Since the renaissance was a transition period between medieval and modern, and since it revived much that was classical, this collection of diagrams throws a slanting light also on those periods.

In all candor, however, I must make it clear that this is not a history of cosmology—not even a history of renaissance cosmography. Rather than a retrospective attitude, I have striven for a synoptic view. What images of the universe were available to the bookish man of the renaissance? It is necessary, of course, to place each diagram in a historical context in order to decipher the sometimes esoteric message that it carries. But I have tried to keep the history severely subordinated to the illustration itself. And I doubt that even a semblance of continuity can be achieved by hooking up the numerous historical moments in the text. One section, dealing with Copernicus and his followers, is arranged with some attention to chronology—but that of necessity, because Copernicus was responding to Ptolemy, Tycho to Copernicus, Galileo to Tycho, Riccioli to Galileo, etc. Moreover, the last paragraph of the book, for the sake of rounding off, does suggest the end of an era. But sequence of events is not the nub of this presentation. At least here, I am only incidentally interested in the development of philosophical schools and scientific theories.

Nonetheless, there are categories that provide a minimal organization for the book. The opening essay serves as an introduction to cosmography, with the hope of orienting the modern reader to a world which might seem strange to him, but should not be dismissed as primitive or even quaint. Like ours, that world has its self-evident truths, carefully supported postulates, and boggling conundrums. It is necessary to understand—even feel—this complex body of thought if we are to respond to the art of the period in the spirit in which it was intended. The art in whatever medium is largely a reflection of these premises.

The remaining figures in the book fall into two major groups. The first group contains diagrams that depict the universe in terms that we observe with our senses, the mode of knowing that sits most easily with us. It includes Series I, which deals with the problems and events and results of creation; Series II, which explains the multitudinous details of Ptolemaic cosmology; and Series III, which sketches the shift from geocentrism to heliocentrism. The second group contains diagrams that depict the universe as an intellectual scheme without reference to any data collected by our senses, a mode of knowing that is contrary to our cultural conditioning as phenomenalists. It includes Series IV, which grounds this group in the presently discredited idealism of the pythagorean-platonic tradition and displays the world-systems that grew out of the Boethian quadrivium; Series V, which exhibits the many forms of the human microcosm, a special case of conceptual thinking;

and Series VI, which demonstrates how widely and rigorously the tenets of the pythagorean-platonic tradition were applied in a variety of ancillary disciplines. Obviously, the first group assumes an ontology in which ultimate reality resides among the objects of physical nature, while in contrast the second group assumes an ontology in which ultimate reality resides at some insubstantial level in a realm of ideas.

In presenting the diagrams, I have tried to resist the temptation of going beyond the precise information each contains, though perhaps I have not always succeeded in doing so. What has required the greatest restraint is the urge to admire the figures as works of art in their own right. Some of them are extremely beautiful, with a meaning that transcends the simple denotation of their subject matter. But by intention I leave the esthetic enjoyment of the illustrations to my reader, unmolested— though I encourage him to look at them with an eye to discover their beauties. These are outstanding examples of the graphic arts, in which the renaissance excelled, and many of the woodcuts and engravings exhibit that distinctively renaissance quality of engaging both the mind and the heart. What I hope is that my prosaic explanations will enhance the appreciation of their artistic merit.

I have similarly refrained from any overarching argument in this book. But one conclusion, I think, is inescapable. This large assortment of diagrams fairly well destroys any notion that there was a prevailing image of the universe in the renaissance. Instead, there was a welter of differing images—many strongly appealing, none convincingly authoritative. In his text, E. M. W. Tillyard gives a fair account of how many components made up his composite abstraction, *The Elizabethan World Picture;* but the title of his popular work has led to a simplistic assumption that there was one world-view which most renaissance Englishmen accepted. There were a few basic principles to which most renaissance men adhered, but even these were being challenged at the time. And as this volume reveals, there was an astonishing range of concrete diagrams reflecting a full array of conflicting thought. Never, in fact, has cosmological speculation enjoyed such a loose rein. In the absence of strong authority, any proposal was given a hearing, and some quite outlandish opinions were given credence.

As a corollary to this conclusion, we might conjecture that the artist, not bound by the constraint of cosmological dogma, felt free to engage in cosmological speculation of his own sort. He assumed a license to create his own universe. The worlds of Hieronymus Bosch, of Leon Battista Alberti, and of John Milton, to name a few notable examples, are the result. We might even go so far as to say that these artists would not have created as they did in a period of cosmological certainty. They are not expressing a prefabricated universe of someone else's making, but rather exercising their art to reach personal conclusions about how the universe is put together and how it works. Their art is a record of their search for a worldview, a product of the times' being out of joint, a compensation for what they did not find ready-made in their culture. Their art for them is a mental construct that took the place of the orthodox view of reality.

But this is to get into the area of hypothesis, which I have disclaimed. I will delay no further than to acknowledge the many sorts of assistance that were needed to bring this volume into being. This is a final pleasure in what has been a most pleasant enterprise.

For the use of their books and the help of their personnel, I wish to thank several libraries. Specifically, for permission to reproduce material in their custody I thank the Curators of the Bodleian Library (Figures 3, 7, 8, 9, 17, 21, 29, 30, 32, 37, 40, 42, 43, 44, 45, 46, 47, 48, 51, 53, 63, 64, 75, 77, 78, 92, 94, 98, 100, 106, 107, 110, 112, 114), the Trustees of the British Library (Figures 5, 41, 54, 55, 65, 93, 97, 109), the Librarian of Duke University (Figures 67, 79, 83), the Director of the Folger Library (Figure 62), and the Director of the Huntington Library (Figures 1, 2, 4, 6, 10, 11, 12, 13, 14, 15, 16, 18, 19, 20, 22, 23, 24, 25, 26, 27, 28, 31, 33, 34, 35, 36, 38, 39, 49, 50, 52, 56, 57, 58, 59, 60, 61, 66, 68, 69, 70, 71, 72, 73, 74, 76, 80, 81, 82, 84, 85, 86, 87, 88, 89, 90, 91, 95, 96, 99, 101, 102, 103, 104, 105, 108, 111, 113, 115 116, 117).

Preliminary study for this project began many years ago while I enjoyed a fellowship from the John Simon Guggenheim Memorial Foundation. Other necessary financial support has come from the University of British Columbia. I hope that I have not turned their gold into dross.

Several colleagues laid aside their own work in order to read through the typescript of this volume. For such generosity I am profoundly grateful to Joseph A. Wittreich, Jr., Lee M. Johnson, Edward W. Tayler, and Robert Westman. I profited enormously from the diversity and depth of their learning. They saved me, if not from all error, at least from that which was most egregious.

This volume was written at the Huntington Library — not always on its premises, but certainly within the aura of its spirit. And in a real sense it is a product of that remarkable institution. My thanks must be distributed wholesale to the many, each an expert in his field, who at one time or another have come to my aid.

Foremost, I must thank James Thorpe, who encouraged me to proceed with this project when I was unsure that so costly a book would ever be published. He has been a constant adviser and friend, as full of good cheer as of good counsel. I can only hope for a way to express my affectionate appreciation.

In the practical business of putting the volume together, I owe an incalculable debt to Betty Leigh Merrell, who has been privy to the plan since its inception. She has remained unflinchingly optimistic through rain, sleet, snow, and dead of night, and I hope that she feels something of the same sense of joy in the book that I do. At our side has been Jane L. Evans, who patted the whole into shape and gave each page its final form. A great deal of the pleasure which the eye derives from this book comes directly from her knowingness.

My deep gratitude goes to the Librarian of the Huntington, Daniel H. Woodward, and to the Curator of Rare Books, Carey S. Bliss, who never blenched no matter how unreasonable my requests. For unfailing helpfulness I am grateful also to those in charge of reader services, Mary Isabel Fry and Virginia J. Renner, and to Mary Wright and her several assistants, who provided an endless supply of books from the stacks. For miscellaneous kindnesses Noelle Jackson, Janet Hawkins, June Wilcox, and Deborah Smith must likewise be thanked. In a special category, I recognize the invaluable aid of Barbara Quinn and Elsa Sink, who labored in the subterranean vaults of the Huntington to produce the numerous xerox copies that prepared the way for the finished volume, and the careful work of Robert Schlosser, whose skill accounts for the clarity of the photographic reproductions. I want to acknowledge also the sustenance and delight taken from other readers, especially Jackson Cope, Stuart Curran, Robert Dent, Daniel Donno, Elizabeth Story Donno, French Fogle, Jean Hagstrum, Richard Ide, Beach Langston, Peter Medine, James Riddell, Lawrence Ryan, Alice Scoufos, Claude Simpson, Hallett Smith, John Steadman, Stanley Stewart, and Paul Zall.

It would be fitting for me to dedicate this book to all those at the Huntington who make such books possible. But they will understand when I say that an even greater debt lies elsewhere.

S. K. H.

Vancouver, B.C.
June, 1976

THE
COSMOGRAPHICAL
GLASS

Fig. 1 *William Cuningham, aged 28.*

Introduction

 ATE IN 1559 the London printer John Day offered for sale in his bookshop at Aldersgate an impressive folio entitled *The cosmographical glasse, conteinyng the pleasant principles of cosmographie, geographie, hydrographie, or navigation*. The care taken in preparation of this book is evident even at a glance. Its pages reveal a variety of handsome types, elegant illustrations in profusion, mathematical tables and marginal glosses and foldout maps — everything to draw attention and win respect. In the prefatory matter, the author makes clear his aim: "I . . . have devised this mirrour, or Cosmographical Glasse, in which, men may behold not one or two personages, but the heavens with her planets and starres, th'Earthe with her beautifull Regions, and the Seas with her merveilous increse" (A2). Without mistake, this is an authoritative treatise on the science of cosmography, a thorough explanation of astronomy and geography as they were practised in England when Elizabeth I came to the throne.

The author of this informative volume was William Cuningham, a twenty-eight-year-old physician who resided in Norwich. His personable portrait, with one hand on a terrestrial globe and with the text of Dioscorides open before him, looks out at us in greeting (**Figure 1**). As this portrait suggests, Cuningham was well versed in the arts of astrological medicine. He had earned degrees from both Cambridge and Heidelberg, and was soon to launch a notably successful practice in London. He dedicated his book to Robert Dudley, already the queen's favorite though not yet earl of Leicester. Dudley had previously rewarded Cuningham and Day, and it is clear that he was instrumental in procuring Elizabeth's patronage for this book.[1]

The elaborate title page, cut especially for Cuningham's *Cosmographical glasse*, gives an indication of the book's importance and its contents (**Figure 2**). The page is not only handsome, but also full of recondite meaning. The printed title is surmounted by a terrestrial globe handled on one side by Ptolemy, the dean of ancient cosmographers, and measured with compasses on the other side by Marinus, an almost legendary Greek cosmographer considered to be the predecessor of Ptolemy. Beside Marinus sit Strabo, drawing a map of England for his *Geography*, and then Polybius, using a cross-staff to locate a comet which presages some changeful event in his *Histories*. On the opposite side flanking Ptolemy are Aratus, best remembered for his long poem on the constellations entitled *Phaenomena*, who is holding a measuring instrument known as the quadratum geometricum, and then Hipparchus, the greatest practicing astronomer of antiquity, who raises a quadrant to take a reading of the sun. Beneath the globe is an apothegm sometimes quoted as a motto by Day, *Vulnere virescit veritas*, "Truth grows stronger from a wound"[2] — or, as an American poet would

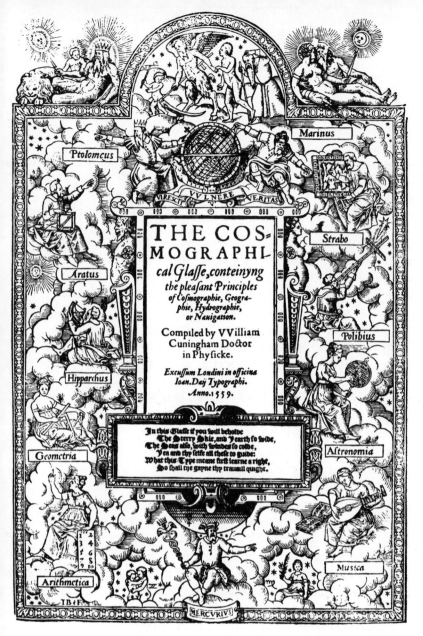

Fig. 2. *The title page of Cuningham's* Cosmographical glasse.

have it, "Truth crushed to earth will rise again."

At the bottom of Cuningham's title page is Mercury with his caduceus and winged hat. By virtue of his role as god of learning, he presides over the four disciplines that make up the quadrivium, the advanced course of study in the tradition of Boethius. On his right are Geometry with a ruler, square, and compass, and Arithmetic with a tablet of digital numbers. On his left are Astronomy with an armillary sphere and Music playing on the lute before an open book with musical notations.[3] Immediately flanking Mercury are two signs of the zodiac, Gemini and Virgo.

So much for the ancient authorities and for the mathematical disciplines to be drawn upon in Cuningham's treatise. Of equal importance, though perhaps not so obvious in meaning, are the figures at the top of the title page, which place the entire subject squarely within the context of time. Dominating the group beneath the central arch is Time itself, personified as a satyrlike Saturn from the Golden Age.[4] His identity is attested by wings and a scythe for mowing. He leads a procession of three human figures depicting man at his different ages: childhood, maturity, and senility. This *tableau vivant* exemplifies the passage of time and our necessary submission to it.

In the uppermost corners of the title page reside two other groups of distinctive figures who are complementary to the central group led by Time. The refulgent halos bestow a quasi-divinity upon these figures, a status confirmed by their high position on the page. The group on the left consisting of an old king and a small boy is identified with the sun. The group on the right consisting of a mature female embraced by an equally mature male is identified with the moon. To paraphrase these icons in a prose statement is difficult, and perhaps an outright affront; if the attempt be made, though, it is best made using terms from the discipline of alchemy.[5] The old king and his child, with the organ of reproduction much in evidence, represent age and youth linked in the succession of generations and thereby embodying the continuity of time. In alchemical terms, they depict the stages within the opus which lead toward the perfection of the philosophers' stone. Thereby they bring into operation the fact of time as a durational process, but a process which leads to the stasis of totally reconciled opposites. The group on the right, the noble lady and her consort, makes much the same statement, though in terms of male and female rather than age and youth.

2

These two, as their voluptuous nudity and their intense scrutiny of one another suggest, are engaged in sexual play, an activity of temporal duration. Simultaneously, however, the group represents the self-sufficiency of the mutually satisfying man-woman relationship, a two-phase system best known iconographically as the alchemical hermaphrodite (see figure 114). So again opposites are reconciled within a single system which is represented as both an action and a stasis. Finally, the lobster beside the woman is there to recall the moon's function as mistress over watery things (e.g., the tides), and being a sea creature may emphasize the sexuality of the scene; while the lion in the other group, being monarch of beasts, gives witness to the sun's supremacy over all creatures here below and emphasizes the power of the king.

To continue the prose paraphrase of these icons, the group under the sun and the group under the moon are interrelated, and the meaning which emerges from this interrelationship adds yet a further dimension to the meaning of each group considered separately. Taken together, the two groups express the notion of time in an even more recondite way —though it is comparably more difficult to translate the visual image into a verbal statement because the simultaneity of the two groups is impaired in the process and their coexistence is the most significant fact.

But terms for an argument can be derived by equating the sun with day and the moon with night. Taken together, the sun and the moon generate a two-phase system that comprises the diurnal unit of time, the twenty-four hours from sunrise to the next sunrise. Milton expresses the thought exactly:

> . . . light and darkness in perpetual round
> Lodge and dislodge by turns, which makes
>   through heav'n
> Grateful vicissitude, like day and night.
>   (Paradise Lost, VI. 6-8)

Furthermore, the diurnal unit of time repeated for 365 cycles produces the annual unit of time, the year. And the annual unit of time is reproduced endlessly as the sun proceeds along his course through the zodiac. Therefore the diurnal unit of time becomes the integer of eternity, the unit which by infinite repetition generates eternity. Hieremias Drexel, who directed small devotional tracts to an eager public in the early seventeenth century, makes the point with conviction:

> They [the ancients] have represented *Eternitie* by the *Sunne* and the *Moon*. The *Sunne* revives every day, although it seems every day to die, and to be buried. It always riseth again, although every night it sets. The *Moon* also hath her increase after every wane.[6]

Consequently, as Drexel implies, the union of sun and moon, the period of one day, is the simplest cryptogram for representing time in the abstract. In alchemy, the conjunction of sun and moon is an icon for the completed opus, another stasis which subsumes all change.

The meaning of the sun and moon in conjugal splendor is concisely explained by an illustration from a proto-alchemical text written by Albertus Magnus and printed in Oppenheim, 1518. In **Figure 3** the sun and moon shine coordinately as the adornment of a ring. The endless circle of the ring is, of course, a common symbol of eternity, a symbol perpetuated in our use of wedding bands. Here, however, the symbol is sophisticated by placing the greater light and the lesser light in the ring's top to give definition to its form. Although the circle is complete, it does have a starting point and a finish. It is a finite item. Nonetheless, its

Fig. 3. *The annual "ring" defined in terms of day and night according to the alchemical tradition.*

alpha and its omega are congruous, so that its end is its beginning, and so on. By uninterrupted repetition of the day-night pattern, it becomes an endless continuum.

Time itself is such a circle measured by the heavenly bodies, as both the Bible and Plato's *Timaeus* tell us. It was argued, in fact, that the word for the yearly unit of time, *annus*, was taken from the world *annulus*, "ring." John Swan, an early seventeenth-century Cantabrigian, states the case for this derivation:

> In Latine the yeare is called *Annus*, because we may say of it, *revolvitur ut annulus*. For as in a ring the parts touch one another, circularly joyning each to other; so also the yeare rolleth it self back again by the same steps that it ever went.[7]

When Andrew Marvell praised Cromwell on the first anniversary of the Commonwealth, it was just this imagery that he chose to convey the unique durability of the Lord Protector:

> *Cromwell* alone with greater Vigour runs,
> (Sun-like) the Stages of succeeding Suns:
> And still the Day which he doth next restore,
> Is the just Wonder of the Day before.
> *Cromwell* alone doth with new Lustre spring,
> And shines the Jewel of the yearly Ring.
> ("The first anniversary of the Government under O. C.," lines 7-12)

Such superiority removed Cromwell from "the weak Circles of increasing Years" (line 4), and placed him above the status of merely human.

It may seem that we have wandered from an explication of the title page for Cuningham's *Cosmographical glasse* and from a delineation of what he saw as the proper limits for his subject. Cosmography has broadened to a discipline of the greatest scope, confronting the largest questions about man and his relation to the universe, to time, and even to deity. Any feeling of uneasiness on our part, however, stems from our own preconceptions about man's position in the universal scheme,

from the conditioning we have received from modern assumptions about science. As post-Baconians we are likely to think of science almost exclusively in its utilitarian aspect as a means of subjugating nature. Those of us who are laymen confine our interest to applied science — to what the renaissance would have called "arts," from the Latin *ars*, meaning "technical skill"; we are excluded from *scientia* itself, meaning "theory." Of course, the renaissance also recognized the practical application of cosmography, and there is little doubt that Dudley and his queen lent their support to Day's printing of Cuningham's work because they saw it as a useful textbook for the instruction of practitioners in the various cosmographical arts. They recognized it as a practical contribution towards the maritime and mercantile success of England. But cosmography held more interest than its mere usefulness. It was a subject of the widest possible appeal and of unequalled seriousness. For most, it was the science sans pareil.

Such was the case with Robert Recorde, at mid-sixteenth century the outstanding physician in London and the most influential scientist in England. For him, cosmography was the very stronghold of truth, approached only after the travail of mastering arithmetic and geometry. Recorde prepared a series of textbooks for the mathematical disciplines: in 1542 he published a treatise of arithmetic entitled *The ground of artes*, in 1551 a treatise of geography entitled *The pathway to knowledg*, and in 1557 a treatise of algebra entitled *The whetstone of witte*.[8] In 1556 he published a corollary textbook for astronomy, *The castle of knowledge*, an important forerunner to Cuningham's *Cosmographical glasse*.

Figure 4 is the title page of Recorde's *Castle of knowledge*, an open avowal of his reverence for cosmography. It shows a queen representing Knowledge reigning supreme atop a fortresslike castle. From turrets at left and right two male figures use a quadrant and an astrolabe to take readings of the heavenly bodies.

This trio is surrounded by stars; and the sun and moon, as on Cuningham's title page, shine in the upper right and left corners. There is little doubt that knowledge is equated with the study of cosmography, and that time is an overriding concern in this treatise.

To corroborate this reading of the central icon, a pair of contrasting figures face one another in the foreground. On the left a handsome female in classical garb holds a measuring compass in one hand and raises an armillary sphere in the other. From the labels (in both English and Latin) supplied for the sphere, we know this figure to be Destiny or Fate, the future that has been decreed by the gods,[9] and she is pledged to knowledge. In contrast, on the right stands another female, disheveled and barefoot, who holds a bridle in one hand and in the other a rope attached to the axle of a wheel. We do not need the labels supplied for this wheel to recognize the second figure as Fortune, the future that is haphazard

Fig. 4. *The title page of Recorde's* Castle of knowledge.

and unpredictable, and maintained by ignorance. She has the customary accoutrements of Fortune: the bridle, the blindfold, and the wheel (suitably inscribed, "Whoever rises will soon fall"). She also stands on a rolling ball, to indicate her continuous motion; while, in an interesting bit of cosmic geometry, her counterpart, Destiny, stands upon a sturdy cube, to indicate stability.[10]

The verse in the cartouche between Destiny and Fortune calls attention to the opposition between them, and makes the useful point, which Recorde reiterates in his preface, that knowledge of cosmography is a way to evade the spitefulness of chance. There is more than a suggestion that the adept astronomer performs the valuable service of prognosticating events to come and thereby allows an opportunity to prepare for those events. Perhaps here, though, the emphasis rests upon the superiority of the celestial spheres over our earth, which is subject to passing time and therefore constitutes the realm of Fortune. Of even greater consequence is the praise of cosmography as the study of the unchanging heavens, the repository of knowledge and truth.

It is clear from Recorde's textbook that renaissance cosmography drew upon a revered tradition that had cumulated through the ages. The title page of Cuningham's *Cosmographical glasse* likewise radiates respect for the subject and cites many authorities from the ancient world. And others could be named with equal justification—for example, Eratosthenes, Posidonius, Philo Judaeus, Manilius, Cleomedes, Pomponius Mela, Solinus Polyhistor, Macrobius, Diadochus Proclus. After the collapse of classical civilization, interest in cosmography continued through succeeding centuries. In the earliest middle ages, Isidore of Seville and the Venerable Bede had written extensively on it. If we judge an authority's importance by his popularity, however, the outstanding medieval cosmographer was Joannes de Sacrobosco, an Englishman at the University of Paris whose treatise on the sphere vied with that of the neoplatonist Proclus for precedence

of place in the schoolroom. Numerous editions of Sacrobosco and of Proclus were published throughout the sixteenth century,[11] despite the fact that the renaissance itself produced authoritative treatises of theoretical cosmography—most notably, perhaps, the *Cosmographicus liber* of Peter Apian[12] and the *De mundi sphaera, sive cosmographia, libri V* of Oronce Finé.[13] The English were eager students of cosmography because of their rampant interest in foreign trade and exploration, and a steady stream of English texts dealt with the subject in various ways. In addition to the treatises by Recorde and Cuningham, particularly noteworthy are Thomas Blundeville's *Exercises*[14] and Joseph Moxon's *Tutor to astronomie and geographie*.[15]

By the sixteenth century, then, cosmography was a highly refined and fully formulated science. In the broadest sense, it was defined as the study of the universe—the study of both the celestial and the terrestrial regions, and of the interaction between them. Blundeville, a learned country gentleman of Norfolk who wrote treatises on morals and logic as well as on navigation, began his "Treatise of the first principles of cosmographie" with this definition: "Cosmography is the description of the whole world, that is to say, of heaven and earth, and all that is contained therein."[16] Cosmography included a wide range of subject matter which on the one hand impinged upon the heavens of theology and the insubstantial realm of metaphysics, and on the other verged upon the borders of natural history.

Given this breadth of range, it is not surprising that learned men subdivided cosmography into particular fields. By the sixteenth century, in fact, it had been specified into four distinct disciplines: astronomy, geography, astrology, and chorography. And each of these disciplines had its individual focus. Astronomy dealt with the celestial spheres that circle our planet and reach to the empyrean. Geography dealt with the terrestrial globe itself, the fixed center of our universe. Astrology dealt with the reciprocal exchange between the celestial and the terrestrial regions, and of course could be turned to the applied science of prognostication (judicial astrology). Chorography — from Greek χώρα, meaning "place" — dealt with the account of a particular locale considered in isolation from the rest of the globe, and usually contained topographical and even antiquarian lore. These distinctions had been instituted as early as Ptolemy (Geographia, I.i), and were perpetuated by such authorities as Peter Apian,[17] Heinrich Cornelius Agrippa,[18] Cuningham,[19] and John Dee.[20] Again Blundeville is useful to quote because of the clarity in his definitions:

> Astronomy is a Science, which considereth and describeth the magnitudes and motions of the celestiall or superiour bodies....
>
> Astrologie . . . is a Science which by considering the motions, aspects, and influences of the starres, doth foresee and prognosticate things to come....
>
> Geographie . . . is a knowledge teaching to describe the whole earth, and all the places contained therein, whereby universall Maps and Cardes of the earth and sea are made....
>
> Chorographie . . . is the description of some particular place, as Region, Ile, Citie, or such like portion of the earth severed by it selfe from the rest.[21]

Despite such tidy distinctions between these sciences, each was embraced by the general name of cosmography, and therefore all were interrelated. And each, of course — even astrology — had an indisputable legitimacy stemming from the parent science.

The word cosmography itself implies an interdependence between the celestial and terrestrial regions. It derives from the Greek κόσμος, which carried for the renaissance, as for antiquity, a heavy freight of scientific and emotional meaning. According to Plutarch,[22] the term cosmos originated with Pythagoras, the greatly revered philosopher from Samos who had inaugurated the long-lived pythago-

rean sect. Pythagoras devised the word to express the beauty and the orderliness of the created world. The corresponding word in Latin is mundus,[23] and in English universe. The seminal text for the study of cosmos is Plato's Timaeus, one of the most fruitful dialogues, which is given over almost entirely to a discourse on cosmography by Timaeus, an astronomer from Pythagoras' Magna Graecia.

The concept of cosmos assumed a beneficent deity, the divine monad of the pythagorean school. This Holy One began the creation with an archetypal idea to which he gave physical extension into a time-space continuum, thereby producing the universe as we perceive it.[24] Because the creating deity is beneficent, his creation is good and beautiful. Because he worked from a rational plan, it is orderly, with the endless variety of the world carefully organized into a systematic arrangement. Each item has its proper place, and is related both to the whole and to every other item — hence universe. The word, in fact, comes from L. unus+versus, and means literally "that which rolls around as one." The heavens continually circle in their course and carry all within them in a regulated movement.

As another important corollary in this theory of cosmos, the pattern of the archetypal idea in the divine mind persists throughout the universe. The original idea of the creating deity literally informs every level of creation. As a consequence, the four seasons, for example, reveal the same pattern of organization as the four elements, which in turn are correspondent to the four bodily humours. The three microcosmoi of annus, mundus, and homo are inextricably interrelated because each is an image of the same central pattern (see figure 66). This corollary is the basis for the macrocosm-microcosm analogy, which applies in every category of existence and which binds each category to every other in a network of correspondences (see figure 74).

From his studies in Plato's Academy, Aristotle absorbed this concept of cosmos, but he chose to restate it in terms which accorded with his own world-view. For Aristotle, ultimate reality did not lie among the ideas in Plato's changeless world of being, but rather it lay among the objects which comprise physical nature.[25] As a result, Aristotle reinterpreted the theory of cosmos as a theory of continuous matter which he called the *plenum*. For aristotelians the creation is a *universe*, but its coherence depends upon the continuity of categories laid edge to edge rather than upon any common pattern that informs each category. There is a scale of being that rises without interruption from stones to plants to animals to man to spirits and eventually perhaps to the deity. The universe is a continuum of matter, rather than a network of correspondent forms. Any conceptualization, in fact, is arrived at by a process of abstraction, by drawing the common quality from a large number of particular examples and then extrapolating this shared characteristic to a universal. For example, by looking at a large number of trees and noting that all have leaves, we may conclude that the quality of leafiness is a universal characteristic of trees.

The subject matter of cosmography, then, could be the *cosmos* for those oriented toward idealism, or the *plenum* for those oriented toward materialism — though usually the distinction was not contentiously advanced. In either case, the science was a worthy subject for human contemplation. Man did not become the proper study of mankind until a later period. The thrust of cosmography, at least as its apologists argued, was to turn man's attention away from the imperfect world and direct it toward the divine and the eternal.

Not surprisingly, the strongest exhortation to study cosmography was based upon the Holy Scriptures — most squarely upon Psalm 19, which asserts: "The heavens declare the glory of God and the firmament sheweth his handiwork." Therefore by studying the secrets of nature, man may discern the attributes of God. In the early renaissance, carrying over from the middle ages, this was the greatest impetus behind physical science. John Dee speaks for the mathematical practitioners of London when he quotes Psalm 19 approvingly and then comments:

> The whole Frame of Gods Creatures, (which is the whole world,) is to us, a bright glasse: from which, by reflexion, reboundeth to our knowledge and perceiverance, Beames, and Radiations: representing the Image of his Infinite goodnes, Omnipotency, and wisedome. And we therby, are taught and persuaded to Glorifie our Creator, as God: and be thankefull therfore.[26]

Cuningham, at least in part, intended his book to be such "a bright glasse." Both scientists may well have had in mind the teaching of Calvin, who had concluded: "This skillful ordering of the universe is for us a sort of mirror in which we can contemplate God, who is otherwise invisible."[27] In fact, no one was more positive than Calvin in reiterating "that saying of the Prophet David, that the heavens though they have no tongue, are proclaimers of the glorie of God: and that this excellent order of Nature in being silent crieth out, howe wonderfull his wisedome is."[28]

This assertion is stated visually in **Figure 5**, which comes from the *Globe du monde*, an elementary textbook of cosmography prepared by Simon Girault and published at Langres in 1592. Reaching down from heaven are the two hands of the *opifex optimus*, which grasp the north and south poles of a celestial sphere. The sphere is girded by the five circles that delineate the traditional climatic zones, and also by the zodiac, which traces the path made by the sun in its annual journey. The top of the sphere is marked "orient" and the bottom "occident"; and a banner at the bottom announces what every schoolboy already knew: "The power of God causes the heavens to turn from east to west, and the heavens make a complete revolution in twenty-four hours." At the top in a suitably ornamental cartouche appears the opening of Psalm 19 in Latin. Girault, who himself had two children, wrote his

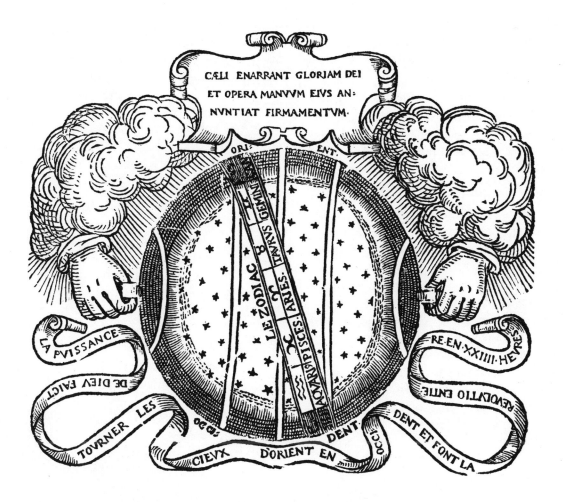

Fig. 5. *A demonstration of Psalm 19.*

discourse as a winsome dialogue between a brother and sister who discover their father's book of cosmography while he is at dinner. The older child, Charles, is careful to instruct Marguerite in the proper uses of the science, and explains to her the numerous technical diagrams in the text.

Besides the Judeo-Christian tradition of the Psalms, another tradition urged study of the heavens as a source of ultimate knowledge. In the *Timaeus* Plato had recounted how the creating deity had placed the heavenly bodies in the sky to measure the passage of time:

> With a view to the generation of Time, the sun and moon and five other stars, which bear the appellation of "planets," came into

existence for the determining and preserving of the numbers of Time. (38C)

Our observation of the celestial movements, Plato continues, has been the origin of natural science, and furthermore through our concern with time has led to the origin of speculative philosophy as well:

> The sight of day and night, the months and returning years, the equinoxes and solstices, has caused the invention of number, given us the notion of time, and made us inquire into the nature of the universe; thence we have derived philosophy. (47A)

Of course, this inquiry *de rerum natura* is more than idle speculation; it has direct application in our personal affairs. By discerning

9

the divine reason that pervades the universe, we obtain a model for our own behavior, thereby realizing our potential as a microcosmic image of the deity:

> We should see the revolutions of intelligence in the heavens and use their untroubled courses to guide the troubled revolutions in our own understanding, which are akin to them. (47A)

According to this instruction in the *Timeaus,* turning one's eyes to heaven provides a means of knowing the divine will, and parallels the introspective quest for personal perfection. Study of the macrocosm reveals the attributes of God, and also reveals the patterns for the microcosm so that we can know ourselves.

This attitude persisted throughout the renaissance. It underlies Giovanni Giovano Pontanus' long poem *Urania*[29] and appears repeatedly in Saluste du Bartas' hexaemeron *La sepmaine.*[30] **Figure 6**, taken from one of the most popular handbooks of cosmography in the sixteenth century, demonstrates the literalness of the injunction to cast our eyes upon the world around us and up to the heavens. Plato's teaching was still current in the middle of the seventeenth century, as evidenced by its echo in the textbook of the practicing astronomer Vincent Wing:

> God Almightly, who is Δημιουργὸς ποιητής, καί πατήρ τοῦ ὅλου, the Creatour, Maker, and Father of the whole Universe, having in the begining, out of his infinite wisdom, created the World, did then most gloriously adorn and beautifie the lower part of the Heavens with those lucid Globes, the *Sun, Moon,* and *Stars;* which are the chiefest parts of the visible created being, as they demonstrate themselves to the Eye of our understanding.[31]

Plato's praise of astronomy retained a following far into the period of modern science.

Along with Psalm 19 and with Plato's injunction to study the skies, another prevalent belief had roots in biblical and classical thought. A common metaphor spoke of creation as a poem written by the supreme *poeta.* In its simplest statement this metaphor becomes "the book of nature" compiled by a gracious deity. Nature as a book for man's spiritual enlightenment is an old notion, by the twelfth century already fully formulated by Alanus de Insulis, who cast the sentiment into a rhyming lyric:

> Omnis mundi creatura,
> Quasi liber, et pictura
>   Nobis est, et speculum.
> Nostrae vitae, nostrae mortis,
> Nostri status, nostrae sortis
>   Fidele signaculum.[32]

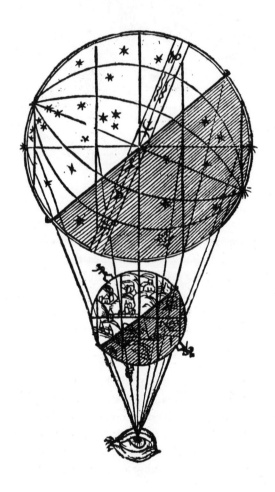

Fig. 6. *Human sight as a means of perceiving the universe.*

10

In the late sixteenth century Pierre de la Primaudaye boldly restated this notion for the generation of serious readers—which included Spenser and Shakespeare—who perused his encyclopedia, *The French academie*. He used the phrase "God his great booke of nature," which he then glossed at considerable length:

> I meane the admirable frame of this Univers, or whole world. Wherein the infinite varieties and sorts of creatures, like so many visible wordes, doe proclaime and publish unto man the eternitie, infinitie, omnipotency, wisedome, justice, bountie, and other essentiall attributes of his dread and soveraigne creatour.[33]

For many, this book of nature which displayed God's intention was a source of revelation carrying authority equal to that of the Holy Scriptures. La Primaudaye, for example, declares that we must consult both books in order to come to a full understanding of the Creator:

> We must lay before our eyes two bookes which God hath given unto us to instruct us by, and to lead us to the knowledge of himselfe, namely the booke of nature, and the booke of his word.[34]

For George Hartgill, a successful astrologer in the 1590s who billed himself as "minister of the word of God," the Bible and physical nature were indeed complementary texts. **Figure 7** shows the title page of his *Generall calendars* (London, 1594), which are really astronomical tables. He stands in a setting like the Garden of Eden with a city in the background and holds the *verbum dei* in one hand and an armillary sphere in the other. Beneath his feet a plaque identifies him as a "Christian philosopher," while a balloon from his mouth announces, "I shall contemplate the word and the works of Jehovah." Above this scene, in a starry sky, shine the sun and the moon, adding their customary suggestion of both time and eternity.

Paralleling this advice to study cosmography as insight into the divine will, and adding force to it by reverse english, was a persistent attitude of *contemptus mundi* that had early been given cosmological dimension by Cicero. In the *Somnium Scipionis* Cicero reports how Scipio, looking down from heaven, is struck by the triviality of the earth compared to the vastness of the panorama spread beneath him. When Macrobius came to this passage in his commentary, he confirmed this sentiment that denigrated man and his habitation. It continued to be a commonplace in the renaissance, and was solemnly cited by Recorde in his address to students encouraging their diligence:

> When Scipio behelde oute of the high heavens the smallenes of the earth with the kingdomes in it, he coulde no lesse but esteeme the travaile of men moste vaine, which sustaine so muche grief with infinite daungers to get so small a corner of that lyttle balle. So that it yrked him (as he then declared) to considre the smalnes of that their kingdom, whiche men so muche did

Fig. 7. *The Christian philosopher, who reads both the Holy Scriptures and the book of nature.*

magnifie. Who soever therefore (by Scipions good admonishment) doth minde to avoide the name of vanitie, and wishe to attayne the name of a man, lette him contemne those trifelinge triumphes, and little esteeme that little lumpe of claye: but rather looke upwarde to the heavens, as nature hath taught him, and not like a beaste go poringe on the grounde.[35]

For Recorde, the study of cosmography is little less than a moral choice. We may grovel as groundlings among the brutes, or we may turn our attention up the scale of being and aspire after angels in the empyrean.

Recorde's words were well heeded, by men of letters as well as by scientists. In 1585, for example, Robert Greene published a collection of prose narratives which he placed in an astronomical framework and titled *Planetomachia*. By way of introduction he provided "A brief apologie of the sacred science of astronomie," which repeats the familiar argument:

Thrise unhappy then we be thought, who are not delighted with this sweete and pleasaunt contemplation, and whose minds are not moved with the wonderfull works of God and Nature. He is a foolish beast, not a man sayth *Plato*, whiche is not delighted with the studie of Astronomie: whereof God himselfe is the author.[36]

Once more the study of cosmography leads to a knowledge of God Himself. In this light, Faustus' crime is a matter of means, not of ends.

The most remarkable lesson to be learned from study of the heavens, in fact, is an understanding of our relationship to the deity and to his handmaid, nature. Most concisely and most meaningfully this relationship was expressed as a conception of time. It is for this reason that Recorde and Cuningham emphasize the importance of time in the iconography of their title pages and accord it considerable attention in their texts. Following their lead,

Blundeville in his very practical manual for navigation introduces the subject of time in the midst of highly technical instruction:

Most men that write of the Spheare, after they have spoken of the ascentions [i.e., the rising and setting of the stars] doe immediatly treate of the diversitie and inequalitie of dayes and nightes, but sith dayes, nights, and houres, are but parts of time, like as be weekes, moneths, and yeares, I mind here therefore first briefly to treat of time, and then of all his chiefest parts in order.[37]

The study of time is the raison d'être of cosmography. No one makes the point more succinctly than Vincent Wing, who refers to astronomy as "this Art, whereby time, and the periods of time are constantly, and continually determined by the heavenly Bodies."[38]

The explanation of time, then, was the final aim of cosmography, the overriding intention that shaped its subject matter. We have already noted how Plato in the *Timaeus* accounts for measured time by the movement of the celestial bodies. Similarly in the Holy Scriptures of the Judeo-Christian tradition, a statement about the origin of time comes early in the book of Genesis:

And God said: Let there be lights in the firmament of heaven to divide the day from the night; and let them be for signs, and for seasons, and days and years. (1:14)

John Dee typified the sixteenth-century scientist when he quoted this passage of scripture to justify his empiricism:

Astronomie, was to us, from the beginning commended, and in maner commaunded by God him selfe. In asmuch as he made the *Sonne, Mone*, and *Starres*, to be to us, for *Signes*, and knowledge of Seasons, and for Distinctions of Dayes, and yeares.[39]

It was clear to Dee that God had filled the heavens with visible signs to raise man from ignorance, and specifically that the greater light and the lesser light in their revolutions

12

have the appointed purpose of marking the passage of time. They are the clocks that mete out mutability.

And yet the empyreal heavens are not subject to the changes that passing time brings in the sublunary world of four elements. The eternity that existed before creation continues to exist untrammeled despite the generation and corruption that proceeds around us. Manifestly, as the renaissance saw it, there are two different coordinates within which time may be considered, one producing a concept of time as stasis, and the other a concept of time as motion. Blundeville takes considerable pains to make the distinction: on the one hand, he identifies "time, without time, that is to say everlasting and infinite, called of the Latines *Eternitas*, ascribed chiefely to God, and therefore not contained within the mooveable Spheares"; and on the other, he identifies "time which is a number measuring the mooving of the first mooveable [i.e., the *primum mobile*, the heavens], and of all other mutable thinges."[40] So while the celestial bodies measure the passage of time, yet they and their patterns are immutable, beyond the reach of *tempus edax*. They are both timely and timeless. In the words of Timaeus, the heavens are a moving image of eternity (37D).

This paradox was the occult wisdom at the center of cosmography, the greatest truth that study of the universe could reveal to man. While it acknowledged two systems for dealing with time, the eternal and the ephemeral, it also insisted upon their synchronization. And thereby it bound together the celestial and the terrestrial, the divine and the human. The changing and the changeless were paradoxically resolved into a single continuum. To share this mystery with us, in his "Preface to the reader" Recorde directs our attention to the heavens:

> There are those pure creatures, whiche waxe not werye with laboure, nother growe olde by continuance, but are as freshe nowe in beutye and shape, as the firste daye of their creation, and as apte nowe to perfourme their course, as they were the firste hower that they began. And thoughe time wholly depend of it, yet time can not utter anye force in it, yea thoughe all other thinges in the worlde by tyme be consumed, and even the moste harde metals freted into drosse, yet the liquide heavens not only governe time it selfe, but utterly stande cleere from all corruption of time.[41]

At this point, Recorde falls before the subject of his discourse in worshipful apostrophe: "Oh woorthy temple of Goddes magnificence!"

I Creation

INCE STUDY of the heavens, God's handiwork, was the noblest inquiry of human mind, the cosmographer inevitably faced the question of how they came to be. Especially since the drift of cosmography was toward some concept of time, much thought was devoted to the origin of our universe. Speculation focused on that moment when the unchanging became corruptible—when the timeless became timely and when the immaterial filled out space. That critical juncture when insubstantial thought in the divine mind became physical fact provides the *terminus a quo* for natural history.

The state of affairs before creation is earnestly characterized by Du Bartas:

> Before all Time, all Matter, Forme, and
> Place;
> God all in all, and all in God it was:
> Immutable, immortall, infinite,
> Incomprehensible, all spirit, all light,
> All Maiestie, all selfe Omnipotent,
> Invisible, impassive, excellent,
> Pure, wise, just, good, God raign'd alone at
> rest,
> Himselfe alone selfes Pallace, hoast and
> guest. [42]

These conditions prevailed "before all Time, all Matter, Forme, and Place," and some explanation was needed to indicate how this conceptual level of absolute being could produce our time-space continuum with its obviously mutable and seemingly haphazard relationships.

No subject has driven the human imagination more relentlessly or stirred it more deeply. The beginning of our world's history holds a fascination that at once intimidates and inspires. The origin of things is the mystery of mysteries, and every civilization that has risen above brute nature has tried to explain it. The renaissance with eager catholicity collected as many cosmogonies as possible, the more ancient the better.

The supreme testimony about creation, of course, resides in the Holy Scriptures of the Judeo-Christian tradition. Especially decretive is the book of Genesis with its explanation of how the generic imperfection known as evil was introduced into the world, consequently separating mortal from immortal. Before the end of the classical period, Philo Judaeus, the proto-cabalist who was readily christianized, had offered an elaborate interpretation of Genesis, replete with mystical rapture and number symbolism. And there were other authorities equally revered. The *Timaeus* of Plato, with its benign deity giving physical extension to an archetypal idea, was known directly as an important text in the newly resurrected Platonic corpus, but had yet greater influence through its early assimilation into the mainstream of Western thought from Macrobius onward. Even earlier, a mythological account of creation had been engagingly recorded by Hesiod, and his story of sexual procreation between cosmic forces and battles between giants was immensely popular. Better known still was the account of how cosmos proceeded from chaos narrated by Ovid as the introductory tale in the *Metamorphoses*. The Bible, Philo Judaeus, Timaeus, Hesiod, Ovid — each of these authorities was honored by innumerable citations, editions, paraphrases, and translations. They were the common currency of educated exchange. Each was available as an independent tradition.

More usually, however, the several accounts of creation were amalgamated to produce a single account which embraced them all. Not only was this the case in the popular mind, where indifference and ignorance might hold sway, but also in the minds of serious scholars. After Ficino, the tendency was decidedly syncretic rather than analytical. The *Heptaplus* of Pico della Mirandola, for example, is an exercise of just this sort. As commentators upon the first book of Genesis, Pico brings forward platonists and peripatetics and stoics as well as the Evangelists and Church Fathers and cabalists, and even Avicenna and Averroes. The thrust was to make creation an inclusive and conclusive narrative that placed our universe in the context of time. Creation, as the renaissance recognized, is a metaphor for time, an attempt to make the paradox of time intelligible to the mortal mind. In this prodigious effort, the various traditional accounts of creation had coalesced into one conglomerate statement.

Typical of this casual syncretism is a reference to creation that Thomas Masterson makes at the opening of the dedicatory epistle in his *Third booke of arithmeticke*:

In the beginning the Omnipotent and ever living God (great architector of all things) out of a heavy lumpe or disordred *chaos*, framed the heavens, the earth, the sea, and all things in them contayned, in number, weight and measure: observing such an harmonie therein, that the Sunne, Moone, and starres, which he placed above (as it were the vault or coverture of his worke) serve for lightes, signes, seasons, yeares, and dayes, to grace, governe, and direct beneath.[43]

Masterson begins in a biblical vein, echoing the *in principio* of both Genesis and St. John, and endowing God with epithets from the Judeo-Christian scriptures. He is "omnipotent" and "ever living." Before the end of the first sentence, however, Masterson repeats an epithet for God from the *Timaeus* (28C), "great architector of all things"; he uses the Greek term χάος, which is especially prominent in Hesiod *(Theogony,* 116) and Ovid *(Metamorphoses,* I.7); he commits the heresy of saying that God did not create *ex nihilo;* he quotes King Solomon, who in the Book of Wisdom (11.21) said that God had created all things, according to number, weight, and measure; and he gives the whole a Pythagorean tinge by talking about the "harmonie therein."

The same sort of syncretizing tendency is observable in **Figure 8**, which illustrates the opening book of Ovid's *Metamorphoses* as it appeared from the press of Jacques Huguetan in Lyons, 1512. This classical narrative of how chaos was transmuted into cosmos is here focused on the line: "God — or kindlier Nature — composed this strife" (Hanc deus et melior litem natura diremit; I.21). But in this illustration God is more like Jehovah than Jupiter, and perhaps more Christ-like than either. What comes to mind, in fact, is the incarnate λόγος of Christian tradition presiding in a Garden of Eden of His own making — as the devotees of St. John's gospel read Genesis. The deer and the rabbit lie down with the lion, and perhaps even the lamb is present in the figure of Christ. Watery creatures and airy creatures inhabit their appropriate realms. From the upper

Fig. 8. *Creation from an early edition of Ovid's* Metamorphoses.

left, Zephyrus blows his nurturing breath into the scene like some divine afflatus; and to align this illustration with the syncretic tradition embracing all knowledge, the sun and moon shine in the sky. Such ambiguity is thoroughly agreeable with the renaissance reading of Ovid. As George Sandys observes in his commentary on Book I of the *Metamorphoses*, Ovid's account of creation is "so consonant to the truth, as doubtlesse he had either seene the Books of *Moses*, or receaved that doctrine by tradition."[44] Figure 8 could adorn the Pentateuch as readily as Ovid's pagan text.

Many philosophical problems were raised about the creation of the world. Best known, perhaps, was the question of whether there was preexistent matter in which the deity merely patted into shape (the view of the *Timaeus*), or whether God created the world out of nothing (the view of Genesis as it was commonly interpreted). **Figure 9** displays the conclusion of Charles de Bouelles, an early French humanist, who in this diagram catches God in the act of creating a time-bound universe from nothing-

Fig. 9. *God creating* ex nihilo.

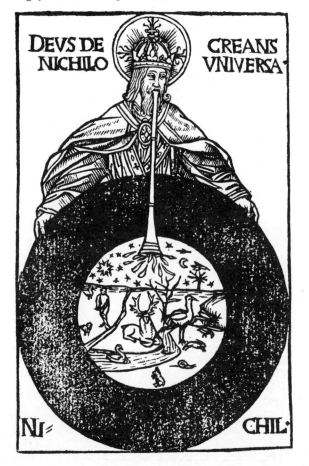

ness, as the caption announces. From the abysmal "nichil" of chaos, He fashions a sphere presided over by the sun and the moon to mark the passage of time. He blows His divine breath through a long tube, thereby literally "inspiring" a multitude of creatures—including a deer, a snail, a rabbit, and a man to represent land creatures, a swan to represent watery creatures, various birds to represent creatures of the air, and several shining bodies in the heavens to represent fiery creatures. Another alternative to *creatio ex nihilo* was the heretical argument that God created the world out of His own being, an argument voiced by Milton: "Because I am who fill / Infinitude, nor vacuous the space" (*Paradise Lost,* VII.168-69). Milton is trying to deal with the truism that since God is infinite, there could be no matter —nor indeed, anything else—outside His being. There could not be space even for chaos, for nothing, for a vacuum.

Equally vexing was the question of whether the world would someday end or whether it would last forever. The two giants of ancient philosophy were in open dispute on this issue. Plato had argued that since the world had a beginning, it must have an end (*Timaeus*, 28B-C). Aristotle, however, had argued to the contrary that the world is ungenerated and indestructible, without beginning or end *(De caelo*, 279b4-283b22).[45] John Swan begins his prose hexaemeron *Speculum mundi* (Cambridge, 1635) by reviewing the arguments on both sides of this question, and he judiciously observes:

> The Philosophers of ancient times were diversly transported in the stream of their own opinions, both concerning the worlds originall and continuance: some determining that it once began; others imagining that it was without beginning, and that the circled orbs should spin out a thread as long as is eternitie, before it found an ending. (page 1)

He cites Plato in the *Timaeus* (28C), "that God was Δημιουργὸς ποιητής καί πατήρ τοῦ ὅλου the Creatour, Maker, and Father of the whole universe." But he also gives Aristotle's contradictory opinion "that the world neither began, nor yet shall end," referring in a marginal gloss to the *De caelo* (I.x-xii; II.i), the *Physica* (VIII), and the *De generatione et corruptione*. Swan exercises both reason and faith like a good Christian, however, and proves that sequential time is finite. Since the world had a beginning in measured time, it must have a foreseeable termination.

Another question, again demonstrating the importance of time in these debates, was whether God created the world instantaneously or in stages distributed over several days. Philo Judaeus had pointed out that days are determined by the sun's course, and therefore time could not be measured in such terms until after the heavens themselves had been established.[46] The Judeo-Christian answer, however, was unequivocal. Although God Himself resides beyond the domain of passing time and had existence prior to creation, He produced our time-space continuum by means of a temporal process. To be specific, He laboured for six days and rested on the seventh.[47]

The details of the hexaemeral operation are laid out day by day in a remarkable series of woodcuts prepared for Hartmann Schedel's *Liber chronicarum* (Nuremberg, 1493), better known as *The Nuremberg Chronicle*. Like Recorde and Cuningham, Schedel was a physician by profession, but also a lover of books. In this compendium he collected the historical anecdotes at his disposal and arranged them in chronological order from the beginning of the world to his own day; and Anton Koberger, an ambitious printer, called upon the considerable talents of Michael Wohlgemut and Wilhelm Pleydenwurff to produce the most profusely and handsomely illustrated book of the fifteenth century. This monumental treasure-house of learning quite naturally opens its door with the biblical account of creation. *In principio*, Schedel begins, *creavit deus celum et terram*.

In **Figure 10a** the hand of God in a beneficent gesture of blessing reaches forth from heaven to separate light, which He called "day," from darkness, which He called "night." This is the first differentiation of the void, not yet involving substance. In **Figure 10b** the hand of God separates the firmament from the waters below, now making a differentiation between substantial components of the void. In **Figure 10c** the same hand gathers together the waters beneath the firmament in one place, so that dry land may appear, and the world is further divided into earth and seas. Until this point,

Fig. 10a. *The first day of creation in* The Nuremberg Chronicle.

Fig. 10b. *The second day of creation in* The Nuremberg Chronicle.

earth and water and the other elements are still inchoate, so that the number of spheres in each diagram is indeterminate — two or five or four according to the whim of the illustrator, who faced the difficult task of making visible to our sight what was still a largely undiscriminated mixture.

With **Figure 10d**, however, sequential time comes into play, and new modes of perception are required of us. Schedel begins his commentary on the work of the fourth day by quoting Genesis 1:14-16:

> God said, Let there be lights in the firmament of the heaven to divide the day from the night; and let them be for signs, and for seasons, and for days, and years: And let them be for lights in the firmament of the heaven to give light upon the earth: and it was so. And God made two great lights; the greater light to rule the day, and the lesser light to rule the night.

On the fourth day the celestial bodies began to turn in their courses and measure the passage of time. At that moment the world is discriminated into recognizable parts. The heavens begin to declare the glory of God and the firmament to show His handiwork. Then we see the fully articulated diagram that is familiar to us as the earth-centered universe publicized by Ptolemy. In the middle is our planet Earth, upside-down but stationary. Next come three undesignated spheres for each of the other three elements: water, air, and fire. Then come seven spheres for the seven planets — beginning with the Moon followed by spheres for Mercury and Venus, continuing with the Sun in the fourth sphere, and concluding with spheres for Mars, Jupiter, and Saturn. The word "planet" <Gr. πλανήτης means "wandering star,"[48] in contradistinction to the fixed stars that keep their relative positions night after night. Since the fixed stars also must be fitted into the scheme, outside the planetary spheres is the sphere

Fig. 10c. *The third day of creation in* **The Nuremberg Chronicle.**

Fig. 10d. *The fourth day of creation in* **The Nuremberg Chronicle.**

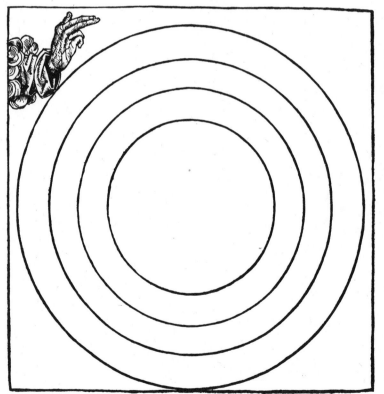

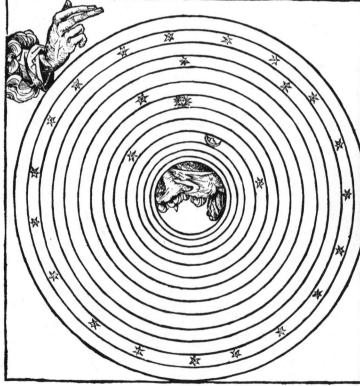

which contains the constellations, decorated with stars equidistantly spaced around it. All of the fixed stars are likewise equidistant from the Earth. Finally there is a sphere representing the *primum mobile,* the cause without an antecedent cause that sets this finite universe apart from the infinite empyrean and keeps it in uniform motion. All in this diagram is orderly and knowable.

Figure 10e displays the creatures of land, sea, and air that God made on the fifth day to populate the Earth. And **Figure 10f** shows God in the act of creating Adam, the culmination of His six days' labor. Heretofore the creating deity has been represented by a faceless hand, a mere instrument to carry out an impersonal scheme. But now God is shown full length, resplendent in solemn majesty as He raises the first man from a lump of dirt with His left hand and blesses him with the other. God and the noble creature fashioned in His image face one another in an approving attitude of *caritas,*

while the beasts of Eden browse in a peaceful nature that stretches undisturbed to a distant horizon.

Having finished His mighty task, God rests in glory in **Figure 10g.** The archetypal idea has been fully extended into dimensions of both space and time. The universe is now "perfect" in a literal sense (from L. *perficere*)—that is, the divine intelligence has worked through its scheme to completion.[49] Beneath God's feet whirls the cosmos that He set in motion on the fourth day. Clearly labeled at the center is the "Earth," surrounded by the "sphere of water," the "sphere of air," and the "sphere of fire." Next come the ten celestial spheres: one each for the seven planets (the Moon, Mercury, Venus, the Sun, Mars, Jupiter, and Saturn), then the "firmament" to contain the constellations of fixed stars (here represented by the twelve signs of the zodiac), next the "cristalline heavens" (an interpolation having no empirical basis but required to bring the heavenly

Fig. 10e. *The fifth day of creation in* **The Nuremberg Chronicle.**

Fig. 10f. *The sixth day of creation in* **The Nuremberg Chronicle.**

spheres up to the divine number 10), and finally the "first mover" of aristotelian tradition. Flanking God's throne and protectively surrounding the universe are the nine orders of angels, neatly enumerated at the left: Seraphim, Cherubim, Thrones, Dominations, Princes, Potentates, Virtues, Archangels, and Angels. From the four corners of the world blow the cardinal winds: Subsolanus in the upper left, Auster in the upper right, Aparctias in the lower left, and Zephyrus in the lower right. This in broad outline is the world-view that the renaissance inherited from the middle ages. God is manifestly in His heaven, and all is right with His world. This sabbath, through God's beneficence, endures without term.

The hexaemeral tradition continued unabated throughout the sixteenth century, finding advocates among Protestants as well as Catholics. When the first edition of Miles Cov-

Fig. 10g. *The sabbath in* The Nuremberg Chronicle.

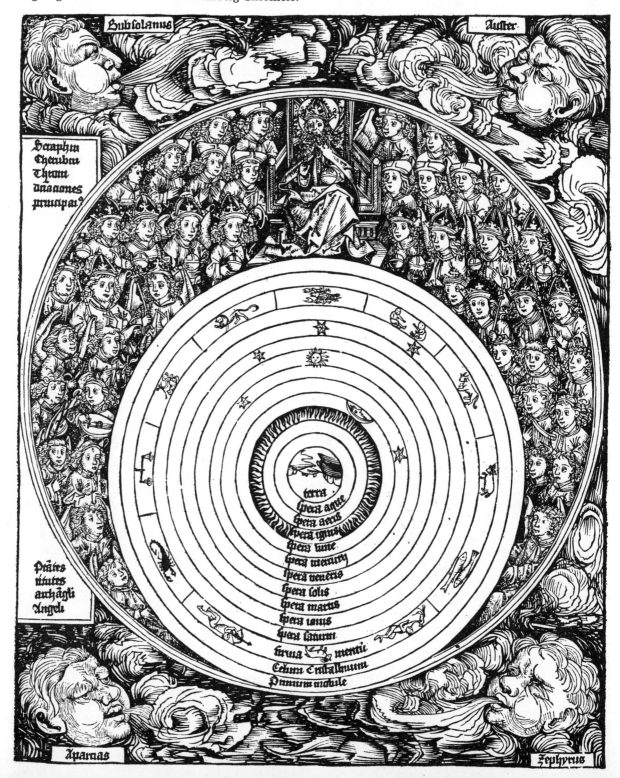

erdale's English Bible was published in 1535, a fine series of woodcuts depicting the six days of creation was printed as a headpiece to the text (**Figure 11**). The work of each day is graphically presented in strict illustration of the account in Genesis. As Coverdale had translated the opening lines:

> In the begynnynge God created heaven & earth: and the earth was voyde and emptie, and darcknes was upon the depe, & the sprete of God moved upon the water.

> And God sayde: let there be light, & there was light. And God sawe the light that it was good. Then God devyded the light from the darcknes, and called the light, Daye: and the darcknes, Night. Then of the evenynge and mornynge was made the first daye.

> And God sayde: let there be a firmement betwene the waters, and let it devyde the waters asunder. Then God made the firma-ment, and parted the waters under the firmament, from the waters above the firmament: And so it came to passe. And God called the firmament, Heaven. Then of the evenynge & mornynge was made the seconde daye.

The work of the other days proceeds uninterruptedly according to the familiar text. The illustration for Coverdale's Bible is noteworthy, however, in two ways. First, the culmination of God's effort in this instance is the creation of Eve from Adam's rib, rather than merely the creation of the first man; and this concern with Eve heralds the Calvinistic obsession with the fall. Second, there is no seventh day on which God rested, no sabbath. Omitted is the joyfulness that leads to the optimistic acceptance of God's bounty. The hexaemeron depicted in this Protestant Bible is more literal, less full and fanciful, than that detailed in *The Nuremberg Chronicle*.

Fig. 11. *The six days of creation in Coverdale's* Bible.

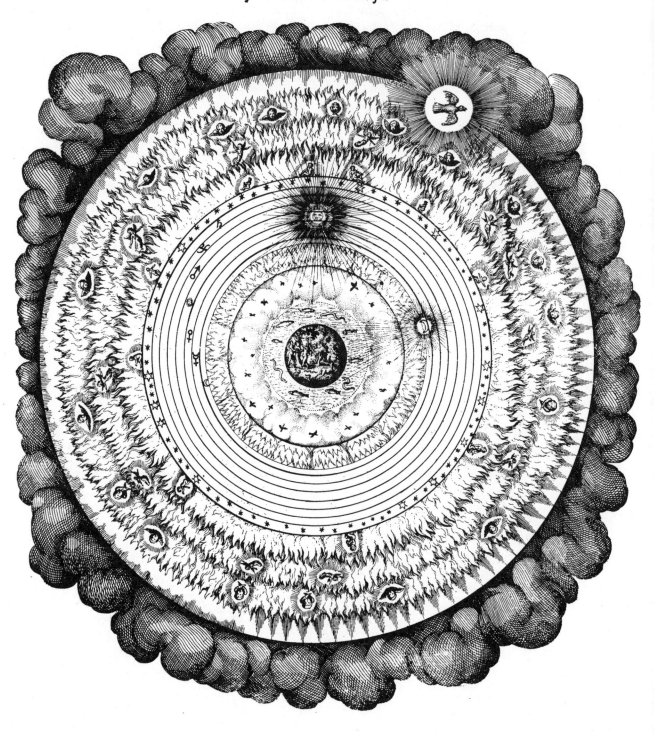

Fig. 12. *The creation according to Fludd.*

In contrast, the author of **Figure 12** felt little Puritanical restraint in his depiction of the *genesis mundi*. Robert Fludd, the most distinguished physician in early seventeenth-century London, published a four-volume encyclopedia of human knowledge which he entitled *Utriusque cosmi majoris scilicet et minoris metaphysica, physica atque technica historia* (Oppenheim, 1617-19). The first treatise in this "metaphysical, physicial and technical account of both worlds, the macrocosm as well as the microcosm" is given an equally grandiose heading, "an account of the structure of the macrocosm and of the origin of its creatures, divided into seven books." The result is Fludd's hexaemeron, a curious blend of physical science and occultism which is visually epitomized by figure 12. There the Holy Spirit carries out God's command, "Let there be light," and circumscribes a finite but fully articulated cosmos identical with figure 10g. The only novel datum is the embellishment of Earth with the scene of the *felix culpa*. At the center of this diagram Adam and Eve partake of the fatal fruit amidst the lush scenery of Paradise.

An even more extravagant illustration of Genesis appears in **Figure 13**, which depicts "the harmony of the nascent world." Athanasius Kircher was a German Jesuit who spent an eventful life teaching in several centers of learning until he died near the age of eighty in 1680 at Rome. Even more important, he was a prodigious polymath, as prolific in his writing as he was wide ranging in his studies. Without doubt, he was one of the most learned men of the seventeenth century—and also one of the most interesting, if his sort of erudition were still in vogue. In 1650, in mid-career, Father Kircher published the *Musurgia universalis*, which in many respects is comparable to Fludd's *Utriusque cosmi . . . historia* and Kepler's *Harmonice mundi*. The title of the publication, which means "The Universal Work-of-the-Muses," indicates the breadth of its intention and the syncretic bent of its method.[50] It

is to our minds a preposterous piece of outmoded pedantry, often building on false assumptions and rising to equally false conclusions; but no one can deny the intellectual energy that went into its compositon.

In one weighty chapter (Volume II, pages 365-67), Father Kircher gives his version of the hexaemeron in musical terms, taking his cue from the pythagorean-platonic tradition that the cosmos is a harmony of discordant components, *concordia discors*. As the chapter heading announces, "The world is compared to an organ" (mundus organo comparatur), and God becomes the organ player (Deus Organaedus). Figure 13 is the result, the "heav'n's deep organ" of Milton's "Nativity Ode." At the top, reminiscent of figure 12, the Holy Spirit implements the divine command, *Fiat lux*, and provides the harmony of the first day. The harmony of the second day derives from the succeeding passage in Genesis: "The waters were gathered together in one place and dry land appeared." And so on through the other four days of creation until we arrive at the climax, the appearance of man. The label in the vignette for the sixth day repeats the passage from Genesis that is of greatest concern to humanists: God said, "Let us make man in our image." Again reminiscent of Fludd's diagram, however, this moment is not a triumphant achievement that elevates man to a lordship over nature and a likeness to deity, but rather it shows the crucial event of man's fall. Adam's moral choice to sin counteracts the generosity of God so evident in Paradise. Nothing more succinctly expresses the melancholy of the seventeenth-century pessimist.

When the creation of the world is extended over a period of six days, it emphasizes the temporal dimension of our environment. There is also, of course, the spatial dimension to be reckoned with. Creation produces a continuum of space as well as of time. **Figure 14**, a full-page woodcut from the first edition of Gregor Reisch's *Margarita philosophica* (Freiburg, 1503), calls attention to space. There we

Fig. 13. *Creation as a heavenly organ according to Kircher.*

Fig. 14. *The birth of Eve in a spatial continuum from Reisch.*

see God in the final act of genesis, producing Eve from Adam's rib. Illustrations of this event were commonplace[51] — the *Margarita philosophica* was no more than a popular encyclopedia of the liberal arts compiled by a studious cleric. What makes this illustration notable, however, is its setting. Very carefully the artist has included each of the four elements: Eden is populated by creatures of the water, the land, and the air, and above is a sphere of fire. Creation has achieved completeness, as the presence of all four elements attests. Furthermore, stratification of the scene into the elements as our senses perceive them directs notice to the extended space consumed by God's work. We are made aware that the void has been wholly filled.

The dimension of space resulting from creation is even more clearly demonstrated in **Figure 15**. Sebastian Münster was a distinguished professor of mathematics and Hebrew as well as an early supporter of Martin Luther, and his *Cosmographia* is a large proto-atlas collecting the geographical lore available to a

scholar in the middle of the sixteenth century. On the first page as a headpiece to the text is this woodcut. God, having completed the task of creation, presides in glory at the top. To represent the dimension of space, the four elements are extended in layers beneath him, each in its proper place. To represent the dimension of time, the sun and the moon shine in a sky filled with stars. Two good angels caress the universe in the upper corners of the diagram, while two demons lurk in the lower corners. The creation is a plenum which stretches from the presence of God to the meanest specimen of His handiwork, and on the moral scale from the highest good to the basest evil.

Despite the fact that creation took six days and fills a vast space, it eventuated in a continuum, extensive but unified. There is diversity, both temporal and spatial; yet from this multeity arises a unity. *E pluribus unum.* Robert Recorde cites Oronce Finé on this point:

Orontius defineth the worlde to be the perfect and entiere composition of all thinges:

Fig. 15. *The creation as a spatial continuum from Münster.*

a divine worke, infinite and wonderfull, adorned with all kindes and formes of bodies, that nature coulde make.[52]

The dimensional quality of the plenum is stressed in **Figure 16**, a diagram that Finé himself drew to illustrate the *Livre singulier & utile, touchant l'art et practique de geometrie* of Charles de Bouelles (Paris, 1542). It makes the same statement about the spatial arrangement of the elements and the heavens that figure 15 makes. But it goes further, as the text explains: "La grande encyclie du monde universel, tient la figure de ronde pyramide ren-

Fig. 16. *The universe as a plenum of four elements plus the heavens.*

versee, ayant la base au ciel, & le poinct capital en la terre" (fol. 52). Looked at from the vantage point of our Earth toward its base in the heavens, this round pyramid expands to include "l'encyclie du monde," the wide compass of a multiplex world. But looked at from the opposite direction, *sub specie aeternitatis*, the pyramid is reversed and the universe narrows down to our insignificant planet. Our earth becomes an infinitesimal point, a dimensionless unit.

Paradoxically, then, infinity is a self-consistent entity, and therefore a monad. The infi-

nite variety of our world coalesces in a *universe*, so that all things roll around as one. This is the paradox expressed by the concept of cosmos, and visually represented in **Figure 17**. As the first emblem in his huge compendium of emblems, the *Mundus Symbolicus* (Cologne, 1694), Filippo Picinelli exhibits an armillary sphere with a gnomic inscription equating "One" with "All" and making both terms interchangeable.

In a particularly well-known passage of the *Timaeus* (28C), the term τὸ πᾶν is used to designate the universe.[53] In figure 17 we see τὸ πᾶν translated into the Latin, *omnes*. It was also translated into English as "the all."[54] In his hymn of praise to God the Father, for example, Spenser describes the firmament as "that mightie shining christall wall, / Wherewith he hath encompassed this All" ("An Hymne of Heavenly Beautie," lines 41-42). Shakespeare speaks of "the all-cheering sun" *(Romeo*, I.i. 140), and Donne refers to the sun as "the Lustre, and the vigor of this All" ("Second Anniversarie," line 5). From this meaning of "all" we can devise a string of synonyms: κόσμος = πᾶν = *omnes* = all = universe = perfection. To this list we might also add "Christ," for English poets equated Πᾶν and God the Son.[55]

We should also note that the antonym of "all," which is "nothing," was commonly used in its cosmological sense as well. This is the "nothing" that God used for the *creatio ex nihilo*. This "nothing" is nonexistence, a void, a conception of chaos as the opposite of cosmos. As Du Bartas observes, adding pun to paradox: "But all this *All* did once (of nought) begin."[56] In the extremity of her grief over Antony's death, Shakespeare's Cleopatra makes the same pun with even greater economy, "All's but naught" (IV.xv.78), thereby paraphrasing Othello's realization that loss of a lover is chaos come again (III.iii.92).[57] Charles de Bouelles deals with these matters in a brilliantly incisive treatise entitled *Liber de nichilo*,[58] and Lear reveals his knowledge of the subject when he threatens Cordelia, "Nothing will come of nothing" (I.i.92).[59]

Looking again at figure 15, we see there just such a comprehensive all created out of nothing. The lower portion of the illustration presents a plenum of the four elements with the creatures appropriate to each. But there is another important point to make about this diagram: above the elemental strata there is an additional area that represents a different level of existence. Beneath is the realm of the four elements, the physical world, mutable nature. Above is the celestial world, the empyrean, the abode of God. Beneath is the sense-perceptible and finite; above is the measureless, aspatial and atemporal. The greater and lesser lights appear in the sky to mark the passage of sequential time in the elemental world below; but the sun and moon, taken conjointly, are an icon for eternity as we have seen, and therefore signify the changeless perfection of the empyrean. It is the realm of essences, pure forms without corruptible substance.

The two levels of existence distinguished in figure 15 derive ultimately from the distinction made by Plato between a world of being and a world of becoming (*Timaeus*, 27D-28A). In the world of being, the data are unchanging ideas (Gr. ἰδέα = "form"), and therefore really *are* themselves. In the world of becoming the data are imperfect objects, each an unstable combination of the elements and therefore continually *becoming* something else. The world of becoming is perceptible to the senses, and consequently is said to be "sensible." The world of being is perceptible to the intellect only, and consequently is said to be "intelligible."[60] The platonic division between these two mutually exclusive realms of human experience in turn derived from the belief propounded in the *Timaeus* that the universe is the extension of an archetypal idea into a time-space continuum. Not only are there two distinct realms — the conceptual and the physical — but also there is posited a correlation between them because the physical is a projection of the conceptual (*Timaeus*, 39E ff.). The objects that comprise the world of becoming are replicas (albeit im-

Fig. 17. *The universe, both one and all-inclusive.*

perfect) of the ideal forms in the world of being.

The division of the universe in these terms, and yet the conjugal relationship between the two halves, is admirably demonstrated in **Figure 18**, a typically magnificent diagram from Fludd's *Utrisque cosmi . . .historia.* Although reminiscent of figure 16, Fludd's drawing is even more explicit. Two opposite poles are identified in the diagram: at the bottom is our planet, the extreme of physicality, represented by a ball labeled "Earth"; at the top is God, the extreme of essence, represented by a refulgent triangle to suggest His trinal capability. Reaching down from God — Who is pure idea — is a "formal pyramid," showing how abstract formality stretches down through the various spheres to the surface of the Earth. It goes through "the highest and more formal part of the empyreal heavens inhabited by the highest

27

angelical hierarchy," through "the middle part of the empyreal heavens assigned to the middle angelical hierarchy," through "the lowest part of the empyreal heavens appropriate to the lowest angelical hierarchy," next through the seven planetary spheres, and finally through the spheres of elementary fire, air, and water. Formality decreases as it descends from God until it diminishes to zero at the surface of the Earth, thereby tracing out a "formal pyramid." Conversely, in the other direction a "material pyramid" (as Fludd identifies it in the text) stretches up from Earth until it diminishes to zero at the presence of God.[61] "Formality" and "materiality" are different orders of existence, the one increasing in proportion as the other decreases. In consequence, absolute symmetry is sustained in this diagram. God and Earth are counterposed, and their opposition continued in the neat balancing of the three angelical hierarchies against the three elements above Earth. Formality and materiality come into

Fig. 18. *The universe dichotomized into material and non-material components.*

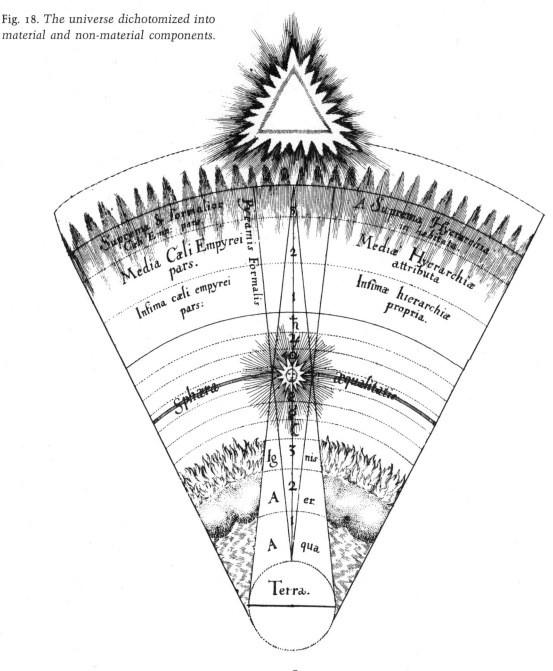

exact equilibrium, each equally strong, along a line labeled "the sphere of equality"; and significantly this median position coincides with the sphere of the Sun. Here formality and materiality are in exact balance; the Sun has a component to be perceived by the intellect which is exactly equivalent to its component to be perceived by the senses.[62]

Plato's distinction between a world of being and a world of becoming—a world of forms and a world of matter—was easily translated into theological terms. Eternal heaven, the habitat of God, could be set apart from time-bound earth, the habitat of men. **Figure 19** works on this assumption while illustrating a discussion of the fallen angels and the origin

Fig. 19. *Immortal heaven set apart from the imperfect and therefore mutable physical world.*

of evil. The *De proprietatibus rerum* of Barthol- omaeus Anglicus is an early product of the encyclopedia tradition that flourished in the thirteenth century, a monument of erudition that transmitted intact the medieval world- view to the renaissance. John Trevisa trans- lated it into English in 1398, and Wynken de Worde published this text at Westminster in 1495 to produce one of the most impressive incunabula printed in England. In figure 19 God reigns in majesty, enthroned between two kneeling angels, who objectify the everlasting praise of Him. The kingdom of heaven is localized by three concentric circles and bounded by a symbolic ring of clouds, the con- ventional division between heaven and earth. Outside this serene tableau, the fallen angels

plunge pell-mell into another area. Quite evi- dently, the divine region of heaven is distin- guished from the corruptible region, full of hurly-burly, that we inhabit below.

The magnanimous act of creation has even- tuated in evil, modifying, if not fully cancel- ing, the divine intention. Passing time is a continual reminder of that universal defect. But still, somewhere, if only in the minds of those who worship Him, God holds eternal sway, dispensing love and mercy and justice— all those positive attributes that knit our uni- verse together beneath the eye of a watchful providence acting through natural forces. Such was the gist of genesis for the cosmogra- pher.

II The Geocentric Universe

RENAISSANCE COSMOGRAPHY enjoined its practitioners to gaze upon the heavens, and often held out hope of discerning the deity by literally speculating upon his handiwork. Nevertheless, most cosmographers, unlike theologians, based their discipline upon what is visible from the earth. In consequence, most cosmographies begin, like Recorde's *Castle of knowledge* and Cuningham's *Cosmographical glasse*, with the practical question, *Quid mundus*, "What is the world?" The favorite answer was a statement attributed to Cleomedes, which Cuningham translates as follows:

The world is an apte frame, made of heaven, and earth, & of thinges in them conteyned. This comprehendeth all thinges in it self, nether is there any thing without the lymites of it visible.[63]

This definition recognizes the two orders of existence, formality and materiality, and it identifies the world with the material—what the Greeks called φύσις and what we call "nature" in the broadest sense. Beyond our finite and sense-perceptible universe there stretches a measureless empyrean, the proper province of metaphysics and of theology. But according to this definition, the world includes everything known or knowable by man, God only excepted.

The world, however, is itself divided into two parts, into "heaven" and "earth," to use the terms of Cleomedes, or into the "celestiall" and the "elementarie," to use the terms of Blundeville.[64] **Figure 20**, taken from Cuningham's *Cosmographical glasse*, shows this division in its most rudimentary form.[65] "The heavenly Region" comprises the celestial

spheres, while the "Elementarye" region is confined to the sublunary realm of the four elements. This distinction is an obvious line of demarcation to draw, but in the schools it derived ultimately from Aristotle's description of the elements. In the aristotelian system the elements, to quote Recorde's definition, are "the fyrste, simple and originall matters, whereof all myxt and compounde bodies be made, and into whiche all shall tourne againe."[66] Aristotle, in accord with prevalent belief, had identified four of them based on their inherent motions: earth, which has an extreme ten-

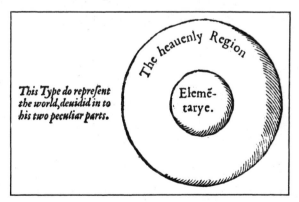

Fig. 20. *The universe divided into the celestial and the mundane.*

31

dency to sink, and therefore is absolutely heavy; water, which has a moderate tendency to sink, and therefore is relatively heavy; air, which has a moderate tendency to rise, and therefore is relatively light; and fire, which has an extreme tendency to rise and therefore is absolutely light. These four elements are restricted to linear motions—up and down, or forward and backward, or left and right. Aristotle had identified also a fifth element, the quintessence αἰθήρ, which follows the perfect pattern of circular motion, a schema for eternity because it has no beginning and no end. The heavenly spheres, from the Moon up, are composed of ether, while the sublunary region is composed of the four base elements.[67] Since earth, water, air and fire continually transmute one into another, the elementary region is subject to mutability; in contrast, the ethereal heavens are unchanging.[68]

Following Aristotle, all cosmographers agreed that the four elements, because of their substantiality, were concentrated at the center of the universe. Plato in the *Timaeus* had also placed them in this central position (31B-32C). Despite agreement on their centrality, however, the arrangement of the four elements in the sublunary sphere was open to various interpretations. Christopher Clavius, a Jesuit who spent most of his illustrious scientific career in Rome during the last quarter of the sixteenth century, distinguished three ways of arranging the elements:[69] first, by their qualities (i.e., hot, dry, moist, and cold), a conceptual arrangement that ignores the physical coordinates of time and space, and leads to a schema for cosmos known as the tetrad (see pp. 102-107, below); second, by their properties (i.e., heavy and light), and again an arrangement arrived at by deductive reasoning rather than empirical observation, but recognizing spatial relationships and leading to a stratified arrangement of the elements; and third, by our sense perception of them, depending upon our response to physical objects, which are unstable mixtures of the elements, the elements themselves in pure form lying beyond our sense perception.[70]

Fig. 21. *Stratification of the four elements including the three regions of air, according to Finé after Aristotle.*

Figure 21 presents the elements in a stratified arrangement according to their heaviness or lightness. It appears in the *Protomathesis* (Paris, 1532) of Oronce Finé, the dedicated professor of mathematics appointed by Francis I to teach in his newly founded Collège de France. At the center of figure 21 is our planet, Earth, comprising the two heaviest elements, "earth" and "water." The land mass is recognizable as a rough map of Europe, Africa, and Asia, a derivative of the T-map that prevailed in the middle ages. According to Finé (and ultimately, Aristotle), earth is absolutely heavy and water is relatively heavy. Fire is the absolutely light element, and so it occupies the outermost sphere in the diagram. Between the sphere of fire and our Earth is the sphere of air, the relatively light element, which is here, as usual, divided into three distinct regions: the "highest region of air," the "middle" region, and the "lowest." The highest region of air is hot because of its proximity to the sphere of fire, while the lowest region of air is hot because of the reflection of sunbeams from the Earth's surface. The middle region of air, however, is

Fig. 22. *Stratification of the four elements according to Cuningham.*

cold because of the two hot layers on each side which act according to a principle of opposition and compact the cold within it. As a result of this coldness, the vapours that rise from the surface of the Earth congeal in this middle region of the air and produce meteorological phenomena, such as clouds and rain and snow.[71] Outside the realm of the four elements is "the heavens," as Finé's diagram unmistakably indicates, the region composed of that incorruptible fifth element, ether. Cuningham took over Finé's diagram for his *Cosmographical glasse,* and we see it again in **Figure 22.**

Figure 23 is an extremely interesting diagram which presents the four elements as our senses perceive them in the generable and corruptible objects of physical nature — and which obviously goes on to present the rest of the universe in the same terms. This illustration appears in an early edition of Konrad von Megenberg's *Buch der natur,*[72] one of the most popular of the medieval encyclopedias (written 1349-50). The numerous components of the universe are arranged in layers, starting with the four elements at the bottom. In the lowest layer we see earth, water, and air, and their creatures. Just above is the sphere of fire, which

being a pure element is not visible, but nonetheless we know it is there. Above the elementary region rise the spheres of the seven planets, which are visible, especially the lesser light and the greater light. Then comes the sphere of fixed stars, also apparent to our eye. Above this level, the limit of the palpable world, lies the empyreal heaven, with the conventional row of symbolic clouds to mark its boundary.

The heavens of course belong to an order of being different from the extended universe below, and consequently require a mode of perception other than our senses. The heavens are perceptible to the intellect alone. Nonetheless, the artist here has ventured to present a picture to our mind's eye, and he images the perfection of the divine region in terms of the three-in-one mystery of God. In the center of the strip representing heaven is God the Son with His crown to signify dominion over the world.

Fig. 23. *The universe as a hierarchy of the elements, the planetary spheres, and the Christian heaven.*

Above Him flies the Holy Ghost in the familiar form of a dove. And beside Him is God the Father, Who for purposes of symmetry is made two figures, just as symmetrical groups of angels are placed at extreme right and extreme left. But remember—we do not perceive this area with our senses, and therefore we do not really "see" two figures of God the Father. We "know" in our minds that God the Father is a single entity, though apparently here divided into two, just as the Holy Trinity is one in conception though three in its modes of operation. Like figure 15, the universe is here dichotomized into sense-perceptible and intellect-perceptible halves.

The details of figure 23 are largely determined by the dominant cosmology devised by the ancient Greeks and transmitted to later centuries by Claudius Ptolemaeus, who wrote his *Almagest* in Alexandria during the second century A.D. As the renaissance knew it in simplified form, the Ptolemaic system consisted of a finite universe with our Earth as its stationary center. Ranging out from this center were the heavenly bodies, located on concentric revolving spheres that extended to the primum mobile—pretty much as we see the world after the final day of creation in figure 10g and figure 12. This system had the virtues of simplicity and completeness, and by the sixteenth century carried the overbearing authority of long tradition. This, if any, was the conventional world-view of the renaissance.

The Ptolemaic system was in essence a mathematical construct. It was based upon the principle of sphericity, upon a belief that the sphere is the standard form in the universal structure[73]—in Aristotle's phrase, "the primary shape in nature" (*De caelo*, 286b11). Recorde expounds the principle at length:

The whole worlde is rounde exactlye as anye ball or globe, and so are all the principall partes of it, everye sphere severallye and joyntlye, as well of the Planetes, as of the Fixed starres, and so are all the foure Ele-

mentes. And they are aptly placed togither, not as a numbre of rounde balles in a nette, but every sphere includeth other, as they be in ordre of greatnes, beginning at the eighte sphere or firmamente, and so descending to the laste and lowest sphere, is the Sphere of the Mone: under which the foure elementes succede: first the fier, then the ayer: nexte foloweth the water: which with the earth joyntlie annexed, maketh as it were, one sphere only.[74]

According to the pythagorean-platonic doctrine, the sphere is the most perfect of solid figures, since all points on its surface are equidistant from its center and since it encloses a maximum volume given its surface area.[75] Therefore, it was assumed, the universe must be spherical because God, working from His archetypal idea, would not have created anything short of perfection. The world's sphericity reflects His justice and bounty and eternality.

In consequence, any respectable description of the universal world begins with proof of its roundness. Several arguments were tenable, and Blundeville summarizes three of them:

How prove you the frame of the world to be round?

By three reasons, First by comparison, for the likenes which it hath with the chiefe Idea or shape of Gods minde, which hath neither beginning nor ending, and therefore is compared to a Circle. Secondly by aptnesse aswell of moving as of containing, for if it were not round of shape, it should not be so apt to turne about as it continually doth, nor to containe so much as it doth, for the round figure is of greatest capacitie and containeth most. Thirdly, necessitie prooveth it to be round, for if it were with angles or corners, it should not be so apt to turne about, and in turning about, it should leave voide and emptie places, which nature abhorreth, for no place by nature can be without a bodie, nor a body without a place.[76]

34

Blundeville's first reason is platonic in reference, his second is grounded in common sense, and his third is taken directly from Aristotle's *De caelo.*

Figure 24 from Recorde's *Castle of knowledge* neatly illustrates Blundeville's third reason

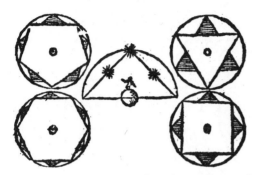

Fig. 24. *Geometrical proof that the earth is spherical.*

and purports to show that the whole world is not a cube or any other solid with angles, but rather a sphere. Aristotle had carried the argument to its logical conclusion:

> Since . . . the whole (τὸ πάν) revolves in a circle, and it has been shown that beyond the outermost circumference there is neither void nor place, this provides another reason why the heaven must be spherical. For if it is bounded by straight lines, that will involve the existence of place, body, and void. A rectilinear body revolving in a circle will never occupy the same space, but owing to the change in position of the corners there will at one time be no body where there was body before, and there will be body again where now there is none. (*De caelo,* 287a12-19)

Recorde's diagram shows the additional space required for the world to rotate if it were a body with pentagonal, hexagonal, triangular, or square faces. His discourse, however, takes a slightly different turn. If some parts of the sky were nearer to us than others, he argues, then the stars would assume different sizes as they move about. Since a star does not change

size from one position to another, it must remain at a constant distance from us; and therefore the heavens are spherical, and congruous with a spherical Earth. The small figure standing on a globe and looking into a triangular sky demonstrates Recorde's point. The star would appear to be smaller when at the apex of the triangle than when at either of the lower positions.

As center of God's perfect creation, the Earth of course conforms to the spherical pattern. However, those who were more scientific — that is, disposed to hypothesize from empirical evidence rather than to reason deductively — offered proof that the Earth is spherical based on the observation of lunar eclipses. **Figure 25**

Fig. 25. *Proof from lunar eclipses that the earth is spherical.*

Hoc Schema demonstrat terram esse globosam.

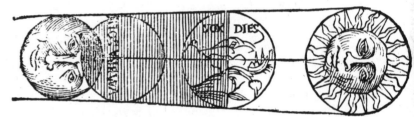

Si terra esset tetragona, vmbra quoq; tetragonæ figuræ in eclipsatione lunari appareret.

Si terra esset trigona, vmbra quoq; triangularem haberet formulam.

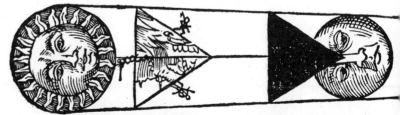

Si terra hexagonæ esset figuræ, eius quoq; vmbra in defectu lunari hexagona appareret, quæ tamen rotunda cernitur.

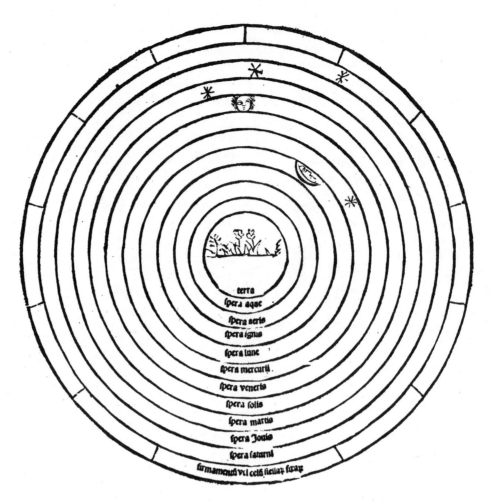

terra
ſpera aqae
ſpera aeris
ſpera ignis
ſpera lune
ſpera mercurii
ſpera veneris
ſpera ſolis
ſpera martis
ſpera Jouis
ſpera ſaturni
firmamentũ vel celũ ſtellaꝝ fixaꝝ

Fig. 26. *The geocentric universe according to Aristotle.*

is a page from the thoroughly professional cosmography of Peter Apian, the *Cosmographicus liber*, as Gemma Frisius edited it in 1533. Apian was professor of mathematics at the university of Ingolstadt and first reported the phenomenon that the tails of comets always stream out in a direction away from the sun. Following the arguments of Aristotle (*De caelo*, 297b23-31), he begins at the top of figure 25 with the declaration: "This diagram shows that the Earth is round." He continues with the next diagram: "If the Earth were four-cornered, its shadow in a lunar eclipse would also appear to be a four-cornered figure." And so on through two other diagrams: "If the Earth were three-cornered, its shadow would also have a triangular shape"; and "If the Earth were a hexagonal figure, its shadow in a lunar eclipse would also appear to be hexagonal, so it is clearly seen to be round."[77] Anyone with an eye to watch the Earth's shadow cross the Moon must conclude that the Earth is spherical.[78]

The geocentric universe focused, then, on a round Earth, frequently articulated, as in **Figure 26**, into four concentric spheres, one for each of the four elements. This diagram comes from an early edition of Aristotle's *De caelo* and typifies the cosmology deriving from the Aristotelian and Ptolemaic tradition. Surrounding the spheres of the four elements are seven planetary spheres, one for each of the seven planets. The outermost sphere is the "fir-

Fig. 27. *The geocentric universe according to Sacrobosco.*

mament or heaven of fixed stars," divided into twelve segments to represent the zodiac and presumably bounded in turn by the primum mobile.

Diagrams of a geocentric universe are legion in the renaissance and testify to a widely accepted convention. **Figure 27** purveys the usual information, and is in fact noteworthy only because it comes from an early edition of Sacrobosco's commonly used textbook — in this instance, an edition prepared by the energetic French humanist Jacques LeFèvre d'Etaples at the turn of the sixteenth century. Again, we have four spheres representing the elements in the center, then seven spheres for the planets, next the sphere of fixed stars indicated by the

twelve signs of the zodiac, and finally the primum mobile. This diagram or derivatives of it appeared in countless editions of Sacrobosco's *De sphaera.*

Figure 28 is another example of the geocentric universe, this one taken from the oft-reprinted *Cosmographicus liber* of Peter Apian. It represents the best thought of a theoretical cosmographer in the early sixteenth century. The sublunary realm can be easily discerned, and the sphere of each element is indicated by a familiar convention. The seven planetary spheres are numbered, and each has the appropriate astronomical symbol for its planet as well as a label — the "heaven" (coelum) of the Moon or of Mercury or of Venus. The "eighth

Fig. 28. *The geocentric universe according to Apian.*

heaven" is labeled "the firmament," and the symbols for the signs of the zodiac (proceeding counterclockwise) as well as numerous stars show that this is the sphere of fixed stars. The "ninth heaven" is the "cristalline" sphere, a transparent orb that nonetheless reflects the signs of the zodiac. Two special markers indicate the vernal equinox at the beginning of Aries and the autumnal equinox at the beginning of Libra. The "tenth heaven" is the primum mobile, the boundary of our finite universe; and outside that double line lie the "empyreal heavens, the habitation of God and all the Saints."

Figure 29 suggests just how commonplace the geocentric diagram had become by mid-sixteenth century. It appears in a wholly practical

handbook for sailors, Martin Cortes' *Arte o, navigation,* as Richard Eden translated it for English seamen in 1561.[79] The dependence of this diagram upon figure 28 is unmistakable, though information about the planets is sophisticated in various ways: by assigning two qualities to each, by designating each as benevolent or malevolent, and by associating each with a metal. This additional lore about the planets had been tabulated by Oronce Finé, the eminent French cosmographer.[80]

Finé had also championed a variant of the Ptolemaic system which disposed of the ninth and tenth spheres, thereby reducing the number of spheres to eight. Early in his career Finé had edited a treatise by Agostino Ricchi entitled *De motu octavae sphaerae, opus mathe-*

38

matica atque philosophia plenum (Paris, 1521), in which Ricchi denies the existence of any sphere that does not contain visible bodies — i.e., the cristalline sphere and the primum mobile. This argument lops off everything beyond the sphere of fixed stars, and then that delimiting boundary necessarily assumes the function of the primum mobile to produce a diurnal rotation of the heavens. **Figure 30**, which appears in Finé's *Protomathesis*, presents a diagram to illustrate the result. After Ricchi and Finé, many scientists inclining toward empiricism, such as Robert Recorde,[81] rejected the notion of spheres they could not see and propounded systems that contained only eight. Even before Copernicus there were revisions of the traditional arrangement of ten geocentric spheres.

So far we have considered the universe from the vantage point of our position on Earth. We have viewed the universe as a complex of concentric spheres surrounding our own stationary residence. But the geocentric system can also be viewed from the outside looking in — or rather, the Earth can be reduced to a point at the center of the universe, and the relationship between that point and the Sun as it revolves about the Earth can be projected outward as a pattern on a hypothetical celestial sphere. The result is **Figure 31**, taken from one of the earliest editions of Sacrobosco, the most frequently consulted authority on "the sphere of the world," as the banner at the bottom labels the diagram.

What we see in figure 31 was known as an "armillary" sphere, from L. *armilla*, meaning "bracelet" or "hoop." It was constructed of metal rings which represented in skeletal form the essential features of the Ptolemaic system. Later when this system was threatened by Copernicans, the armillary sphere became the distinctive instrument used in explanation and defense of it. At the center is a black ball representing the Earth, and an axis or "pole" extends vertically through it, touching the *sphaera mundi* on top at the *Polus Arcticus*

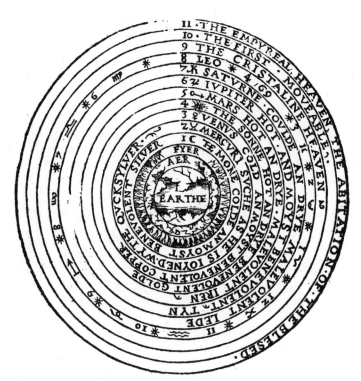

Fig. 29. *The geocentric universe according to Martin Cortes.*

Fig. 30. *The geocentric universe of only eight spheres according to Finé.*

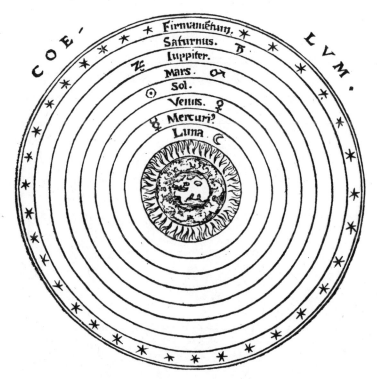

39

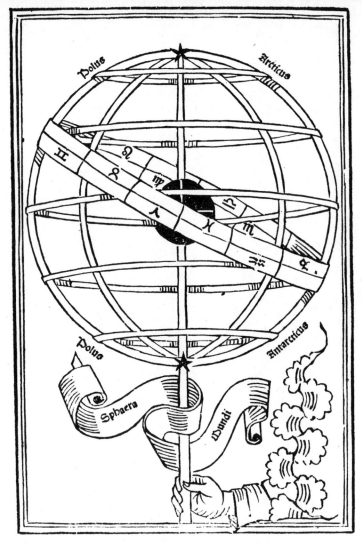

Fig. 31. *The armillary sphere from Sacrobosco.*

and on bottom at the *Polus Antarcticus*.[82] In this system the Sun, of course, travels around the Earth, and its oblique path, called "the ecliptic,"[83] is marked by the zodiac,[84] appropriately divided into the conventional twelve signs. The equator of the sphere provides one great circle; and two other great circles, known as "colures,"[85] are at right angles to the equator and at right angles to one another. As we shall see, the colures mark the two equinoxes and the two solstices. The northernmost position of the Sun on the zodiac designates a smaller circle known as the Tropic of Cancer, and the southernmost position of the Sun designates a second smaller circle known as the Tropic of Capricorn.[86] There are also two still smaller circles parallel to the equator and the two Tropics, one near the Arctic Pole and another near the Antarctic Pole. The Arctic Circle is defined as a boundary for all those stars that in our hemisphere never set (such as the North Star),[87] and the Antarctic Circle as a boundary for all those stars that never rise in our hemisphere. At the bottom of the illustration the hand of God stretches from a cloud to hold this armillary sphere, offering reassurance of His continuing providence. This diagram was the standard illustration of Sacrobosco's sphere in printed books.

Figure 32 depicts the sphere of Proclus, the other prominent authority on the subject. Proclus was a late classical neoplatonist who enjoyed renewed popularity in the renaissance. His treatise *De sphaera* was translated into Latin by Thomas Linacre late in the fifteenth century, and thereby made readily available to schoolboys. Figure 32 is the title page of the Greek text printed by Jacques Bogard in Paris, 1547, to accompany an edition of Linacre's translation printed at the same time and with the same woodcut on the title page. It displays an armillary sphere comparable to figure 31. But a sun and moon shine at the top of this diagram, a repeated motif in this period, as we have seen, to emphasize time.

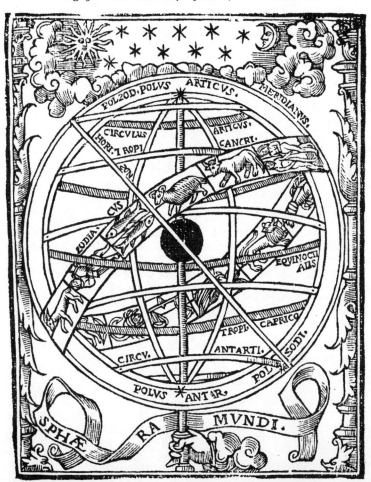

Fig. 32. *The armillary sphere from Proclus.*

Often an armillary sphere was suspended in a mounting to produce a celestial (as opposed to terrestrial) globe such as that in **Figure 33**, taken from Apian's *Cosmographicus liber*. There the regular features of the armillary sphere are easily recognizable despite the clutter of labels and numbers. The Earth appears in the middle as a terrestrial globe with land masses among the seas and its own equator marked off in degrees. It is tilted on its pole, though, so that the *axis mundi* points to the North Star. In this position the "horizon,"[88] the line that divides the globe in equal halves, is in a horizontal position with "south" on the left and "north" on the right. The "Arctic Pole" and the "Antarctic Pole" are labeled, as is the "Equator." The two colures are similarly designated: the "equinoctial colure," which passes through the two equinoctial points, and the "solsticial colure," which passes through the two solstices. Furthermore, there are rings for the Tropic of Cancer and the Tropic of Capricorn, and for the smaller Arctic Circle and Antarctic Circle. The zodiac is depicted in elaborate form: degrees are marked off (30 degrees for each sign) and each sign is labeled. Moreover, an "axis of the zodiac" is indicated,[89] and also a "zenith" (the high point of the Sun) and a "nadir" (the low point of the Sun). All this mechanism is placed within a circle calibrated in degrees to permit angular measurement and labeled "the moveable meridian,"[90] and it rests above a fixed base line labeled "the meridian line." Displayed for our view is the celestial globe in all its detail, the macrocosm made momentarily static.[91]

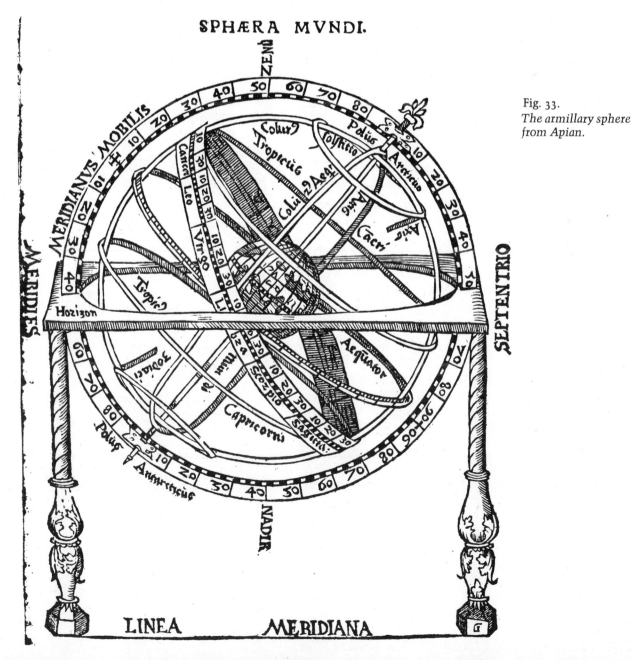

Fig. 33.
The armillary sphere from Apian.

It was traditional from the most ancient of times to divide the Earth into five climatic "zones,"[92] determined by the five circles that run in parallel courses about the armillary sphere. Above the Arctic Circle and below the Antarctic Circle were two frigid zones; between the Arctic Circle and the Tropic of Cancer, and between the Antarctic Circle and the Tropic of Capricorn, were two temperate zones; and between the Tropic of Cancer and the Tropic of Capricorn was a torrid zone which lay in equal parts on each side of the Equator.[93] Plutarch attributed the designation of these climatic zones to Pythagoras,[94] and many classical authors discussed them.[95] Vergil offered a graphic description of the *quinque zonae* (*Georgica*, I.231-39), and Ovid gave them salient notice in his account of creation (*Metamorphoses*, I.45-51).

The *locus classicus* for their description, however — at least their scientific description — was the *Commentarius in somnium Scipionis* by Macrobius (II.v.1-17). **Figure 34** comes from an early sixteenth-century edition of Macrobius, though similar diagrams can be found in most editions of his *Commentarius* since printing began. The text is complete in detail:

> The earth . . . is divided into regions of excessive cold or heat, with two temperate zones between the hot and cold regions. The northern and southern extremities are frozen with perpetual cold, two belts, so to speak, that go around the earth but are small since they encircle the extremities. Neither zone affords habitation, for their icy torpor withholds life from animals and vegetation; animal life thrives upon the same climate that sustains plant life. The belt in the middle and consequently the greatest, scorched by an incessant blast of heat, occupies an area more extensive in breadth and circumference, and is uninhabited because of the raging heat. Between the extremities and the middle zone lie two belts which are greater than those at the poles and smaller than the one in the middle, tempered by the

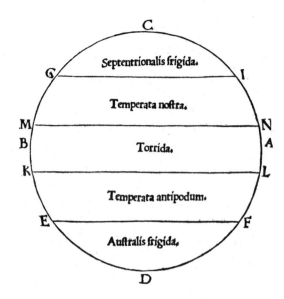

Fig. 34. *The five climatic zones according to Macrobius.*

> extremes of the adjoining belts; in these alone has nature permitted the human race to exist.[96]

Expatiating upon Cicero's text, Macrobius gives a lively picture of which zones are habitable and which are not, and then he offers explicit directions for constructing the climatic zones on a sphere. Sacrobosco repeats much of this information as a conclusion for his second chapter.

The movement of the Sun determined the location of the Tropic of Cancer and the Tropic of Capricorn, and furthermore it produced the changing seasons as it sped in its annual course, crossing and recrossing the equator. Sacrobosco's treatise on the sphere is largely a discourse of these phenomena, as **Figure 35** reveals. There we have the annual movement of the Sun plotted on a plane surface rather than a sphere. It moves from left to right in a sine curve, starting from a position on the equator at the beginning of the natural (as opposed to the Christian) year and returning to its initial point at the end of twelve months. Thus the zodiac is perfected. The northernmost position of the Sun defines the Tropic of

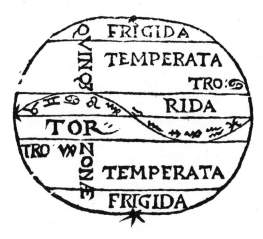

Fig. 35. *The five climatic zones plus the zodiac according to Sacrobosco.*

Cancer and its southernmost position defines the Tropic of Capricorn. When the Sun crosses the equator in its northward movement—that is, at the extreme left of the diagram—the daytime is equal to the night, and hence this occasion is called an "equinox." This marks the beginning of spring, and consequently is the "vernal" equinox. This was the new-year day in the pagan calendar. When the Sun reaches its northernmost position—that is, touches the Tropic of Cancer—the day is the longest of the year, and hence this occasion is called a "solstice," since the Sun seems to stand still.[97] The solstice in June is the summer solstice. When the Sun recrosses the equator going southward, the autumnal equinox occurs, and of course there is a winter solstice when the Sun touches the Tropic of Capricorn at its southernmost position in December. In figure 35 the climatic zones are also labeled.

The same information about the seasons is displayed in **Figure 36**, where their relation to the zodiac is even more clearly manifest. In this illustration from Cuningham's *Cosmographical glasse*, the new year begins at the mid-point of the equator ("Th'equinoctial"), when the Sun crosses the equator going northward. This is the vernal equinox, when the Sun enters the sign of Aries. It proceeds to the

right through the signs of Taurus and Gemini, and reaches the summer solstice as it enters the sign of Cancer. It continues through Leo and Virgo, and crosses the equator again at the autumnal equinox—which necessitates picking up again at the far left of the diagram with the sign of Libra. The Sun passes through Scorpio and Sagittarius, reaches the winter solstice as it enters the sign of Capricorn, and completes its course by traversing Aquarius and Pisces. In this fashion the Sun determines the four seasons that prevail in the macrocosm. Moreover, in their variety and plenitude the seasons represent a four-in-one microcosm in their own right (see figures 65-68). The fact that each of the four seasons is distinct, and yet interdependent with the others, is underlined by the four cardinal winds that blow from the corners of the diagram. They bring to bear the concept of the cosmic tetrad, as we shall see.[98] At this point, however, we can perhaps do no more than note that Subsolanus, the southeast wind, is depicted as a death's head because the pestilential plague was thought to come with his warm, moist breath.

We should also note an error in the labels for the four cardinal directions in this diagram. "East" and "West" should be trans-

Fig. 36. *The climatic zones plus the zodiac according to Cuningham.*

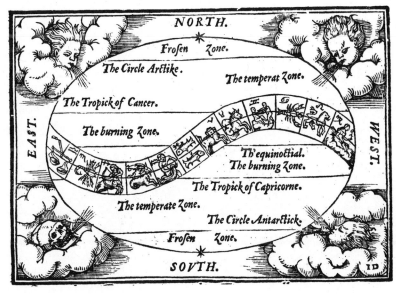

43

posed; "West" should be at the left and "East" at the right. John Day, the printer for *The cosmographical glasse*, was also the designer for this woodblock, as his initials in the lower right corner indicate. He knew that the Sun travels from east to west in its *daily* journey, and apparently in the confusion of this fact he erroneously assumed that the Sun travels from east to west in its *annual* journey. But of course in the Ptolemaic system the Sun goes from west to east in its progress through the zodiac. Recorde summarizes the appropriate principles with admirable succinctness:

> The heavens do move continually from the easte to the west, and that motion is called, The dayly motion: and is the measure of the Common day. . . . The Son also hath a peculier motion from the west toward the easte, whiche he accomplisheth in a yeare, and of that course the yeare taketh his measure and quantitye.[99]

The modern reader trying to accommodate himself to a geocentric universe can no doubt sympathize with John Day's error. We shall pay more attention to this point in our discussion of figure 83.

The orthodox world-view in the renaissance, then, consisted in a finite universe set apart from the infinite empyrean. At its center were the four elements, comprising our stationary residence, surrounded by celestial spheres that carried the seven planets. The fixed stars were imbedded in the underside of yet another celestial sphere and were grouped to form the well-known constellations, including the signs of the zodiac. The Sun in its sinuous annual journey determined five climatic zones, only two of which were habitable, and controlled the changing seasons in a prescribed pattern. Surrounding the whole and giving it definition was the primum mobile, which maintained its sphericity and imparted regular motion. In this system, our Earth stood still while the heavens made a complete revolution from east to west every twenty-four hours. There was no doubting that the Earth is still and the Sun moves about it. Our senses attest to this fact.

III Copernicus and His Consequences

HE GEOCENTRIC SYSTEM gives the appearance of neatness and accounts readily for the casually observed phenomena in the world around us. Nonetheless, it proved unwieldy to the professional astronomer. His job was to chart the actual movement of the planets, rather than construct a perfect model of the universe; and often, in order to provide information required by astrologers and physicians, he was obliged to predict the planets' positions at a given moment. Moreover, the practicing astronomer was aware of data accumulated from centuries of observations. These empirical data made it clear that when the Earth is taken as the fixed point of reference for plotting the movements of the planets, their courses are anything but simple. They do not move at constant speed, and retrograde motion must be accounted for as well as forward motion. Rather than being outrightly circular, as figures 26-30 suggest, the orbits of the planets when plotted against the Earth are convoluted configurations that are recurrent, and therefore predictable, but outrageously cumbersome. The Ptolemaic system when put into practice depended upon a complicated geometry of deferents and epicycles and equants.

In order to clarify the mathematics of the Ptolemaic system, profesional astronomers in the mid-fifteenth century began to subject it to intensive review. Prominent among those who worked for improved exactness and greater ease in computation were Georg Peurbach, a professor of mathematics at the university of Vienna, and Johannes Regiomontanus (i.e., Johann Müller of Konigsberg), Peurbach's pupil and later a much respected mathematical practitioner among the affluent burghers of Nuremberg. Regiomontanus established his own printing house there and brought out a series of almanacs as well as Peurbach's major work, *Theoricae planetarum novae* (c. 1474). This textbook was a massive effort to bring Ptolemy up to date. It sought to explain the geocentric universe in terms of mathematics that was becoming increasingly sophisticated.

Nicolaus Copernicus, today highly touted as the father of heliocentrism, represents the culmination of this thrust to revise Ptolemaic astronomy. He should be seen, however, not as a radical innovator, one who struck out boldly in new directions, but rather as one who worked modestly and self-consciously within the established tradition. Copernicus' aim was to render plain what had become unmanageably clumsy in applied astronomy, and to reinstate a world-view that emphasized simplicity and wholeness. He wished to recognize as a primal force an inherent tendency in nature toward coherence and order—what he called "a certain natural appetency implanted in the parts by the divine providence of the

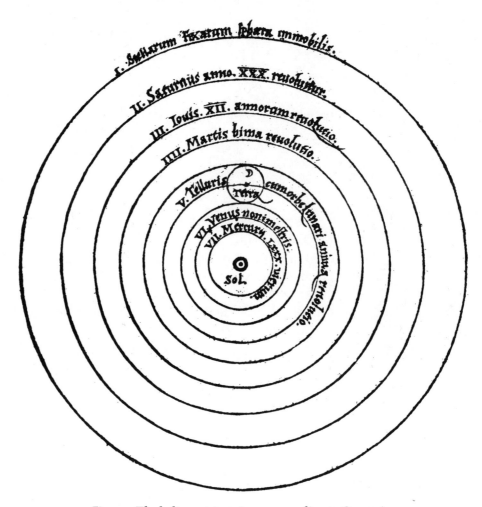

Fig. 37. *The heliocentric universe according to Copernicus.*

universal Artisan, in order that they should unite with one another in their oneness and wholeness and come together in the form of a globe."[100]

No renaissance platonist could have stated the basic thesis of Timaean cosmology with greater fidelity. There is no doubt of Copernicus' deference to the traditional astronomy, a deference that stemmed not so much from fear of punishment by ecclesiastical authorities as from his own firm commitment to the revered principles of cosmos. In the *De revolutionibus orbium coelestium*, written in Frauenburg at a safe distance from controversy, Copernicus demonstrates his orthodoxy in a number of ways. First, in the dedicatory epistle to Pope Paul III he eagerly acknowledges his recourse to authorities, especially the pythagoreans who had proposed a central Sun with the Earth moving about it ([*]3ᵛ-[*]4). He also begins with the fundamental premise that the world is spherical, and bases his subsequent hypotheses upon this initial assumption.[101] Furthermore, he accepts as a donné that the courses of the heavenly bodies are circular or compounded of circular motions, and are therefore regular (a2ᵛ-a3). Finally, he never casts doubt upon the Ptolemaic assumption that the world is finite, bounded by a sphere of fixed stars (c1).

At the risk of verging upon the facetious, we might say that Copernicus did no more than a bit of tinkering with the existing world-view. At most he made a minor adjustment in the Ptolemaic system, which had held sway for two millenia. Copernicus merely made the

Sun the center of the system instead of the Earth, and this done for the conservative reason of returning the universe to a state of mathematical simplicity. But he retained the sphericity and the regularity and the finiteness of the orthodox cosmology.

The conservatism of Copernicus is immediately evident when we compare his diagram of the universe with figure 26, a diagram from a text of Aristotle's *De caelo* printed for use in the schools. Copernicus' diagram, **Figure 37**, is manifestly at pains to reflect the tradition. And in his description of the diagram, Copernicus begins with the outermost sphere, the sphere of fixed stars, to emphasize the finiteness of his system:

> The first and highest of all is the sphere of the fixed stars, which comprehends itself and all things, and is accordingly immovable. In fact it is the place of the universe, *i.e.*, it is that to which the movement and position of all the other stars are referred. . . . Saturn, the first of the wandering stars follows; it completes its circuit in 30 years. After it comes Jupiter moving in a 12-year period of revolution. Then Mars, which completes a revolution every 2 years. The place fourth in order is occupied by the annual revolution in which we said the Earth together with the orbital circle of the moon as an epicycle is comprehended. In the fifth place, Venus, which completes its revolution in 7½ months. The sixth and final place is occupied by Mercury, which completes its revolution in a period of 88 days. In the center of all rests the sun.[102]

This diagram repeats figure 26 except for one detail: the Sun is placed at the center, and the Earth with the Moon revolving about it is placed between Venus and Mars. Thereby the orbit of the Moon is made an epicycle; but the orbits of the other planets, which heretofore had been described only by the use of intricate epicycles and eccentrics, are returned to simple circularity.[103]

The distance between the ambience of Co-

pernicus and the scientism of modern heliocentrism is enormous, and the differences are far more significant than the similarities. For example, as a continuation of the passage quoted in the paragraph above, Copernicus offers his reason for placing the sun in the middle of the universe. Characteristically, he makes his statement in the form of a rhetorical question: "For who would place this lamp of a very beautiful temple in another or better place than this wherefrom it can illuminate everything at the same time?" The argument in this passage proceeds from the premise of cosmos, that the universe is beautiful and ordered, and from the dogma that the sphere is the perfect solid because all points on its surface are equidistant from its center. No support is offered from the actual observation of phenomena, and the indifference to empirical data is not an oversight. Copernicus consolidates his assertion by citing a string of well-known epithets for the sun:

> As a matter of fact, not unhappily do some call it the lantern; others, the mind and still others, the pilot of the world. Trismegistus calls it a "visible god"; Sophocles' Electra, "that which gazes upon all things." And so the sun, as if resting on a kingly throne, governs the family of stars which wheel around.[104]

This does not sound like someone who might change the course of intellectual history. Copernicus is looking backward, not forward. He is reflecting the age-old beliefs of the pythagorean-platonic tradition as it had often formulated itself in sun worship.

Of course, Copernicus did put forward proposals that had far-reaching effects in the work of later scientists. As a result of placing the sun at the center of the universe, he necessarily assigned motion to the earth as it revolved around the sun. This was an annual revolution of the earth. He also assigned to earth a diurnal rotation about its own axis, and this was a proposal of prime importance. If the earth spun around every twenty-four hours, then the heavens could cease their turning. Copernicus stopped the celestial spheres from their whirling about in daily circuit, and thereby prepared for new coordinates of astronomical calculation.

But Copernicus himself thought in terms of simplifying the old, not in terms of introducing the new. And the real break with Ptolemaic astronomy did not come until the ancient concept of cosmos was discarded — until the pythagorean dislike of the limitless was laid aside and the universe was proclaimed to be infinite. Kepler still actively propounded a mathematically ordered (and therefore limited) universe and circumscribed it within a clearly defined sphere, as we shall see. Galileo never publicly engaged with the question of whether our world is infinite.[105] In any case, the so-called Copernican revolution would have been anathema to the modest canon of Frauenburg Cathedral, and in any practical sense was delayed until the late seventeenth century, when Newton made it possible to explain the movements of the planets in terms of celestial mechanics. Only then did description of the universe break out of its sanctified mold of cosmos.

Certainly Copernicus was not seen by his contemporaries and immediate followers as a revolutionary, or even an adventurous innovator. They saw him more in the role of revivalist, as one who had resurrected and reasserted an ancient world-view first proposed by certain pythagoreans. Copernicus himself gave evidence toward this conclusion in his dedicatory epistle to Pope Paul III.[106] For Kepler, writing a foreword to the reader of his *Mysterium cosmographicum*, Copernicus was in direct line from Pythagoras — in the same mathematical tradition, though perhaps "a better observer of the universe."[107] For Galileo addressing the reader of his *Dialogo . . . sopra i due massimi sistemi del mondo*, Copernicus had expounded "the Pythagorean opinion of the mobility of the Earth."[108] It was the gradually solidifying opinion of reactionaries that eventually denounced a theory of terrestrial

motion and drove Copernicus from the ranks of conservative thought. Increasing religious and intellectual orthodoxy in certain circles in time forced the adherents of Copernicanism to become more and more separatist. But only in retrospect does Copernicus assume the role of an intellectual radical.

Nonetheless, Copernicus' work was rapidly recognized as an important hypothesis that offered a viable alternative to Ptolemaic geocentrism. It was, in fact, largely the interest of Georg Joachim Rheticus, a young astronomer from the university of Wittenberg, that brought the *De revolutionibus orbium coelestium* into print. And after 1543, the date of its publication, it received immediate and widespread recognition. Already in 1556 Robert Recorde was referring to it in England,[109] and the intrepid John Dee went so far as to be its advocate.[110]

The strongest advocate of Copernicanism in England was Thomas Digges, the talented son of Leonard Digges, one of the most respected mathematical practitioners in mid-sixteenth-century London. Since 1553, Leonard Digges had issued successive editions of a practical handbook of astrological lore entitled *A prognostication everlastinge of righte good effecte*. To the 1576 edition of his father's perennial almanac, and to the several subsequent editions, Thomas appended a lengthy exposition of the Copernican hypothesis, which he entitled rather aggressively: "A perfit description of the cælestiall orbes according to the most aunciente doctrine of the *Pythagoreans*, latelye revived by *Copernicus* and by geometricall demonstrations approved" (N1).

As a prologue to this treatise, the first extended treatment of terrestrial mobility in English, Thomas Digges offered some comments to clarify his circumstance. He begins by recognizing the wide acceptance of the Ptolemaic system, which was taught in all universities in accordance with the authority of Aristotle. But soon he turns to Copernicus, a "rare witte" who has recently proposed that "the Earth resteth not in the Center of the whole world, but . . . is caried yearely rounde about the Sunne" (M1). Digges then, echoing the very words of Copernicus, proceeds to extoll the sun: "which like a king in the middest of all raigneth and geeveth lawes of motion to the rest, sphærically dispearsing his glorious beames of light through al this sacred Cœlestiall Temple." Moreover, in addition to the annual motion of the earth, there is a daily motion, with the earth "tourning everye 24. houres rounde upon his owne Center." This hypothesis, Digges contends, has been proved by Copernicus, "with demonstrations Mathematicall most apparantly by him to the world delivered." Finally, with extraordinary audacity, Digges maintains that Copernicus intended for his proposal to be taken as an actual description of the physical arrangement of our universe, not merely as an abstract mathematical theorem as some had suggested:

> I thought it convenient together with the olde Theorick [of Ptolemy] also to publishe this, to the ende such noble English minds (as delight to reach above the baser sort of men) might not be altogether defrauded of so noble a part of Philosophy. And to the ende it might manifestly appeare that *Copernicus* mente not as some have fondly excused him to deliver these grounds of the Earthes mobility onely as Mathematicall principles, fayned & not as Philosophicall truly averred. (M1)[111]

Digges is taking the heliocentric system out of the insubstantial realm of theoretical geometry and asking that we make it our physical reality.

The whole-hearted commitment of Thomas Digges to Copernicanism is boldly asserted in **Figure 38**, a diagram of the universe which he placed as an extra-size foldout before the "Perfit description of the cælestiall orbes" appended to his father's perennial almanac. There we see the sun shining resplendently in the center of the diagram, the fixed point about which the earth and planets move. First among the celestial spheres is "the orbe of Mercury" with a period of revolution of 80 days. Next comes "the orbe of Venus," and it "rouleth round in 9 monethes." And then comes an orb for the earth, which is notably larger than the others because the moon travels around it in an epicyclic pattern with the sun as its center. The globe representing the earth is depicted in detail with each of the four elements included, and a label identifies its orb in terms recalling the mutability that characterizes it: "the great orbe carreinge this globe of mortalitye." The revolution of the earth—its "circular periode"—of course determines our year. Then follows in the usual sequence a sphere for each of the remaining three planets: "the orbe of Mars makinge his revolution in 2 yeares," "the orbe of Jupiter makinge his periode in 12 yeares," and "the orbe of Saturne makinge his revolution in 30 yeares."

The salient feature of Digges' diagram, however, is his treatment of the sphere of fixed stars. He recognizes this component of the traditional cosmology, but gives it a most daring interpretation. In the Ptolemaic system the fixed stars were placed on the underside of a single celestial sphere, so that all of them were equidistant from the center of the universe. Digges, however, without precedent for such an innovation, removes the limit of a single sphere for the fixed stars. Instead, he proposes that the region of stars extends outward to infinity, and he illustrates this proposition by placing a large number of stars randomly in space beyond the boundary of the planetary orbs.

Digges came to a conclusion about the infiniteness of the heavens as a result of his belief in the earth's mobility. In his text, which is largely a redaction of Copernicus,[112] he reviews the arguments that aristotelians had made for thinking the earth rests immobile in the center of the heavenly spheres (N4-O3). In the aristotelian arrangement of the elements, earth is absolutely heavy and naturally moves toward the center, so that our earth is central

A perfit description of the Cælestiall Orbes,

according to the most auncient doctrine of the
Pythagoreans. &c.

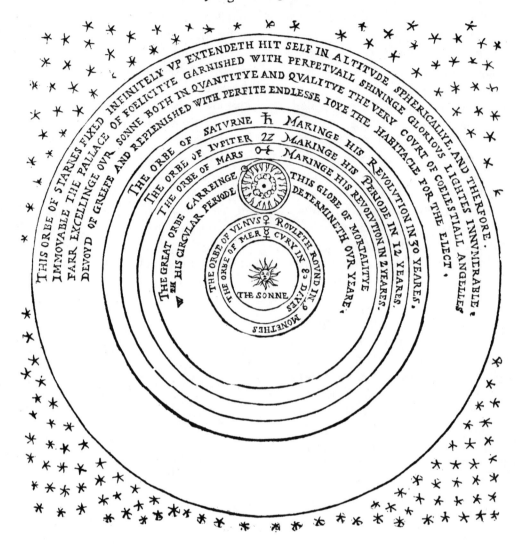

Fig. 38. *The heliocentric universe according to Thomas Digges.*

and fixed by virtue of its inherent heaviness. In such a system the heavens must be finite because they are the components in motion, and that which is infinite cannot move. When the earth is made the component of the system that moves in daily rotation, however—as it does in Copernicus' system—then the heavens stand still, and the heavens can be allowed to become infinite. The primum mobile is no longer necessary to provide motion from an extraneous source, and consequently it is discarded. With the removal of the primum mobile also goes the rigid demarcation between a finite cosmos and an empyrean representing a different and discontinuous order of being. The result is a system like Digges', with an outer sphere that defies confinement and consequently defies regular measured motion. As

50

the label on Digges' diagram announces: "This orbe of starres fixed infinitely up extendeth hit selfe in altitude sphericallye, and therfore [is] immovable."

Digges' argument is basically scientific and doubtless his prime concern is to confirm the hypothesis of Copernicus. He concludes his treatise, in fact, with a confident *probatum est*: "So if it bee Mathematically considered and wyth Geometricall Mensurations every part of every *Theoricke* examined: the discreet Student shall fynde that *Copernicus* not without great reason did propone this grounde of the Earthes Mobility" (O3). Nonetheless, there is another factor in his argument that we should note. Digges is working toward a premise that incorporates the abode of deity into the physical structure of the universe. In the orthodox pythagorean-platonic cosmology, with its unremitting dichotomy between the sense-perceptible world and an empyrean that does not submit to observation, the godhead was placed in a category beyond human knowledge, and at best we can infer his attributes by studying his creation, nature. In the aristotelian adaptation of that system, the deity was denied a suitable habitat: the heavens, though composed of the ethereal quintessence, were nevertheless finite and constantly moving. To Digges' mind, it is more appropriate to place God in an infinite and unmoving heaven. No other habitat suitably accords with His attributes of omnipotence and steadfastness. With a religious fervor, therefore, Digges continues his label for the outermost sphere of his diagram:

... the pallace of foelicitye garnished with perpetuall shininge glorious lightes innumerable, farr excellinge our sonne both in quantitye and qualitye the very court of coelestiall angelles devoyd of greefe and replenished with perfite endlesse joye. . . .

Digges is thankful for the insight that led him to this discovery, and with uplifted spirit he reports upon this divine mystery. With more than a tinge of Calvinism, he concludes his praise of the starry heavens with the most approbative of epithets: "the habitacle for the elect." But what Digges has done, of course, is to incorporate the blessed seat of divinity— "the very court of coelestiall angelles . . . [and] the habitacle for the elect"—into a physical system dependent upon mathematical laws. He has conflated the infinite and the finite into a single continuum. He did not foresee that such naïveté would soon bring into conflict the scientists and the theologians.

The renaissance man who for us has come to symbolize the innocent victim in the life-and-death struggle between religion and science is Galileo Galilei. His fearless assertion of scientific discoveries and the resultant persecution by the Church have been legendized. His courage and wisdom as well as his sufferings are well known. The facts are somewhat different from the legend, but that is another matter. What concerns us here is Galileo's crucial role in gaining acceptance for the Copernican theory.

With some justification Galileo may be seen as the first thoroughgoing man of science who worked through his discoveries and hypotheses to arrive at a comprehensive world-view that we recognize as our own. He was an empiricist, reliant upon observation and experiment, and the subject of his inquiry was the measurable world about us. He sought to quantify and reduce to mathematical laws what had heretofore been explained largely by authority and logic. He showed no restrictive deference to the orthodox cosmology, as did Copernicus. He had no mystical inclinations, as did Kepler. Unlike Tycho, he was not induced to compromise in the face of political and theological pressures. His aim was to reveal truth by the scientific method, and to make knowledge available and understandable to all.

For Galileo the truth of the Copernican theory as physical reality became increasingly self-evident, and the major effort of his mature years was to establish this conviction as an ac-

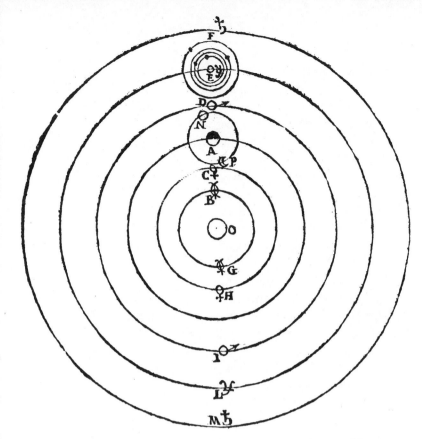

Fig. 39. *The Copernican system from Galileo.*

cepted premise not only in the laboratories of science, but in educated circles everywhere. To this end, he worked for decades on a carefully reasoned defense of the heliocentric system, what eventually he published in 1632 as the *Dialogo . . . sopra i due massimi sistemi del mondo tolemaico, e copernicano.* Galileo presented his opinions in the form of such a dialogue for several reasons. First, the new is often best delineated by contrasting it with the old, and Copernicanism is most clearly defined by pointing to its departures from Ptolemaic astronomy. Second, Galileo had cause to fear indictment by ecclesiastical authorities, and a dialogue allowed some pretense of offering a balanced argument, of presenting alternatives between which the reader can make his choice. Finally, the dialogue form gave opportunity for Galileo to display his considerable literary talent, and consequently to reach the largest number of his educated contemporaries. The *Dialogo* is a masterpiece on any terms: rhetorical, scientific, or literary. It is

both informative and entertaining—urbane, artful, lively—the platonic dialogue in modern dress.

Already in the 1590s Galileo had accepted the Copernican hypothesis, a conclusion that he communicated to his distant colleague, Kepler, in 1597. Subsequent discoveries unalterably confirmed this early belief. When Galileo looked through his telescope in 1609, he could see that the surface of the moon is mountainous, not perfectly spherical, making the moon very much like our earth; and he could see four satellites revolving about Jupiter. These observed data render untenable the Ptolemaic assumptions about the unique quintessence that comprises the heavens, and they demonstrate that some point other than the earth can be the center of circular motion in our universe. Next year the discovery of spots on the sun contributed to rejecting the aristotelian distinction between a corruptible earth and the unchanging heavens. The observation that Venus went through phases similar to those of the moon also fitted with a heliocentric system. Everything pointed to the validity of Copernicus' theory, and Galileo was eager to propound it.

The *Dialogo* proceeds, in mock-platonic fashion, through four successive days, and involves three speakers: Filippo Salviati, a young friend of Galileo from Florence and an avowed Copernican; Giovanni Francesco Sagredo, a Venetian gentleman who professes neutrality but usually supports Salviati; and Simplicio, a fictional character with allegiance to the debased aristotelianism then taught in the schools. In the brief preface Galileo explains with a straight face that "Simplicio" comes from Simplicius, a well-known commentator on Aristotle—thereby demonstrating the sort of double-edged foolery that runs through most of the work. The argument itself, though, is serious, and only a simpleton more simple than Simplicio could miss Galileo's point. The earth and the heavens are bound together in one physical continuum, as Thomas Digges had argued; and the sun, not the earth, is the center of its motion.

The high point of the *Dialogo* comes on the third day when Salviati undertakes to demonstrate the annual motion of the earth about the sun. As so often in the conversation, Salviati sounds like a patient schoolmaster and Simplicio becomes an accomplice in his own refutation. Simplicio complains of difficulty in understanding such a complex configuration, so Salviati suggests that he take a sheet of paper and a pair of compasses, and they go through the construction of a diagram step by step. The result is **Figure 39**. Simplicio begins with A to represent the terrestrial globe, and O to represent the sun. Then according to Simplicio's drawing—at Salviati's prompting—the circle CH about the sun represents the orbit of Venus, and the circle BG represents the orbit of Mercury. Next Simplicio draws a circle DI to represent the orbit of Mars, and then follow two circles, EL and FM, to represent the orbits of Jupiter and Saturn, respectively. Simplicio, now with very little help from Salviati, includes an orbit for the moon about the earth, the circle NP; and though not mentioned in the text, the four satellites of Jupiter also appear in orbit about that center of motion. At this moment—with a barely suppressed "Ah, ha!"—Salviati triumphantly proclaims, "We have all this while, Simplicius, disposed the mundane bodies exactly according to the order of Copernicus."[113]

After publication of Galileo's *Dialogo*, the widespread acceptance of a heliocentric system was assured. Salviati's arguments, and the overweening respect for Galileo's scientific achievements, swept away all but the most stubborn opposition. Despite the immediate placement of the *Dialogo* on the index of prohibited books—the Church had earlier prohibited Copernicus' *De revolutionibus orbium coelestium* in 1616—there was no chance of keeping the earth fixed as the hub of a tidy universe. The earth moved, and the mechanical laws that govern its motion became the next concern of astronomers.

It should be noted again, however, that Galileo does not follow the Copernican hypothe-sis to its logical conclusion and advocate an infinite universe. He broaches the subject in a gingerly fashion at the end of the discussion pertaining to figure 39, but ultimately begs the question. After Simplicio has constructed all of the planetary orbits and the orbit for the moon, Salviati asks pointedly:

> Now, Simplicius, what shall we do with the fixed stars? Shall we suppose them scattered through the immense abysses of the Universe, at different distances from one determinate point; or else placed in a surface spherically distended about a centre of its own, so that each of them may be equidistant from the said centre?

This is the question that Thomas Digges had asked himself, and his daring answer is evident in figure 38. He opted for the first alternative and scattered the stars through the immense abyss of space. But Digges was far ahead of his time—ahead, even, of Galileo. For Simplicio replies to Salviati's question with a colossal hedge:

> I would rather take a middle way and would assign them a circle described about a determinate centre and comprised within two spherical surfaces, to wit, one very high and concave, and the other lower, and convex, betwixt which I would constitute the innumerable multitude of stars, but yet at diverse altitudes. (page 339)

Simplicio allows for some variation in the distance of stars from the center of the universe, but not much; all of the stars are compressed between two fixed limits, between two concentric spheres. And there Galileo lets the matter drop. While insisting upon a heliocentric universe, he refuses to argue for its infinitude.

Once Copernicus had posited both a diurnal and an annual motion for the earth, there were others who suggested variations and adaptations of his theory. Most prominent among these was Tycho Brahe, a brilliant though contentious nobleman of Denmark

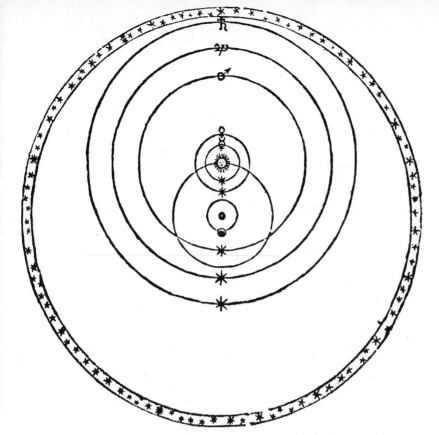

Fig. 40. *The world-system of Tycho Brahe.*

who dominated the science of astronomy for the last few decades of the sixteenth century. Tycho's forte was the manufacture of measuring instruments and the recording of observations. His data were methodical and remarkably accurate, the result of thoughtful planning. His hypothesis about arranging the planets, however, is at best an expedient compromise.

Already in the 1570s Tycho had reason to discredit the aristotelian tenet that the celestial spheres are incorruptible, in contrast to the terrestrial realm of mutable elements. In 1572 he observed a nova in Cassiopeia, and in 1577 a widely discussed comet. Aristotelian physics decreed that such events be confined to the sublunary regions, which are variable. But both the nova and the comet, Tycho concluded after careful calculation, were considerably more distant from the earth than is the moon, and therefore transpired in what had previously been held to be the invariable realm of quintessential ether. Unquestionably the heavens are not immutable, as Aristotle and his followers had insisted.

Tycho inevitably inclined toward the Copernican hypothesis in lieu of the Ptolemaic, because Copernicus had introduced significant simplifications of utmost importance to the practicing astronomer. But there were two objections to the Copernican theory that Tycho could not ignore. First, the earth is manifestly ponderous, palpably heavy and steadfast, and not likely to move either at the speed or with the variety of motions that Copernicus requires. Second, since Tycho could detect no parallax in his observation of the stars, it would appear that the distance between the sphere of Saturn and the stars is enormous, thus leaving a vast and puzzling void in the system.[114] Therefore with doggedness — or should we say industry? — Tycho devised a world-system that accepted as much as possible of Copernicus' hypothesis, but nonetheless took into account these two objections.

Tycho sets forth the principles of his system in a book on the notorious comet of 1577, *De mundi aetherei recentioribus phaenomenis*, printed on his own press at Uraniborg in 1588. This volume reporting on "recent phenomena in the celestial world" was intended as part of a multi-volume series that considered the whole subject of astronomy in the light of recent discoveries. **Figure 40** appears as illustration of the conclusions that Tycho had reached. The earth is stationary in the center with the moon revolving about it. The sun also revolves about the earth in an annual movement, and its orbit is indicated by a circle. The other planets, however, revolve about the sun. Mercury and Venus revolve in orbits whose radii are shorter than the distance between the sun and earth; but the radii of the orbits of Mars, Jupiter, and Saturn are greater than the distance between the sun and earth. The orbit of Mars, in fact, intersects the orbit of the sun at two points, so that there is a possibility of collision. The whole system is firmly enclosed within a traditional sphere of fixed stars, thereby making it unequivocally finite. And since the earth is fixed without any motion of its own, the entire heavens must spin completely

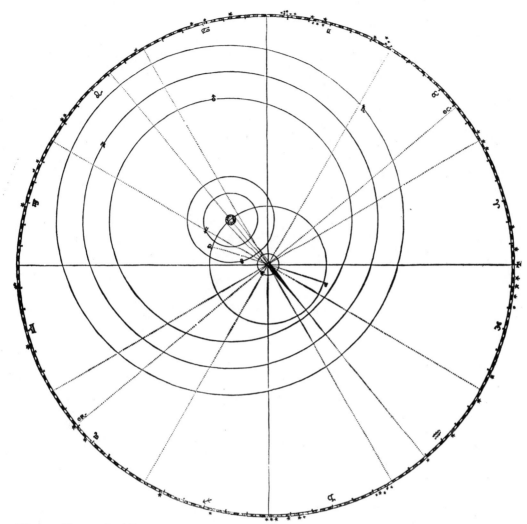

Fig. 41. *The world-system of Reymers.*

around every twenty-four hours to account for
the diurnal changes that we see. While Tycho's
hypothesis may seem a shameless compromise
to us, a falling between two stools, it gained a
large number of adherents in its own day by
dint of its reasonableness and avoidance of
controversy. For many, it replaced the Ptolemaic system as the most formidable rival to
Copernicanism.

A world-system similar to Tycho's was proposed at about the same time by another practicing astronomer Nicolaus Raimarus, or Reymers, also known as Ursus (the Bear).[115] Reymers was a man of low birth who through intelligence and hard work made a name for

himself as a man of learning. He rose to be professor of mathematics in Prague and a protegé
of Emperor Rudolph II, and it required the
combined efforts of Tycho and Kepler to impugn his authority. In 1588 at Strasbourg, Reymers published his remarkably competent
Fundamentum astronomicum, a manual of advanced trigonometry, to which he appended
*Hypotheses novae ac verae motuum corporum
mundanorum* (fol. 37-40ᵛ). In this treatise, dedicated at least in part to John Dee, Reymers sets
forth twenty original *theses astronomicae* and
several annotations that clarify his "new and
true hypotheses concerning the motions of
cosmic bodies" (**Figure 41**). He claims to have
derived his system from an ancient authority,

Apollonius Pergaeus, and he dedicates it to that noble patron of astronomers, Wilhelm IV, Landgrave of Hesse.

According to Reymers, the earth is in the center of the universe, and it rotates diurnally on its own axis to produce night and day. Circling the earth is the moon, whose radius of revolution is quite short, and the sun, whose radius of revolution is considerably longer. The other planets, as in the system of Tycho, then circle around the sun. First come Mercury and Venus, whose radii of revolution are shorter than the distance from the sun to the earth; and next come Mars, Jupiter, and Saturn, whose radii of revolution are greater than twice the distance from the sun to the earth. The entire system is bounded by the familiar sphere of fixed stars, which is divided into twelve equal parts and identified with the zodiac. This outermost circle is also marked off in 360°. In addition, perpendicular lines crossing at the earth indicate the horizon—labeled or[iens] for "east" on the left and oc[cidens] for "west" on the right—when the sun is in its zenith at noon.

One particularly noteworthy feature of this diagram is the outer circle which delimits it. The stars are not imbedded in this sphere— that is, all stars are not equidistant from the earth. Some fall within the circle, and even more fall without. Furthermore, Reymers makes some effort to arrange the stars in constellations appropriate to each sign of the zodiac. Like Thomas Digges (see figure 38), Reymers may be suggesting, however cautiously, that the universe is not firmly bounded by a single sphere of fixed stars. At least in his Thesis XVIII he is willing to entertain the possibility (fol. 38^v).

Regardless of his conclusion about the finitude of the universe, there are two definite and highly significant differences between the system of Reymers and that of Tycho. First, the orbit of Mars is plotted so that it clears the orbit of the sun and does not intersect it, thereby removing the unsettling possibility of col-

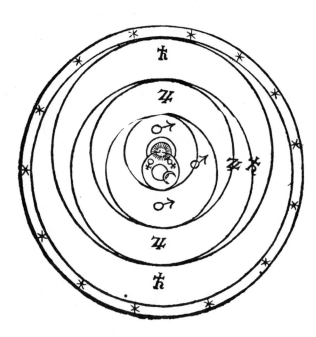

Fig. 42. *The world-system of Röslin.*

lision. Second, and even more important, Reymers argues for the daily rotation of the earth, and consequently does away with the need for the whole celestial apparatus to circle around each twenty-four hours. In this respect, Reymers' system comes closer to that of Copernicus than does the system of Tycho.

Egoist that he was, Tycho was infuriated by the publication of Reymers' hypothesis and determined to destroy its author. Tycho charged Reymers with having pilfered a manuscript while on a visit to Uraniborg in 1584, and Reymers indignantly lodged a counter-charge that Tycho had stolen the idea from him. The two men, the outstanding astronomers of Europe in the 1590s, carried on the acrimonious argument to their dying breaths. When Tycho was joined by Kepler at Prague in 1600, he set his young assistant the odious task of writing a definitive refutation of the hated rival. It is not a happy chapter in the history of astronomy.

Yet another world-system even closer to

Tycho's was put forward by Helisaeus Röslin, a German doctor and sometime astronomer with a mystic bent. His hypothesis (**Figure 42**) was published in the *De opere dei creationis seu de mundo hypotheses* (Frankfurt, 1597), a curious little volume that well illustrates the inextricable fusion of science, religion, and occultism in the renaissance. Röslin places earth in the center of the universe, and like Tycho (but unlike Reymers) he deprives it of all motion, diurnal as well as annual. The moon and the sun revolve around the earth. The other five planets, however, revolve around the sun (though the orbits of Mars, Jupiter, and Saturn in some unexplained way are also conceived as concentric circles centering upon the earth). As in the system of Reymers, the orbit of Mars clears the path of the sun, but just barely. Reymers was utterly scornful of Röslin's hypothesis; and in the *De astronomicis hypothesibus seu systemate mundano tractatus astronomicus et cosmographicus* (Prague, 1597), written when Reymers was at the height of his career, he disparages Tycho as well as Röslin, claiming that Röslin has followed Tycho like one monkey imitating another (C3).

To say the least, by the turn of the seventeenth century there were several alternative world-systems to choose among. Copernicus had been repeated, refined, and respected by many, not least of all by Englishmen. And Galileo was standing in the wings, ready for his entrance as the champion of heliocentrism. Although the Ptolemaic system itself was largely discredited, there were compromises that still preserved its salient features: the immobility of the earth and the delimiting fixity of the outermost sphere. Tycho and Reymers, and even Röslin, had argued their cases persuasively. Kepler just a few years before had published his startling *Mysterium cosmographicum* (Tübingen, 1596), in which he enhances the new mathematics at the same time he confirms the old notion of cosmic harmony by finding the key to the universal structure in the proportions between spheres circumscrib-

ing the five regular solids (see figure 78). This was a harbinger of the curious alliance, yet contretemps, between science and religion that characterizes the early seventeenth century, an interaction between disparate disciplines that produced a mind as mercurially complex as that of Sir Thomas Browne.

For lesser men, however, confusion is an understandable result. And it is confusion that the prosaic Robert Burton professes:

Nicholas Ramerus will have the Earth the Center of the World, but moveable [i.e., rotating on its axis], and the eighth sphere immoveable, the five upper Planets to move about the Sun, the Sun and Moon about the Earth. Of which Orbs, Tycho Brahe puts the Earth the Center immoveable, the stars immoveable, the rest with Ramerus, the Planets without Orbs to wander in the Air, keep time and distance, true motion, according to that virtue which God hath given them.[116] Helisæus Rœslin censureth both, with Copernicus (whose Hypothesis concerning the motion of the earth Philippus Lansbergius[117] hath lately vindicated, and demonstrated with solid arguments in a just volume . . .).[118]

Burton has obviously read widely in the raging debate about whether the earth is a moving or a stationary body. He is remarkably well informed, and continues to ruminate upon the possibilities:

Rœslin(I say) censures all, and Ptolemy himself as unsufficient: one offends against natural Philosophy, another against Optick principles, a third against Mathematical, as not answering to Astronomical observations: one puts a great space betwixt Saturn's Orb and the eighth sphere,[119] another too narrow. In his own hypothesis he [Röslin] makes the Earth as before the universal Center, the Sun to the five upper Planets, to the eighth sphere he ascribes diurnal motion, Eccentricks and Epicycles to the seven Planets, which had been formerly exploded.

Despite his diligence, though, Burton can

come to no conclusion, and his net response is annoyance with the astronomers: "The World is tossed in a blanket amongst them, they hoist the Earth up and down like a ball, make it stand and go at their pleasures."

As a result of this conflict in world-systems —proposals passionately formulated by zealous prophets—it proved necessary to compare one hypothesis with another. It became a frequent practice to line up diagrams of the possibilities, so that a reader could see at a glance the distinguishing features of each, or how many share a particular feature. The Ptolemaic system sits beside the Copernican, which in turn brings forward the Tychonic—and so on, for as many alternatives as the author can muster. The number of such comparative series during the seventeenth century bears witness to the interest in cosmology and to the uncertainty about it. This was a period not so much of doubt as of questioning—not so much of skepticism as of inquiry.

As early as 1573 Valentinus Nabodus, or Naiboda, had published in Venice a sequence of diagrams that compare world-systems in his *Primarum de coelo et terra institutionum quotidianarumque mundi revolutionum, libri tres.* Naiboda served as professor of mathematics at Cologne and later at Padua, and called himself "physicus et astronomus" (fol. 1). In this volume, as the title indicates, he reviews the first principles of both the heavens and the earth, and the arguments for the daily rotation of the world. Clearly he is writing in the backwash of Copernicus. To illustrate his discussion, Naiboda provides three woodcuts: first, a diagram of the traditional geocentric system, then a diagram of the system described by Martianus Capella, and finally a diagram of the Copernican hypothesis.

Naiboda's diagram of the geocentric system (**Figure 43a**) is largely conventional. As the caption announces, this is "a system of the major parts of the cosmos by which, authorities generally claim, everything in the entire universe is interconnected." The Earth, of course, is at the center, surrounded by a sphere for each of the seven planets, and by a sphere of fixed stars. This makes a total of only eight celestial

Fig. 43a. *The geocentric system from Naiboda.*

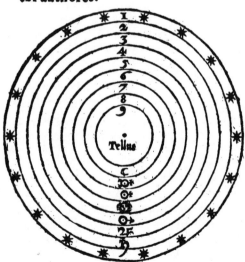

Fig. 43b. *The world-system of Martianus Capella from Naiboda.*

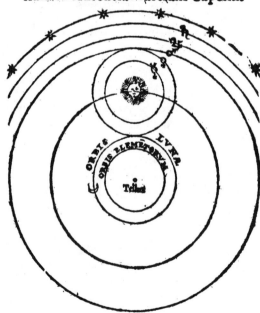

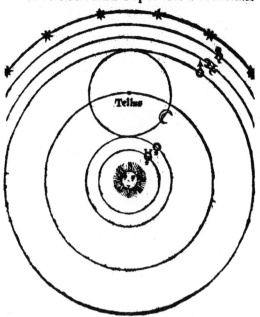

Fig. 43c. *The world-system of Copernicus from Naiboda.*

spheres. Naiboda had omitted the cristalline sphere and the primum mobile, probably under the influence of Agostino Ricchi. In the *De motu octavae sphaerae, opus* (Trino, 1513), Ricchi had argued that no sphere should be given credence unless it carries a visible body, a condition not met by the thoroughly transparent cristalline sphere or the primum mobile (see figure 30).

Naiboda's "System of the major parts of the universe from the writings of Martianus Capella" (**Figure 43b**) puts in visual form the cosmology enunciated by this early fifth-century encyclopedist in his *De nuptiis Philologiae et Mercurii libri novem* (VIII.853-55). The last seven books of this much-read school text are devoted one each to the seven liberal arts—the trivium and the quadrivium—as they had maintained their identity through the middle ages and well into the renaissance. In Book VIII, dealing with Astronomy, Martianus sets forth a world-system, and here is one of the few depictions of it. Earth is again the center, surrounded by a sphere of the four elements, our elementary world. Next comes the sphere of the Moon, which circles about the Earth, as

does the Sun. The planets Mercury and Venus, however, circle about the Sun; and the radius of Venus' orbit is just a mite shorter than the distance between the sphere of the Moon and the sphere of the Sun, and also shorter than the distance between the sphere of the Sun and the sphere of Mars. Spheres for the three superior planets—Mars, Jupiter, and Saturn—then follow, and each of them centers on the Earth. Finally, the entire system is bounded by a sphere of fixed stars. Naiboda advances this system because Martianus had argued that the Sun is the center for the spheres of Mercury and Venus—in other words, some center other than the Earth is the hub for celestial motion. Copernicus had similarly cited Martianus to make the same point.[120] When Galileo reported on the moons of Jupiter after looking through his telescope, it was exactly this point, of course, that he incontrovertibly proved.

Naiboda's "System of the universe according to the opinion of the great man Nicolaus Copernicus of Thurn" (**Figure 43c**) is evidently taken from the *De revolutionibus orbium coelestium* (figure 37). The sun is in the center, surrounded by orbits for Mercury, Venus, Earth, Mars, Jupiter, and Saturn, while the moon circles about the earth. A sphere of fixed stars determines the outer limit of this finite system.

Despite Naiboda's early example, publishing a methodical comparison of all recognized hypotheses really begins with Helisaeus Röslin in the slim quarto mentioned above (page 57). An appendix is given over to a series of diagrams for the universe according to various authorities. There are diagrams of the Ptolemaic system, the Copernican hypothesis, the hypothesis of Reymers, the hypothesis of Röslin himself, and the hypothesis of Tycho Brahe. It may well have been this volume that Robert Burton had in hand when he wrote the passage quoted on page 57, above.

"The system of the universe according to the hypotheses of Ptolemy and the ancient

SYSTEMA MVNDI SECVNDVM PTOLOMÆI ET VE-
terum Philofophorum Hypothefes.

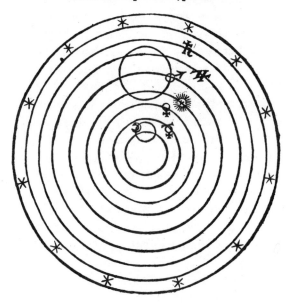

Fig. 44a. *The Ptolemaic system from Röslin.*

Fig. 44b. *The world-system of Tycho (wrongly titled)*
from Röslin.

philosophers" (**Figure 44a**) is fairly straightforward. The Earth presumably occupies the center, though it is not precisely designated, and the other seven planets revolve around it. An epicycle for the Moon is indicated, and also Mars is shown with an epicyclic orbit to account for its retrograde motion. Otherwise all is familiar, with a sphere of fixed stars coinciding with the primum mobile to give the system an outer limit.

In printing this volume, an error was made in the placement of diagrams. "The system of the universe according to the hypotheses of Nicolaus Copernicus" (**Figure 44e**) was transposed with "The system of the universe according to the hypotheses of the noble Dane, Tycho Brahe" (**Figure 44b**), as the printer confesses to his embarrassment in figure 44e. But making the transposition that the printer requests, we see that the Copernican diagram closely repeats the heliocentric diagram in the *De revolutionibus orbium coelestium* (figure 37), while the Tychonic diagram is a reasonable reproduction of the diagram in Tycho's *De mundi aetherei recentioribus phaenomenis* (figure 40).

Fig. 44c. *The world-system of Reymers from Röslin.*

SYSTEMA MVNDI SECVNDVM NICOLAI COPERNICI
Hypothefes.

SYSTEMA MVNDI SECVNDVM RAY-
mari Vrfi Dictmarfi hypothefes.

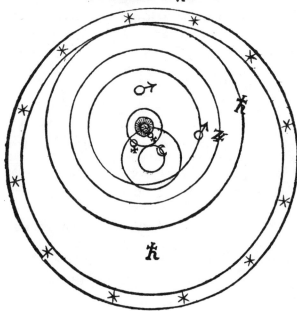

"The system of the universe according to the hypotheses of Reymers (the Bear) from Ditmarschen" (**Figure 44c**) is somewhat simplified from the original diagram (figure 41), but accurate enough. And "The system of the universe according to Dr. Helisaeus Röslin" (**Figure 44d**) we have already discussed. As in the other diagrams (except the Copernican), the earth is assumed to be the center of the system, but is not specifically indicated.

In the year before Galileo published his *Dialogo*, Jean-Baptiste Morin officiously offered a survey of the best-known theories about the motion or immobility of the earth up to that time: *Famosi et antiqui problematis de telluris motu, vel quiete; hactenus optata solutio* (Paris, 1631). Morin had trained as a physician, and in 1631 was the newly appointed professor of mathematics at the Collège de France, the celebrated institution in Paris that had been a center for scientific studies since Francis I had founded it a century earlier. For some time, however, Morin had pursued a lucrative career as an astrologer, and for forty years was emi-

nently successful in catering to the rich and powerful in France. He was, for example, more than disinterestedly implicated in several maneuvers with Cardinal Richelieu — altogether a fascinating figure in this lively period of intrigue, though hardly a champion of truth and progress.

In astronomical matters, Morin was *au courant*, but adamantly conservative. Consequently, in his treatise, "A pleasant solution of the famous and ancient problem of whether the earth moves or is still," he concludes in favor of the latter alternative. The earth does *not* move, he argues, for the biblical and scientific reasons that had become commonplace among the orthodox. At best, Morin countenances the compromise of Tycho, which kept the earth at the center of the universe, although it made the sun the center of all the planetary spheres except that of the moon.

The three diagrams dispersed through Morin's argument are collected in **Figures 45a-c**. "The system of the world according to Ptolemy" is wholly conventional except for one item: the cristalline sphere is omitted, and in-

Fig. 44d. *Röslin's own world-system.*

Fig. 44e. *The world-system of Copernicus (wrongly titled) from Röslin.*

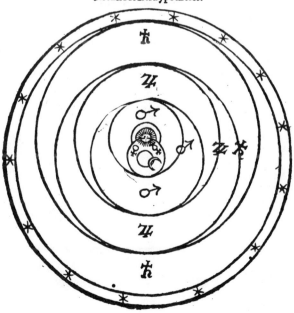

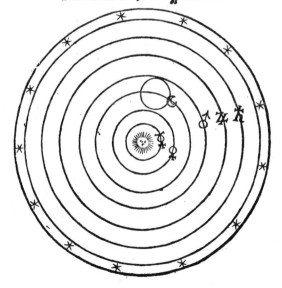

Syſtema Mundi iuxta Ptolemæum.

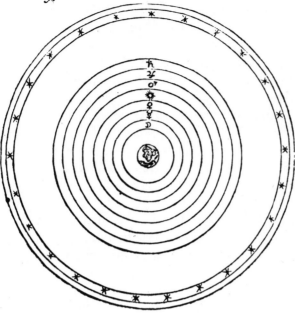

Fig. 45a. *The Ptolemaic system from Morin.*

stead a large space intrudes between the sphere of Saturn and the sphere of the fixed stars, presumably to account for Tycho's inability to observe stellar parallax (see page 54, above). "The system of the world according to Copernicus" is honestly presented without distortion, though here again there is a large space between the sphere of Saturn and the sphere of fixed stars; and the primum mobile, distinctly present in the other two diagrams, does not appear. "The system of the world according to Tycho" is faithfully reproduced (see figure 40), though the moons of Jupiter observed by Galileo are now inserted about that planet, and a separate sphere representing the primum mobile is drawn around the entire system to emphasize its finitude.

A Frenchman situated on the scale of respectability at the end opposite from Morin was Pierre Gassendi, an eminent philosopher and serious astronomer—a true savant. Known for his probity and deep thought, he was patronized by the highest men of the realm, in-

Syſtema Mundi iuxta Copernicum.

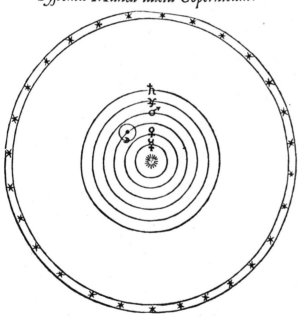

Fig. 45b. *The Copernican system from Morin.*

Syſtema Mundi iuxta Tychonem.

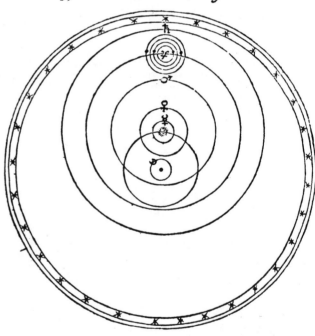

Fig. 45c. *The Tychonic system from Morin.*

COELVM EMPYREVM IMMOBILE.

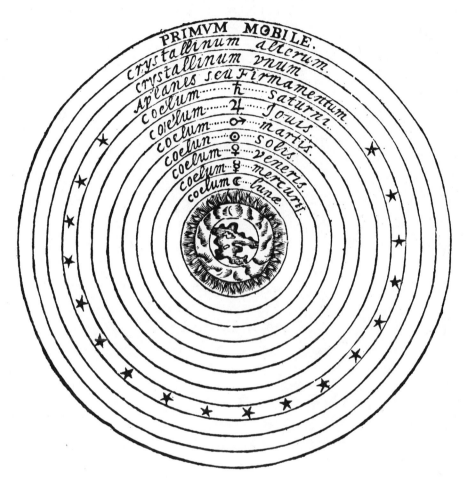

Fig. 46a. *The Ptolemaic system from Gassendi.*

cluding the king. As a reward for honest service, he garnered two honorable titles: Dean of the Cathedral Church in Digne and Regius Professor of Mathematics. Gassendi contributed to the anti-aristotelian movement of the seventeenth century, and through his reconstruction of Epicurus' philosophy provided groundswell for the cresting wave of empiricism. As an innovative thinker, he is worthy of sharing honors with Descartes, whom he often opposed in disputations of considerable consequence.

Gassendi was one of the first men to have a sense of science as a developing corpus of knowledge, a cumulative effort of the human spirit that involves generations of investigators. He was a *philosophe* with an interest in the history of science as a record of achievement rather than as an authority to be resurrected or a straw man to be demolished. In consequence, he wrote carefully researched biographies of several astronomers who had preceded him in the discipline, including Peiresc, Peurbach, Regiomontanus, Copernicus, and Tycho. Even more important, he published what may be considered the first history of

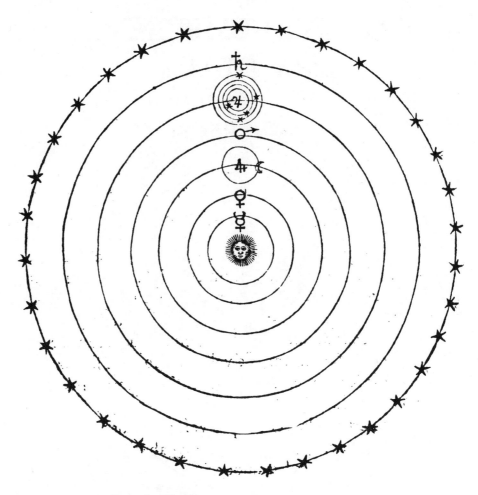

Fig. 46b. *The Copernican system from Gassendi.*

astronomy, *Institutio astronomica juxta hypotheseis tam veterum quam Copernici, et Tychonis* (Paris, 1647).[121]

This exhaustive treatment of astronomical principles according to the major authorities was enormously influential in England as well as on the Continent. A revised reprinting was carried out in London in 1653, and other editions appeared in the Netherlands. In the *Institutio astronomica* Gassendi, as the title suggests, deals in a fundamental way with the principles of astronomy. The first book is devoted to those definitions and propositions concerning the terrestrial and celestial globes that are necessary to making the following books intelligible. Gassendi then methodically discusses the hypotheses of the ancients (i.e., the geocentric system), of Copernicus, and of

Tycho—the three world-systems that Morin had compared. But Gassendi is much more thorough. Furthermore, unlike Morin, Gassendi as a practicing astronomer sees the advantages of heliocentrism. By implication at least, he supports Copernicus. In the final analysis, however, he defers to the literal meaning of the Holy Scriptures, and grudgingly gives the nod to the Tychonic hypothesis. Joshua could not have commanded the sun to stand still unless it moves about the earth.

Scattered through this lengthy treatise are diagrams of each of the three world-systems that Gassendi has chosen to concentrate upon, shown here in **Figures 46a-c**. First comes the standard Ptolemaic diagram (figure 46a) with its "immobile empyreal heaven"—what poets after Milton refer to as "the empyrean." Only

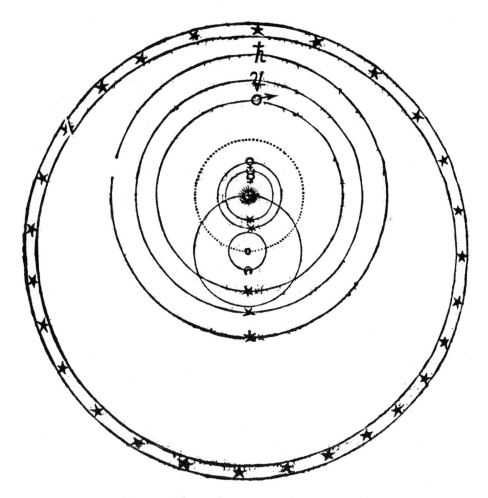

Fig. 46c. *The Tychonic system from Gassendi.*

two things here are worthy of special note: the sphere of fixed stars is given a Greek name, ʾΑπλανές, as well as a Latin name, *firmamentum;* and the cristalline sphere, to allow for what was known as "trepidation of the spheres," is divided into a "primary" and a "secondary" cristalline sphere. Otherwise, however, all is in proper place, with the four elements clearly in their central position and God in His *coelum empyreum immobile.* Appreciably later in the text comes the diagram for the Copernican proposal (figure 46b), obviously taken from Galileo (figure 39), though Gassendi has cautiously enclosed it within a sphere of fixed stars. Finally, some fifty pages later comes the diagram for the Tychonic proposal (figure 46c), copied directly from Tycho (figure 40).

Earlier, in 1642, Gassendi had published two letters to refute those who denied the movement of the earth. Morin, with the self-centered pomposity of a fool, took these letters as a personal attack, and proclaimed a vendetta. What saves this episode from rightful oblivion is a comic error. The fashionable astrologer ostentatiously predicted Gassendi's death in 1650 — but to his own detriment. Gassendi, though in notoriously poor health, enjoyed a particularly good year and did not die until 1655.

More seriously, the two letters arguing against a stationary earth aroused the concern of Church authorities. When pressed on the matter, however, Gassendi discreetly chose to hedge. He had long been a friend of Galileo, and had written letters to aid in Galileo's defense as well as personal letters of condolence. In consequence, Gassendi was acutely aware of how an encounter with the Inquisition might go. Remembering these difficulties, he reserved final judgment about the motion of the earth.

Gassendi was helped in this by Giovanni-Battista Riccioli, a Jesuit who had lectured in philosophy and theology at Parma and Bologna for several decades. After the condemnation of Galileo, Father Riccioli was appointed by his superiors to counter the Copernicans on their own grounds — that is, according to principles of mathematics and astronomy, rather than Church doctrine. When discussing Gassendi, Father Riccioli fell back upon the time-tested sophistry—as old as Andreas Osiander, who had supplied the apologetic preface to Copernicus' *De revolutionibus orbium coelestium* — that Gassendi had presented his arguments as a theoretical hypothesis only, and not as a physical fact.[122] Father Riccioli, for his own purposes, was eager to retrieve Gassendi from the ranks of the Copernicans and claim him as an ally.

Father Riccioli's industry on behalf of the Holy Congregation is preserved in a magnificent two-volume work that stands as a major monument to seventeenth-century erudition: *Almagestum novum astronomiam veterum novamque complectens* (Bologna, 1651). Although later developments in astronomy have bypassed this colossal effort to provide "a new almagest comprising both the old and the new astronomy," it rises with indestructible grandeur like some baroque palace, outdated and visibly chipped, but secure in its very flamboyance. Later scientists have disagreed with Father Riccioli in most of his conclusions, but his graciousness and the fullness of his exposition remain intact.

Figure 47 reproduces the engraved frontispiece of Father Riccioli's *Almagestum novum*, which appears before each of the two volumes. A few hints in the Preface (I.xvii) suggest a general outline of the elaborate allegory in this frontispiece, though it is largely self-evident. A winged figure identified as Astraea and representing Astronomy stands on the right. She wears a classical costume and buskins adorned with stars, and the zodiac serves as her belt. She assertively quotes Psalm 104: "[The foundations of the earth] should not be removed forever." In her left hand she carries an armillary sphere, though her attention is fixed upon the pair of scales held in her right hand. On these she carefully weighs the Copernican system against Father Riccioli's own (see figure 48f), which outweighs its adversary. Across the balancing beam is a Latin inscription: "Weighed in His scales."

Facing Astraea is another mythological figure identified as Argus of the hundred eyes, a denizen of allegory uniquely well qualified to practice astronomy. He is additionally identified as an astronomer by the telescope he holds. In the spirit of the engraving, Argus represents the astronomer in search of Divine Truth, since the light of the sun shines through his telescope. He is covered with eyes by which to see, and he casts his own eyes up towards heaven. Most tellingly, he quotes Psalm 8: "When I consider thy heavens, the work of thy fingers. . . ."

Lying on the ground between these two figures is the ancient astronomer Claudius Ptolemaeus, who rapturously exclaims: "I am extolled and at the same time improved." Ptolemy is extolled by Father Riccioli in the sense that the Jesuit, like his Alexandrian predecessor, maintains the earth at the center of a finite universe, but Father Riccioli has also made adjustments to accord with the times. At Ptolemy's feet lies a diagram of his system, still prominent though evidently subordinate. His left hand rests upon a large coat-of-arms belonging to the Prince of Monaco, to whom the *Almagestum novum* is dedicated. His right hand rests upon another shield displaying two spheres, presumably a fanciful *impresa* for Ptolemy himself.

The upper third of this frontispiece is given over to an exposition of Father Riccioli's own

Fig. 47. *The frontispiece of Riccioli's* Almagestum novum.

67

world-system. At top center is the tetragrammaton, surrounded by an expansive aureole. Immediately below is a divine hand with three outstretched fingers, referring to the number, measure, and weight by which God created our universe. The product of that exercise is displayed by the cherubs who wing their self-conscious way toward the middle of the page from both margins. Those on the right bear the three planets that according to Father Riccioli revolve around the earth below: the moon, half of whose pock-marked surface is lit by beams reflected from the sun; Jupiter, surrounded by its four satellites; and Saturn, in its reported three-part form (the ring had not yet been described as such). Beneath these three planets a comet sweeps in from the right, still contained, as Aristotle had taught, within the orb of the moon. From the opposite side, a cherub bears the sun, which despite its brilliance nonetheless circles around the earth. Three other cherubs, however, carry the planets that according to Father Riccioli revolve about the sun: Mercury, Venus, and Mars. Mercury and Venus appear in their crescent form to indicate that they undergo phases, a recently observed phenomenon. Over this busy scene flutter two banners, which together comprise the second verse of Psalm 19: "Day unto day uttereth speech, and night unto night sheweth knowledge." The same injunction to study astronomy is operative here as at the beginning of the renaissance: by observing the heavens, we discern the attributes of our maker.

Copernicans such as Philippe van Lansberge had complained with justification that the Church opposed the heliocentric hypothesis on theological grounds alone, without examining the evidence and the scientific arguments in its support. In order to counter this complaint, Father Riccioli set himself a course of arduous study and mastered the science of astronomy. He scrupulously compiled the arguments in favor of Copernicus' system, and with the same care devised arguments to disprove it. With as much impartiality as he could manage, he conceded it to be the best unified and most beautiful of all the world-systems that had been proposed. He openly admired Copernicus' conception. He preferred it even to that of Tycho because of its elegant simplicity. Nonetheless, Father Riccioli felt compelled to uphold a literal reading of the Holy Scriptures, and therefore maintained the immobility of the earth in the center of a finite universe, an arrangement decreed and sustained by divine intention. No less than Milton, Father Riccioli asserted eternal providence; and in the process, he offered a painstaking critique of heliocentrism.

Figures 48a-f suggest the thoroughness of Father Riccioli's critique. Chapter vi of Book III bears the heading: "On the location of the sun and of the earth in the universe, upon which occasion the more notable world-systems are presented." Six separate diagrams then follow in rapid order, each with an explication and with a full list of authorities.

Fig. 48a. *The geocentric universe from Riccioli after Pythagoras and Ptolemy.*

Fig. 48b. *The geocentric universe from Riccioli after Plato and the platonists.*

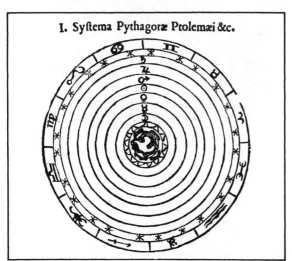

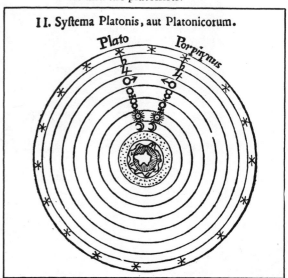

Figure 48a is "The system of Pythagoras, Ptolemy, etc."—the well-known geocentric system of the ancients. It had become customary by this time, however, to remove the cristalline sphere and the primum mobile, thereby constricting the system to eight celestial spheres (see figure 30).

Figure 48b is "The system of Plato and the Platonists"—a representation of the geocentric system that derives from the *Timaeus* (38C-E). The Moon is of course the planet closest to Earth. But then, for some reason not given in the text, the sphere of the Sun is immediately adjacent to the sphere of the Moon. As further anomalies, after the sphere of the Sun come the spheres of Venus and Mercury in that order. Plato does not mention the other planets by name, but it is implied that the spheres of the three superior planets (Mars, Jupiter, and Saturn) follow in the usual order. Porphyry and other neoplatonists, however, differed from their master on at least one point, and reversed the arrangement of Venus and Mercury. For them, the order of the planets (ranging outward from Earth) comprised the Moon, the Sun, Mercury, and then Venus. Some later commentators, misinterpreting a passage in the *Timaeus* (34A), assumed that in this platonic hypothesis the Earth rotates upon its own axis.

Figure 48c is "The system of the Egyptians, Vitruvius, Martianus Capella, Macrobius, Bede, etc."—a system already discussed in connection with figure 43b. Vitrivius does indeed hint at such a system in the *De architectura* (IX.v-vi), while Macrobius in the *Commentarius in somnium Scipionis* is more explicit and ascribes it to the Egyptians (I.xix.1-6). Bede discusses the order of the planets in his *De natura rerum* (xiii), but does not place Mercury and Venus in orbit about the Sun, though one of the several scholia might suggest such an arrangement.

Figures 48a-c were the major hypotheses of those ages that derived their cosmologies without benefit of extensive observational data. Coming into the renaissance, **Figure 48d** presents "The system of Philolaus, Aristarchus, and Copernicus"—the heliocentric system that Copernicus was seen as having revived from the early pythagoreans, Philolaus and Aristarchus of Samos. The sun is of course in the center. Mercury comes next with a periodical revolution of eighty days, followed by Venus with a periodical revolution of nine months. Then comes the earth, circled by the moon, and the orbit of this combination is completed in one year. The amount of space required between the orbit of Venus and that of Mars to allow the moon to revolve about the earth is indicated by dotted circles. Beyond the earth and moon appear the three upper planets: Mars with a periodical revolution of two years, Jupiter with a periodical revolution of twelve years, and Saturn with a periodical revolution of thirty years. Finally, a sphere of

Fig. 48c. *The geocentric universe from Riccioli after the Egyptians, etc.*

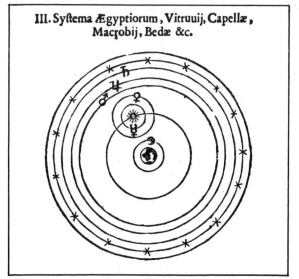

Fig. 48d. *The heliocentric universe from Riccioli after Philolaus, Aristarchus, and Copernicus.*

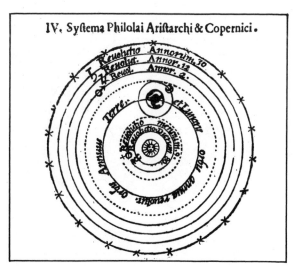

fixed stars provides the outermost limit for the diagram.

Figure 48e presents "The system of Tycho," which by this time was commonplace. The diagram could have come directly from Tycho himself (see figure 40), or perhaps from Gassendi (see figure 46c). But there is an innovation here: a relaxed concept of the sphere of fixed stars. This diagram allows for the stars to escape from the fixity of a sphere and to range at some varying distances between two limits, as Galileo had tentatively proposed (see page 53, above).

Figure 48f is Father Riccioli's own system, as the caption announces. It is basically a geocentric system similar to Tycho's, with the moon and the sun revolving around the earth. Three planets—Mercury, Venus, and Mars—revolve about the sun, as in Tycho's system. The two uppermost planets, however, fix upon the earth as their center of motion. Father Riccioli argues that Jupiter and Saturn, since they have satellite bodies of their own, are planets of a different order from Mercury, Venus, and Mars, and therefore require the earth as an adequately steadfast point about which to wheel. He confirms his conservative view by placing a definite sphere of fixed stars around the circumference of his system.

Despite the steady formulation of important new theories, Father Riccioli's *Almagestum novum* remained a respected source-book of astronomy throughout the seventeenth century. Until the accumulation of a considerable body of fresh data, it was not likely to be replaced. Not surprisingly, the six diagrams of Father Riccioli reappear in the work of a fellow Jesuit, the equally erudite Athanasius Kircher. In 1656 Father Kircher published his account of an imaginary journey through the heavens which supposedly resulted from a dream, but which of course is a literary device as time honored as Cicero's report of Scipio's dream. On the journey Father Kircher has the benefit of two angelic guides, Cosmiel and Theodidactus, who proceed by dialogue to instruct him about the various regions of the universe. The author, like his friend Father Riccioli, is learned and up-to-date in his information, but more than the format of the work is conservative. His universe is basically aristotelian, comprising the four elements below and the quintessential spheres above, with an astrological overlay of planetary influences. The later editions of Father Kircher's *Iter exstaticum coeleste* contain **Figure 49,**[123] which is no more than an epitome of figures 48a-f.

Across the Channel, Father Riccioli's diagrams received an extremely handsome redaction in a volume that stands as a landmark in English neoclassicism. In 1675 in London, Sir Edward Sherburne published his translation of Manilius' *The sphere*, dedicated to his benefactor, Charles II. As part of his learned critical apparatus, Sherburne added an appen-

Fig. 48e. *The Tychonic system from Riccioli.*

Fig. 48f. *Riccioli's own world-system.*

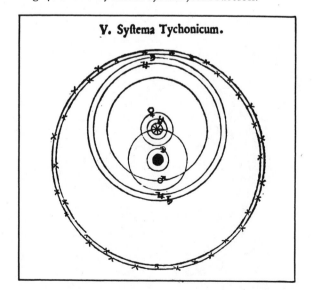

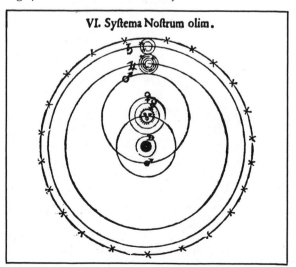

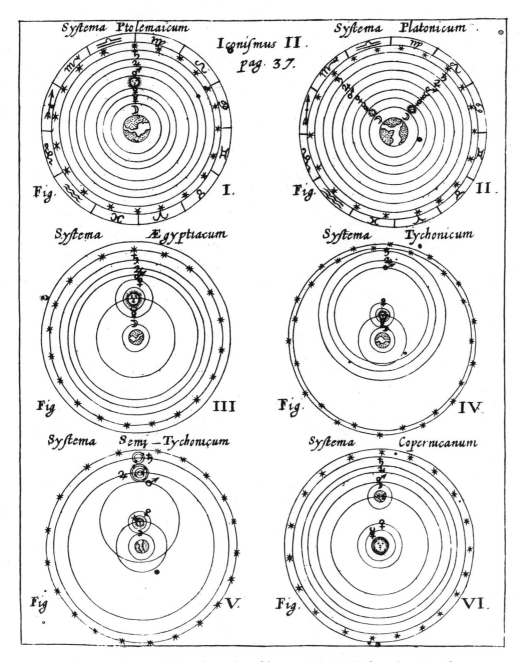

Fig. 49. *A comparative chart of world-systems from Kircher after Riccioli.*

dix that includes a treatise entitled "The original and progress of astronomy" (pages 1-5) and also a lengthy "Catalogue of the most eminent astronomers, ancient & modern" (pages 6-126). Next comes an essay entitled "Of the cosmical system" (pages 127-37), in which, as Sherburne declares, he sets out "to explain and illustrate this Subject, by representing the several Opinions, as well of the *Ancients* as *Moderns*, touching the same" (page 127). Father Riccioli's *Almagestum novum* was undeniably open on Sherburne's study table as he wrote; it is gratefully cited on almost every page.

Illustrating Sherburne's historical survey of cosmology, the famous artist Wenceslaus Hollar supplied a large engraving for each of the six world-systems that Father Riccioli had distinguished. This series is the most beautiful as well as the easiest to study of all renaissance diagrams of the universe.[124] The best way to appreciate the completeness of this achievement is to see the pages whole (**Figure 50**, following), so that Hollar's engravings are enhanced by Sherburne's text.

Fig. 50. *The major world-systems from Sherburne's translation of Manilius.*

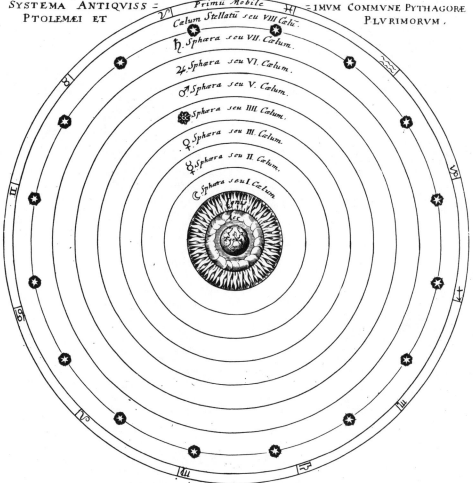

In this Syftem the Terraqueous Globe is feated in the midft or Centre; about it, the Elementary Region; next above that, the *Moon*; then *Mercury*; next above him, *Venus*; the Sun, as Moderator of all, being placed, as in a Throne in the midft of the Planets, environed not only by the three foregoing, called the Inferiour, but by *Mars* likewife, *Jupiter*, and *Saturn*, called the Superiour Planets. Above Saturn is the Sphere of the Fixed Stars, called 'Απλανη, i. e. *Aplane*, or Unerring; by fome, the Firmament. The reafon of this Syftem is thus explained by *Pliny*, *Lib.* 2. *c.* 22. *Pythagoras ex Mufica ratione appellat Tonum quantum abfit à Terra Luna*, &c. i. e. Pythagoras *from Mufical Reafon*, *calls the fpace between the* Earth *and the* Moon, *a Tone*; *the fpace from the* Moon *to* Mercury, *he will have to be half a Tone*; *as much in a manner from him, to* Venus; *from* Venus *to the* Sun, *as much and half again*; *but from the* Sun *to* Mars, *as much as from the* Earth *to the* Moon, *that is a Tone*; *from him to* Jupiter, *half a Tone*; *from* Jupiter *to* Saturn, *another half Tone*; *and from thence to the fixed Stars, as much and a half again*. *Thus are compofed Seven Tones, which Harmony they call Diapafon, that is, the generality or whole ftate of Confent or Concord.* Now a Tone is by fome interpreted the fame as an Unite or Integer, and contains in Meafure according to the Opinion of *Pythagoras* 125000 *Stadia*; according to which Meafure; not only the foregoing fpace, but extent of the whole Syftem, may be computed. And this was the firft *Pythagorean* Syftem, embraced by *Archimedes*, the *Chaldeans*, *Ariftotle*, *Cicero*, *Livy*, *Ptolemy*, *Alphonfus*, *Purbachius*, and the greateft part of Aftronomers, untilthe time of *Maginus* and *Clavius*.

The next Syftem is that which is called the *Platonick*. Touching which, thus *Ricciolus*, Lib.9. c. 3. *As Difcord oftentimes produces Concord ; fo on the other fide Concord often begets Difcord. For between* Pythagoras *and* Plato, *there was thus far a wonderful Concordancy, that they both conceived the Intervals and Order of the Planets ought to be conftituted according to the Laws of Mufick. But from their agreement fprung their diffent ; by reafon the* Platonifts *and* Pythagoreans *differed in their Opinions about the Harmonical Diaftem.* And as *Plato* differed from *Pythagoras*, fo fome of his own followers differed from him, as (among others) *Porphyrius, Apuleius,* and *Marcilius Ficinus.* Whofe difference will appear in the following Scheme.

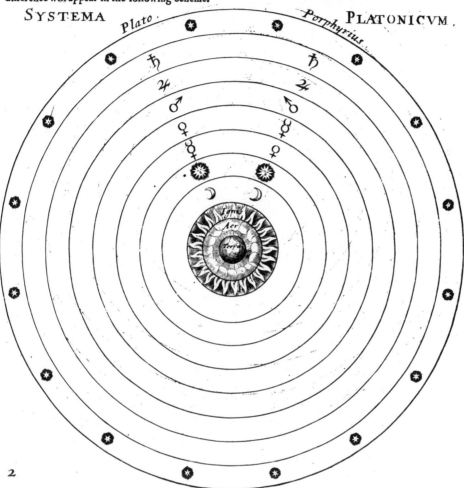

In which, in the firft place, according to *Plato*, the *Earth* with the Elementary Region is placed ; above that, the *Moon*, and immediately above that, the *Sun* ; above him *Mercury*, then, *Venus* ; above Her, *Mars* ; then *Jupiter* ; laftly *Saturn*. In the fecond place is that of *Porphyrius*, and fome other *Platonifts* beforementioned, agreeing in all but this, That whereas *Plato* immediately above the *Sun*, placed *Mercury*, and then *Venus*, they immediately, above the Sun, placed *Venus*, and then *Mercury* above her. Of which laft, *Macrobius lib.1.in Somn.Scip.c.3.* gives this accompt. *The late Platonifts (fayes he) repudiated the Dimenfions of Archimedes, as not obferving double and triple Intervals. For, they held, that what was the Diftance, or Interval, from the Earth to the Moon, the fame was double from the Earth to the Sun ; and the Diftance from the Earth to Venus, was triple, to that from the Earth to the Sun ; and from the Earth to Mercury four times that from the Earth to Venus ; and how far the Diftance was from the Earth to Mercury, nine times that was the Diftance from the Earth to Mars ; and the Diftance from the Earth to Jupiter, eight times that from the Earth to Mars ; and the Diftance from the Earth to Saturn, feven and twenty times that from the Earth to Jupiter.* The fame Order is likewife afferted by the Author of the Book *De Mundo.* Thefe three foregoing Syftems are compofed all of Concentrick Orbs. The next, which is the *Egyptian*, fol-

Kk   lowed

lowed by *Vitruvius*, *Martianus Capella*, *Macrobius*, *Beda*, and *Argol*, is compofed partly of Concentrick Orbs, partly of Excentrick, as may appear by the fubfequent Scheme.

SYSTEMA   ÆGYPTIVM

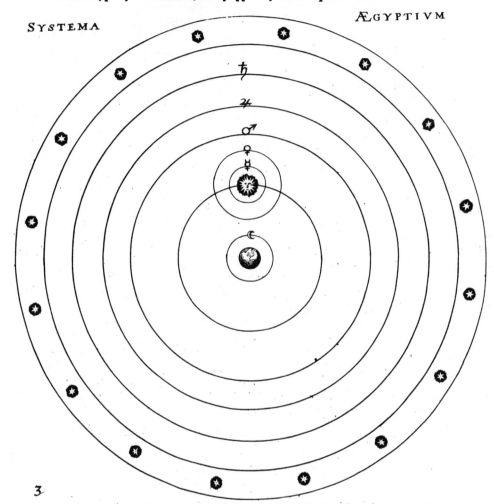

3

Wherein we may perceive the *Earth* feated in the midft of the World, with the Elements, and immediately above them the *Moon*, then the *Sun*, about whom, as their Centre, firft *Mercury*, then *Venus* are fuppofed to move in *Epicycles*; above thefe *Mars*, next *Jupiter*, and then *Saturn*. Of this Syftem, thus *Macrobius, in Somn. Scipion. l. 1. c.* 19. *The Egyptian fubtlety is not without reafon, which is this; the Circle wherein the Sun runs his courfe is furrounded with the Circle of* Mercury, *as Interior, and by that of* Venus *as Exteriour. And hence it is that thefe two Stars, when they are in the upper part of their Circles, are underftood to be above the Sun; but when they are in the inferiour part of their Orbs, or Circles, the Sun is held to be above them. Thofe therefore who affirm the Spheres of thefe Planets to be under the Sun, are perfwaded to believe it, from this Appearance of their Courfe, when they run in the Inferiour part of their Orbits, which is more remarkable and more clearly difcernible, for when they are in the upper part of their Circles, they are more concealed. And therefore this perfwafion of theirs hath prevailed, and accordingly the Order of thofe Planets hath been received almoft by all Perfons; but more perfpicacious Obfervation difcovered this better Order.* And juftly does he ftile it a perfpicacious Obfervation, which fo many Ages fince by the only Sagacity of Wit fo clearly difcovered, what we find now really detected by the help of the Telefcope. And therefore *Ricciolus* fayes of this Syftem, that it is *Pulcherrimum, ac pro hac quidem parte, Veriffimum Syftema.*

We come now to the moft celebrious, and at this day moft generally received Mundane Syftem, from it's Reviver, called the *Copernican*, but owing it's original to the *Samian* and *Italick* School, as being propofed and afferted, in the one, by *Philolaus*, of *Crotona*, in the other, by *Ariftarchus Samius*,

Samius, both *Pythagoreans,* whence it is called the second *Pythagorick* System, as differing from the former before described; That, fixing the Earth immoveable in the midst of the World; This, on the contrary giving to the Earth, not only a Diurnal Motion about its Axis, but also an Annual, about the Sun, as the Centre of the Universe. An Hypothesis not unknown to the *Romans;* and therefore *Seneca,* in his Natural Questions (*Lib. 7.*) proposes it as a thing necessary to be discussed; *To know whether the Earth standing still, the Heavens be moved about it; or the Heavens standing still, the Earth be carried round.* And again, *It is a thing worthy contemplation to be assured,* sayes he, *in what condition We are; whether in a Seat of all others most slow, or the most swift? Whether God turns all things about us, or we our selves are turned about?* This System, about two Ages since, was resuscitated from Oblivion and the Grave, by Cardinal *Cusanus,* but imperfectly, until *Copernicus* came and gave it a perfect consummation, followed by the greatest Wits of this and the foregoing Age, to wit, *Georgius Joachimus Rheticus, Mæstlinus, Rothmannus, Stevinus, Kepler, Galilæo, Schickardus, Jordanus Brunus, Cælius Calcagninus, Didacus Astunica, Foscarinus, Herigonus, Renatus Des Cartes, Lansbergius, Bullialdus, Antonius Laurentius Politianus, Wendelinus* and *Gassendus; Lansbergius* and *Bullialdus,* only differing in this from *Copernicus,* that they allow to the Fixed Stars a proper Motion, which *Copernicus* denies. Take the same represented in the following Scheme.

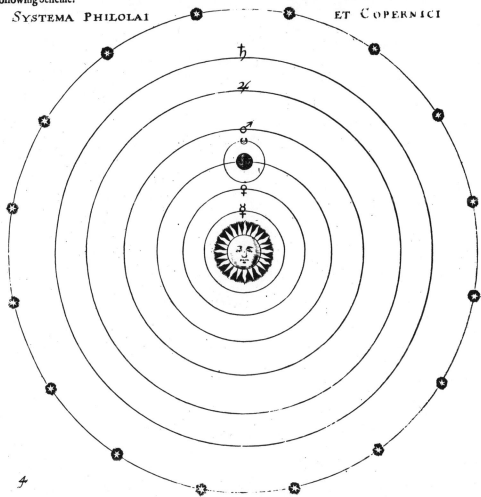

SYSTEMA PHILOLAI   ET COPERNICI

In this System, we may perceive the *Sun* placed in the Centre of the World; next above him, *Mercury,* finishing his Course in the space of eighty dayes, or thereabouts; then *Venus,* making her Revolution in nine Moneths time; above her, the *Earth,* with the Elementary Sphere, in the Annual Orb, which it runs through in 365. dayes and half, by a Motion from West to East; that is in the same Circle, wherein the *Egyptian* and *Ptolemaick* System place the Sun. Besides which

Annual

Annual Motion, *Copernicus* aſſigns to the Earth a Diurnal Revolution, in which it turns about its own Centre and Axis, inclined in the Plane of the Ecliptick, in the ſpace of 24. hours, from Weſt to Eaſt: The *Moon* by a Menſtrual Revolution being carryed about the *Earth*, as in an *Epicicle*; *Mars* running about the *Sun*, as the Centre of the Univerſe in two years; *Jupiter* above him in twelve; and *Saturn* in thirty. The Sphere of the Fixed Stars being diſtant by ſo vaſt an Interval from the Sphere of *Saturn*, that the Annual Orb, in which the Earth moves, appears, in reſpect to it, no other than a Point.

This Syſtem, though, in appearance, of all others, the moſt rationally grounded, could not yet give ſo general a ſatisfaction to the Curious, but that ſome of them conceived it might admit of Alteration, or Emendation. And thence the illuſtrious *Tycho* took occaſion to introduce the following Syſtem of his, which is no other than a certain Tranſfiguration of the *Copernican*, after this manner.

SYSTEMA   TYCHONICVM

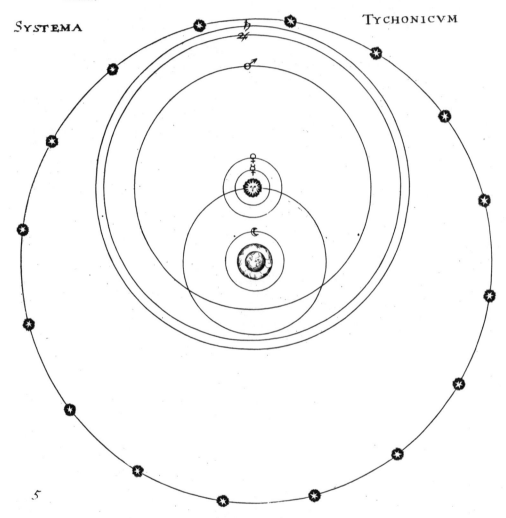

First, the *Earth* is ſuppoſed fix'd without Motion in the Centre of the Univerſe, Concentrick to which is, firſt the Sphere or Circle of the *Moon*'s Motion; next, that of the *Sun*'s Annual Courſe; then the Sphere of the Fixed Stars. The *Sun* being placed as the Centre of the other Planets, in whoſe Orb (as it were two *Epycicles*) are drawn the Circles of *Mercury* and *Venus*. At a greater Diſtance is that of *Mars*, interſecting, when in Oppoſition to the *Sun*, part of the Solar Sphere, and therefore being Achronical is nearer to the Earth than the Sun. Above *Mars* is the Sphere of *Jupiter*; above *Jupiter*, that of *Saturn*; above that, the Fixed Stars. So that, in this Syſtem, the Sun is the Centre of five Planets; that is, not only of *Mercury* and *Venus*, according to the *Egyptian* Syſtem, but alſo of *Mars*, *Jupiter*, and *Saturn*, according to the *Copernican*; which
likewiſe

likewife it refembles, as fuppofing fewer Converfions, and rejecting the Solidity of the *Ptolemaick* or *Purbachian* Orbs. But the *Copernican*, even in the Opinion of *Ricciolus*, feems to carry with it a greater fimplicity and concinnity. *Nicholaus Raimarus Urfus* feemed to challenge this Syftem, as firft introduced by him, afcribing the Original of the Hypothefis, to *Apollonius Pergæus*. But *Tycho*, in his Epiftles, hath vindicated and afferted his own Right, and hath gained for his Followers *Longomontanus* (who yet gives to the Earth a Motion about its Axis) *Scheinerus*, *Blancanus*, and generally the Aftronomers of the *Jefuitical* School. And the Reafon of their adherence to this Syftem, rather than to the *Ptolemaick* or *Copernican*, is given by *Caramuel*, in his *Interim-Aftronomicum*; which is, *that Demonftration condemns the Ptolemaick, fhewing it to be impoffible and inconfiftent with Modern Obfervations; and as for the Copernican, that it ftands condemned by a congregation of Cardinals, who have (if you will believe them) defined the fame to be repugnant to the Sacred Scriptures.*

Among the feveral Syftems either of the Ancients or Moderns which are grounded upon the Earth's Immobility, there are two (befides the *Tychonick*) which feem to *Ricciolus* the moft probable; the One is *Semi-Ptolemaick*, the other *Semi-Tychonick*.

The Form of the firft, admits the Centre of the Earth as the Term from whence the Excentricity of the feveral Orbs are meafured, fuppofing *Venus* and *Mercury* to be carried about the Sun in *Epicycles* and the Excentricities of the other five Planets, as alfo their *Epicycles*, not to be alwayes of the fame Quantity, which may be apprehended by the Figure of the *Egyptian* Syftem already defcribed, fuppofing only that *Mars* in Oppofition to the Sun, be made to approach nearer to the Earth, than the Sun does.

The Form of the fecond is reprefented in the following Scheme, and ows its Invention to *Ricciolus*, wherein the Sun is fuppofed to be the Centre of the Sphere of *Mercury*, *Venus* and *Mars*; And the Earth, the Centre of the Circle of the Moon's Motion, and of the Fixed Stars, as alfo of thofe of *Saturn* and *Jupiter*. The Reafons impelling him to embrace this Hypothefis, being thefe.

Firft, he obferved that *Saturn* and *Jupiter* had Secundary Planets moving about them, but *Mars*, *Venus*, and *Mercury* none; whence he conceived it probable that *Saturn* and *Jupiter* exercifed as it were their proper Monarchies in the Heavens; and were no Attendants or Satellites of the Sun; but moving about the Earth as their Centre. That *Mars* was one of the Sun's greateft or utmoft Satellites, including within his Sphere that of the Earth; but *Venus* and *Mercury* his nearer and more interiour Gaurds.

Secondly, Becaufe in the Variation of the Excentricities of the Planets, he obferved a greater Connexion of *Mars*, *Venus*, and *Mercury* with the Sun, then of *Saturn* and *Jupiter*.

Thirdly, Becaufe he conceived *Saturn* and *Jupiter*, being more flow and ponderous Planets, to have a greater Affinity to the flow Sphere of the Fixed Stars; and to refpect (as do the Fixed Stars) the Earth rather than the Sun as the Centre of their Motions.

Fourthly, Seeing that *Mars*, *Venus*, and *Mercury* in their Courfes or Circumgyrations enter into the Solar Heaven, he conceived it more probable that thofe Planets fhould have the Sun for the Centre of their Motions, and not to have any Diftinct Æthereal Regions affigned them, but to move All in one common Region. But *Saturn* and *Jupiter* to have their Diftinct Dominions and Regions allotted them.

Fifthly, Becaufe it feems very probable that among the Planets there fhould be one as it were a Mean or Middle, between the Superiour and the Inferiour, and which in his Motions fhould have fome things common with *Saturn* and *Jupiter*, and fome with *Venus* and *Mercury*; to wit *Mars*. But fee the Scheme it felf.

LI   In

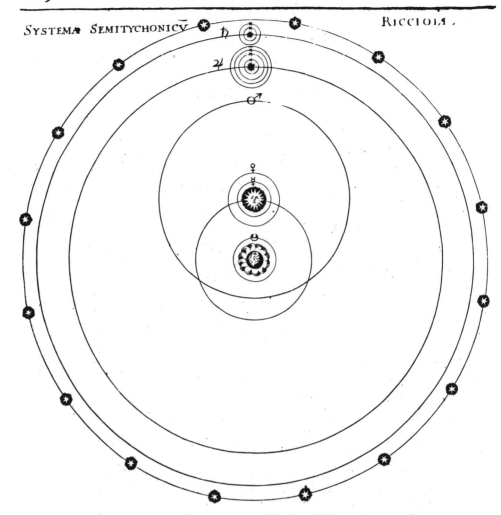

Systema Semitychonicу   Ricciola.

In which is to be noted that the Intervals of the several Orbs are so ordered, that the lowest of the Concave Heaven of *Saturn*, does not touch the upper part of the *Convex* of *Jupiter*, or the lowest of *Jupiters*, the uppermost of *Mars*, as in the *Ptolemaick*, but there is a voyd Interval between the Fixed Stars, and the uppermost *Convex* of *Saturn's* Orb, of 9824 *Semidiameters* of the Earth, and between the *Concave* of *Saturn* and the *Convex* of *Jupiter*, an Interval of 10045 of the like *Semidiameters*, and between the *Concave* of *Jupiter* and *Convex* of *Mars*, an Interval of 5310 such *Semidiameters*, and between the *Concave* of *Venus* and *Convex* of the *Moon's* Orb 1850 *Semidiameters*. Besides, the Thickness of the whole Heaven of *Saturn* computed together with his *Satellites* is supposed 32454 *Semidiameters*, and that of *Jupiter* with his *Satellites* 21361 *Semidiameters*; That of the *Sun, Mars, Venus* and *Mercury*; being but as one *Heaven*, is supposed to contain 19091 of the *Earth's Semidiameters*.

These three last Systems suppose the Heavens, or the Ætherial Region to be pervious, fluid, and of a thin, liquid, and transparent Substance like the Air, but more pure, and not consisting of Solid Orbs, as the *Peripateticks*, and those of the *Ptolemaick* School affirm. This Fluidity of the Heavens being manifested, by the *Maculæ Solares*, whether they be considered as Planets moving tumultuously about the Sun, or as Clouds, Vapours, and Fumosities issuing from the Solar Body; Likewise by the Librating Motion of the Firmament it self, in which the Sun moves, as also by the Libration of the Moon; and by the *Satellites* of *Jupiter*, not long since discovered to move about that Planet, as also those about *Saturn*, and the Extravagant Motion of *Mars*, as also that of *Venus* and *Mercury* running now above, now beneath the Sun. No less evidenced by the Production of Comets, and their divers Motions, which beginning in One, make their Progress through several Ætherial Regions; which they could not do if the Celestial Orbs through which they pass were

were folid; from which fuppofition feveral other Inconveniencies would likewife enfue by rea-fon their *Convexities* and *Concavities*, as alfo thofe of fo many *Epicycles* and *Excentricks* would neceffarily produce a Multiplicity of various Refractions of the feveral Rayes of the Sun, of the other Planets, and of the Fixed Stars.   Laftly, it feems as incongruous that the Stars and Planets fhould be carried about in fuch vaft folid Orbs, (to which they bear no other proportion than a drop of Water to the Ocean) as it is for the Earth to be imagined to move only to carry about a Fly or a Pifmire.   Neither do thofe Celeftial Bodies gravitate or need any Support, but move regularly within their feveral Sphericities, as having no Appetency of Motion beyond thofe Bounds.   See *Tycho Brahe*, *Progymnafm. Tom.* 1. and *Ricciolus* repeating the feveral Arguments to this Purpofe (of *Kepler*, *Lansbergius*, *Maginus*, *Galilæo*, *Gaffendus* and *Bulialdus*) *Almag. Nov. Tom.* 2. *p.* 242 and 243.

Sherburne's essay on cosmology shows a comprehensiveness and depth of learning that is not unusual for his time. Such were the views of a cultivated Englishman when *Paradise Lost* was a recent addition to the growing library of cosmic speculation.

At the end of the seventeenth century, mathematical practitioners as active and current as William Leybourn were still using Father Riccioli as the point of reference. In 1690 Leybourn published in London his compendious textbook, *Cursus mathematicis. Mathematical sciences, in nine books.* There we find **Figure 51**, essentially a repetition of the diagrams that Father Riccioli had set forth. Although the immediate source of Leybourn's page is Sherburne's discourse "Of the cosmical system" (see figure 50) — as Leybourn readily admits in his text (page 429) — the authority behind both these English cosmologists is unmistakably the Italian Jesuit who at mid-century had mounted the most sweeping arguments against the heliocentric theory.

What we find in the century and a half after Copernicus, then, is a fluid debate about the arrangement of the planets. This debate focused on the central issues of whether the earth or the sun moves, and whether the universe is infinite or delimited by an enclosing sphere. Gradually, the heliocentric hypothesis won acceptance. That the earth revolves daily around its own axis and moves in annual orbit about the sun was more easily conceded than the disturbing proposition that space is limitless. In any case, at the end of the seventeenth century the matter was far from settled in the public mind, despite fair agreement among the scientists. And the implications of heliocentrism had just begun to be explored.

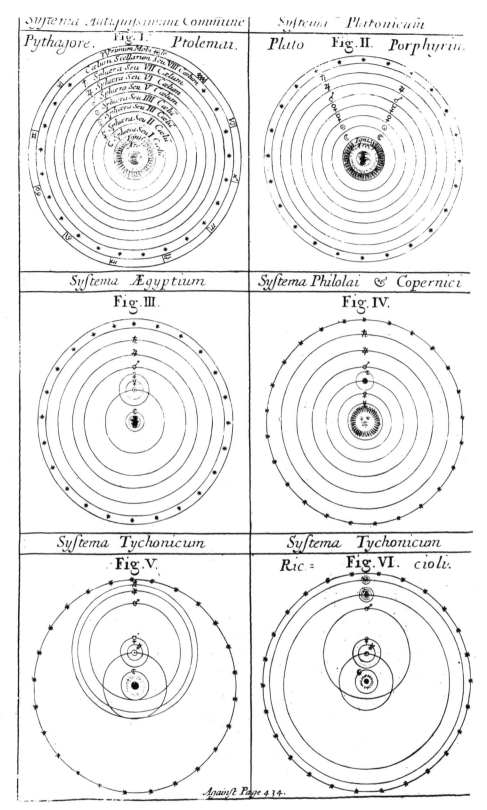

Fig. 51. A comparative chart of world-systems from Leybourn
after Riccioli and Sherburne.

IV The Pythagorean–Platonic Tradition

LL THE DIAGRAMS of world-systems that we have looked at so far have dealt with the universe as an object to be perceived with our sense faculties. We have considered the universe in terms of its spatial dimension, as an extended body filling a time-space continuum. We have been concerned with determining its constituent parts and with defining the temporal and spatial relationships between them. The hexaemeral series which lay out the works of each day during the week of creation begin at some inchoate stage before matter can be identified as such, but even they eventuate in an indisputably visible universe. God's heaven itself is assigned a definite place and a distinct appearance. This is our world as we observe it, maintained by providence perhaps, but unabashedly physical. We have, of course, exercised our cultural bias as modern readers in a scientific age. Like historians of science, we have traced the history of cosmology as it shifted from geocentrism to heliocentrism.

We must recognize, however, that an even more fundamental shift in modes of thought took place during this same period. At the beginning of the renaissance, carrying on from the middle ages, the prevalent world-view placed ultimate reality among the essences in Plato's world of ideas, to use a familiar philosophical system, or with the deity in a Christian heaven, to use the dominant theology. Very early through the efforts of such men as Pico della Mirandola and Johann Reuchlin the cosmological mix was enriched by the addition of cabalism, with its deity and cosmogony based upon the book of Genesis and its similar transcendental values. In either instance — Platonism, Christianity, cabalism (and they were commonly conflated) — ultimate reality lay at some level beyond perception by mortal senses. In fact, that discontinuity is what separated mortal from divine.

The prevalent ontology locating ultimate reality among philosophical or theological absolutes also dictated the prevalent epistemology, how the mere mortal can ascertain knowledge of the divine. There are three possibilities: (1) through revelation, a direct statement of truth offered by God in the Holy Scriptures or in some similar supernatural way; (2) through intuition, an immediate apprehension of truth through introspection, so that by knowing oneself one also knows the deity in whose image he has been created; and (3) through study of physics, an indirect but reliable route to truth made correspondent with revelation by its description as "reading the book of nature." By any of these three methods, a man can seek knowledge, though of course he can never achieve total knowledge because that would be an intrusion upon the godhead. As Cuningham reminds us with the customary ambivalence of the period: "Wherein dothe he [man] so neare approche unto God

81

in likenesse: as by Science, and Knowledge? for this thing is proper to God only, to know all thinges."[125] The proper limits of human knowledge were frequently fretted over and heatedly debated. Adam's transgression, especially as Milton details it, lies precisely in this area.

But out of the third possibility, as we have seen, there developed the scientific method. The study of physics was pursued more and more arduously for its own sake. It was divorced from its original purpose: to reveal the attributes and intentions of the Creator. And markedly after Bacon, it was seen as a means of controlling nature and of subjugating the environment to our wishes. Eventually — and it is difficult to say which came first, the shift in epistemology or the shift in ontology—ultimate reality came to be placed in the objects of physical nature, in those data which the scientific method took to be the subject matter of its inquiry. Ultimate reality no longer resided among insubstantial absolutes, but rather among the mutable items spread before our unreliable sense perception. The renaissance can be defined as the transition period in this shift, and the modern era is its result.

Before the scientific method, though, the prevailing way to contemplate our universe was to *conceive* it rather than to *perceive* it. It was thought of not as a datum to be studied empirically by using more and more precise measuring instruments, but rather as a potential which may or may not be realized as a physical entity. Then our object of inquiry becomes that potency, rather than its realization. Our inquiry focuses upon the ideal plan of the universe, what the middle ages would have called its *schema*. We seek to study it as the archetypal idea in the mind of the creating deity before it took on qualities dependent upon time and space. Under these conditions, it becomes a static concept, atemporal and aspatial, motionless, permanent, eternal. It is a form only, not subject to accidents of time or defects of matter. It is an idea, which can be imposed upon matter and thereby rendered

substantial, but which in its original state has no body. Nor can it be divided into constituent parts, nor put through successive stages of development. To use platonic terms, it is intelligible rather than sensible: it can be *conceived* by the mind, but not *perceived* by the senses.

The basis of this earlier ontology was a belief in cosmos (see pages 7-8, above), a belief that looked to Plato's *Timaeus* as a sacred text. The Church Fathers adopted the Timaean cosmogony, and thus it passed into the mainstream of Western thought, where it dominated until the time of Newton. According to Timaeus, the creating godhead had begun with an archetypal idea that he then proceeded to realize in physical terms by extending it into a time-space continuum. Pierre de la Primaudaye in his sixteenth-century encyclopedia states the principle succinctly:

Each worke liveth in the minde of the workeman before he puts it in practise. So had the worlde perfect being, in the thought of God before it was builded, and the very Idea thereof was contained in it, by which this great architect, when it pleased him, performed his outward worke.[126]

The universe emerged from the potential of a divine concept. This prehistory for creation persevered with remarkable tenacity throughout the classical period, the middle ages, and the renaissance, and it still surfaces in unexpected quarters in our own time. Minds as disparate as Carl Jung and James Jeans have been touched by it.

Figures 52a-b neatly illustrate how the universe is the projection of an idea in the mind of God, if not the idea of God Himself. Once again Robert Fludd, though writing in Bacon's London, recapitulates the lore of previous centuries and transmits it intact to later generations of Rosicrucians and Freemasons. Exercising the hermetic mode, Fludd explains that just as a triangular form has three distinct angles but nonetheless maintains a unified coherence, so in God there exist three distinct persons without fragmenting His unity. **Figure 52a** demonstrates the point and translates it into a scheme that is intelligible. The equilateral triangle ABC is God. Since of all plane figures the triangle encloses the least area per a given circumference, the triangle ABC represents God at His greatest deformation—that is, the farthest He departs from the perfection of unity. As a triangle He displays the greatest possible distortion from the circle, which is perfect (the circle encloses the maximum area per a given circumference), though even in the triangle His unity is not actually violated. But to represent God in His ideal form, a circle labeled "the heaven of the trinity" circumscribes the triangle ABC, thereby indicating the perfection of God in His full extension. The divine triangle ABC in turn encloses the three regions of the palpable universe: "D. the empyreal region"; "E. the ethereal region"; and "F. the elemental region," with the earth at its center. This arrangement demonstrates how God contains within Himself all things, and the concentric spheres D, E, and F show how these three parts of the universe are interdependent and unified just like the three angles of the Trinity, ABC. This is cosmic geometry that is at once simplistic and sophisticated— to be viewed as a diagram of ideas without reference to physicality.

Figure 52b makes explicit the relationship between figure 52a and the deity. In the top half of the diagram the tetragrammaton appears as the innermost and least substantial of a series of radiant triangles. Along one side a caption announces: "that most divine and beautiful counterpart visible below in the flowing image of the universe." In the bottom half of the diagram, the three regions of the universe— empyreal, ethereal, and elemental—are again shown correspondent to the triangular form of the trinitarian deity, and this triangle is a mirror image of the top half of the diagram. Along one side a caption announces: "A shadow, likeness, or reflection of the insubstantial triangle visible in the image of the universe." Evident-

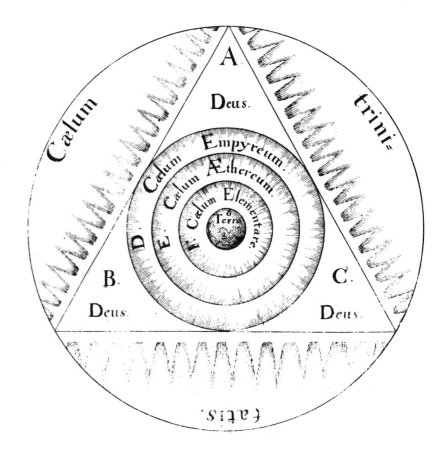

Fig. 52a. *The universe as an insubstantial idea in the mind of God from Fludd.*

Fig. 52b. *The universe as a mirror image of God.*

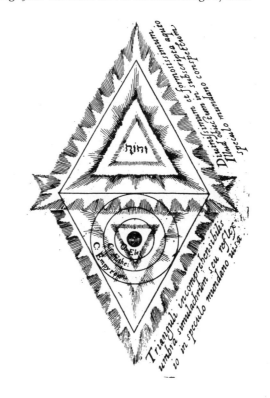

ly, the lower triangle is a projection of an idea that resides with God. The palpable universe preserves the perfection of its heavenly model and maker — indeed, is a shadow or reflection of Him.

In this tradition, ultimate reality resides with the deity, whether platonic or Christian — or, as more usual, both. He is infinite and unchanging, outside of space and time. He is the absolute, and ultimate reality resides among the ideas in his mind. He is the creator of our time-space continuum, and moreover its nurse. He is both progenitor and continuing context for creation. Our world, though finite and mortal, exists paradoxically within his eternal being.

Therefore our world, as Fludd's diagrams propose, reflects the perfection of the deity. And the paradox of his being three-in-one explains the paradox of our world being diverse and yet unified. La Primaudaye in his *French academie* calls upon ancient authority to make the point:

> The learned and venerable antiquitie figureth, and maketh the universall world (to be) one, and threefold, as signifying and representing (though very farre off and much behinde) the omnipotent, triple-one, most wise, and most good worker, by whom it hath been created, formed and ordained.[127]

The antiquity of this doctrine in the Christian tradition is affirmed by a passage from Byrhtferth dating from the early eleventh century in England. After speaking of God the Father, God the Son, and the Holy Ghost, Bryhtferth proclaims:

> This Trinity and Indivisible Unity penetrates all things with its divine majesty, and in penetrating it embraces, and in embracing it fills, and in filling it controls, and in controlling it guides all creatures, upper, middle and lowest.[128]

According to theologians and scientists, then, the trinal aspect of the deity is reflected directly in creation, as figure 52 attests (see also figure 101). And as La Primaudaye continues to explain, elaborating the final words of Byrhtferth, it is manifested in a hierarchy of three distinct levels:

> There is the uppermost world of all, which Divines name, the Angelicall, and philosophers call the intellectuall world: which (as *Plato* saith) was never yet sufficiently praised. Then is there the celestiall world, or that of the spheres, which succeedeth and is next the first: and the third and last is the elementarie world which we inhabite, under the concavitie of the moone.

There is, then, first and highest a level called "the intellectual world" — Fludd's *caelum empyreum* — which is the habitat of angels. At the bottom is a level called "the elementarie world" — Fludd's *caelum elementare* — the physical and sense-perceptible region beneath the sphere of the moon which is our abode. And in the middle is a level called "the celestiall world" — Fludd's *caelum aethereum* — which includes the spheres of the planets and fixed stars. The celestial world, as Fludd's epithet for it reminds us, is composed of Aristotle's quintessential ether, the meta-element which fills the gap between physicality and conceptuality — that is, it is perceptible to our sense of sight, yet has no material substance. Therefore the planets and fixed stars are visible to us, though their spheres are perfect forms and their motion unending.

Our universe as three levels of creation projecting the trinal aspect of deity is shown in **Figures 53a-b**, taken from Charles de Bouelles, *Physicorum elementorum . . . libri decem* (Paris, 1512). At the bottom of **Figure 53a** we see the elementary world inhabited by an assortment of creatures from land, water, and air. This is the *sensibilis mundus* because it is perceptible to our senses. Encompassing "the sense-perceptible world" is the *caelestis mundus*, where God the Son presides over His handiwork of the several heavenly spheres. That the sun and the moon shine concurrently indicates

84

DIVINVS

Intellectualis Cælestis

Senſibilismundus.

Fig. 53a. *The three levels of creation as a continuum reflecting the Holy Trinity according to Bouelles.*

Métal' mūd'

DEVS

Intellectualismūdus

Seraphin.
Cherubin
Throni
Dominatiões
Virtutes
Poteſtates
Princid patus
Archágeli
Angeli

Numerus vigintiquinqǂ quīntus qͭia dͬatus

Celeſtismūdus

Eſſentiale celū
Intellectuale
Rationale
Firmamétūm
Cęlū Satūm
Iouis
Martis
Solis
Veneris
Mercurii
Lunę

Senſibilis

Iguis
Aer
Aqua
Terra

Fig. 53b. *The hierarchy of beings.*

the timelessness of this region, and therefore its incorruptibility. Above "the celestial world" rises the *intellectualis mundus,* the habitat of angels and saints. Finally—literally, "finally," *in fine,* as a limit—God the Father presides over all. He contains the three levels of creation within His trinity, so that the universe, though finite and inconstant, approaches perfection under His ministry. Belief in this cosmology generates optimism despite the corruptive evil evident in the world around us. The Fall itself becomes fortunate. Sin is only a temporary aberration in the divine plan, a passing accident that prepares us for salvation.

In a supplementary diagram, **Figure 53b,** Bouelles helpfully unfolds the three levels of creation and specifies the various categories that make up each. At the top, of course, and incorporating the entire scheme—His perfection is indicated by His circular form—rests God, the *mentalis mundus.* Below Him comes "the intellectual world," comprising the well-known nine orders of angels. Next comes "the celestial world," comprising three spheres that are not visible ("the essential," "the intellectual," and "the rational"), the sphere of fixed stars, and the seven planetary spheres. Last comes "the sensible world," comprising the region of the four elements. This is the hierarchy that persists as a plenum from the lowest stone to the throne of God. As the accounting along the right side indicates, the number of items is 25—that is, 5^2—a number perhaps significant to Bouelles since 5 in numerology represents both marriage and justice.

The opening paragraph of one of the most famous books of the sixteenth century provides an excellent gloss on Bouelles' illustrations:

> Seeing there is a three-fold World, Elementary, Celestiall, and Intellectuall, and every inferior is governed by its superior, and receiveth the influence of the vertues thereof, so that the very original, and chief Worker of all doth by Angels, the Heavens, Stars, Elements, Animals, Plants, Metals, and Stones convey from himself the vertues of his Omnipotency upon us, for whose service he made, and created all these things: Wise men conceive it no way irrationall that it should be possible for us to ascend by the same degrees through each World, to the same very originall World it self, the Maker of all things, and first Cause, from whence all things are, and proceed.[129]

With those words, Agrippa begins his *De occulta philosophia libri tres* (Antwerp, 1531), the most informative treatise on magic and related arts that the renaissance produced.

No commentary on figure 53 could be more cogent and precise, however, than Spenser's opening stanzas for "An Hymne of Heavenly Beautie." In this last of those poems grouped together under the title *Fowre Hymnes*, the poetical pilgrim concludes his ascent from earthly love to contemplation of the Most High. With something of the mystic's fervor, in the proem of this final hymn Spenser divulges his aim of delineating "those faire formes" that reside in heaven. After the proem, the hymn itself opens with the poet flying away on the viewless wings of poesy, as Keats might have said, to survey creation from bottom to top:

> Beginning then below, with th'easie vew
> Of this base world, subject to fleshly eye,
> From thence to mount aloft by order dew,
> To contemplation of th'immortall sky,
> Of the soare[130] faulcon so I learne to fly.

Starting with the "base world"—which submits to inspection by the "fleshly eye," the *mundus sensibilis*—the cosmic voyager mounts to the *mundus divinus*. In the role of vatic poet, he details the progress of such a journey through "the frame / Of this wyde *universe*" with its "endlesse kinds of creatures":

> First th'Earth, on adamantine pillers
>   founded,
> Amid the Sea engirt with brasen bands;
> Then th'Aire still flitting, but yet firmely
>   bounded
> On everie side, with pyles of flaming
>   brands,
> Never consum'd nor quencht with mortall
>   hands;
> And last, that mightie shining christall
>   wall,
> Wherewith he hath encompassed this All.

> .   .   .   .   .   .

> . . . Affixe thine eye
> On that bright shynie round still moving
>   Masse,[131]
> The house of blessed Gods, which men
>   call *Skye*,
> All sowd with glistring stars more thicke
>   then grasse,
> Whereof each other doth in brightnesse
>   passe;
> But those two most, which ruling night
>   and day,
> As King and Queene, the heavens Empire
>   sway.

> .   .   .   .   .   .

> . . . Farre above these heavens which
>   here we see,
> Be others farre exceeding these in light,
> Not bounded, not corrupt, as these same
>   bee,
> But infinite in largenesse and in hight,
> Unmoving, uncorrupt, and spotlesse
>   bright,
> That need no Sunne t'illuminate their
>   spheres,
> But their owne native light farre passing
>   theirs.

86

And as these heavens still by degrees arize,
Untill they come to their first Movers
    bound,
That in his mightie compasse doth com-
    prize,
And carrie all the rest with him around,
So those likewise doe by degrees redound,
And rise more faire, till they at last arive
To the most faire, whereto they all do
    strive.

Spenser ascends with grandiloquent certainty through each of the three levels of creation — the elementary, the celestial, and the intellectual — pausing to describe each in memorably poetic phrases. Eventually he arrives at the presence of God Almighty, "the most faire" of "those faire forms," an aristotelian "first Mover" or a platonic circle with circumference nowhere and center everywhere—"That in his mightie compasse doth comprize, / And carrie all the rest with him around."

Concurrent with this cosmology from platonism and the Church Fathers, and taken to be confirmation of it, was the extensive Hebrew commentary on the Old Testament included under the general term "cabala." This tradition, like that of the cosmology in figures 52 and 53, came directly out of the middle ages after a long and revered, if somewhat obscure, history. The cabala as the renaissance knew it originated in the thirteenth century with the purported discovery of a spuriously ancient manuscript, the *Zohar*, or "Book of Splendor." Actually, the *Zohar* is a collection of widely disparate texts compiled between 1280 and 1286 by a Spanish Jew, Moses ben Shem Tov de Leon of Guadalajara. From this rich source, medieval cabalism developed rapidly, though outside the orthodox rabbinic tradition.

The cabala consists in a fusion of Jewish theology, philosophy, and science, made congenial by the common solvent of mysticism. It seeks to train the worshipper to acquire knowledge of creation largely through study and introspection. Thereby the individual achieves communion with the fountainhead of his existence. The basic tenet of the cabala maintains that ultimate reality resides in the One, superior to and beyond being, Ein-Sof ("Infinite"). Ein-Sof is perfection itself, a unified infinite that admits no distinctions or differentiations. He is boundless, and hence unknowable to mortal minds, and certainly ineffable. Very much as in the ontology of neoplatonism, however, a knowable system — values, ideas, forms, objects — flows from the One as successive waves of emanations. And just as inexorably, everything returns to the One as its source. Consequently, although the One is Himself inscrutable, His effects are discernable in graduated degrees of clarity. Furthermore, as a corollary, each item in addition to its palpable qualities also possesses an esoteric aspect, an entity stretching toward ultimate reality and constituting various planes of existence. This theory led to the view that physical objects are symbols of transcendent meanings, like hieroglyphs.

The first wave of emanations from Ein-Sof was codified as ten "sefirot," or levels of understanding. The first sefirah (Keter, or *corona* in Latin — i.e., the Crown) represents the intention of Ein-Sof to make Himself manifest in a palpable creation, and therefore it is coeternal with deity, always present in His presence. The Crown, furthermore, contains *in potentia* the other nine sefirot, and they proceed to emanate from it, one succeeding another until the full complement of ten is perfected. But neither the Crown nor Ein-Sof is diminished by this emanation; rather, the process is described as though ten candles were lit from one another in series, so that the light is increased without detracting from its source. The ten sefirot therefore produce a self-consistent system that, although it remains in the realm of spirit, nonetheless describes the first stage of the deity's descent into materiality. Moreover, each of the sefirot is distinct from each of the others. Yet each is simply a different effect from the same source, a different manifestation of the same underlying oneness, so that taken together their totality reflects the unified infinity of Ein-Sof. In this scheme there is a dominant motif of multeity in unity, as well as an attempt to explain how that which is entirely conceptual transmutes to physicality. The deity is both transcendent and immanent. Paradox is the heart of the mystery.

The visual depiction of the system of the sefirot is varied, and complex symbolism accompanies it. One common scheme is known as "the tree" because it has a main stem and branches. An example of this formalized structure appears in **Figure 54**. This woodcut serves as title page for the *Portae lucis* (Augsburg, 1516) of Paulus Ricius, an erudite Jew converted to Christianity. After his conversion, Ricius became professor of Greek and Hebrew in the university of Pavia in 1521 and worked hard to convert other Jews. He moved in prominent circles as physician to Emperor Maximilian I, and at one time or another was an opponent of Johann Eck and an ally of Erasmus. Actually, "the gates of light" is an abridged Latin translation of a much older manuscript, the *Sha'arei Orah* of Joseph ben Abraham Chiquatilla (or Gikatilla), a treatise on the names of the deity and the ten sefirot.[132] Gikatilla had been a disciple of the almost legendary Abraham ben Samuel Abulafia, and his writings formed the basis for most dependable knowledge of the cabala in the early sixteenth century.

Within the gateway shown in figure 54 sits an old Jew holding the sefirotic tree, a structure that interconnects the ten sefirot.[133] At the top is the first sefirah, Keter or the Crown. Below to the right is the second sefirah, Hokhmah or Wisdom, while below Keter to the left is the third sefirah, Binah or Intelligence. Keter, Hokhmah, and Binah comprise the first sefirotic triad. Hokhmah is considered masculine, while Binah is considered feminine, and from them proceed the fourth sefirah (on the right), Gedullah or Love, which is masculine, and also the fifth sefirah (on the left), Gevurah or Justice, which is feminine. Gedullah and Gevurah join to produce the sixth sefirah, Tiferet

or Beauty. Gedullah, Gevurah, and Tiferet comprise the second sefirotic triad. Next proceed the seventh sefirah (on the right), Nezah or Firmness, and the eighth sefirah (on the left), Hod or Splendor. Nezah, which is masculine, and Hod, which is feminine, similarly couple to produce the ninth sefirah, Yesod or Foundation. Nezah, Hod, and Yesod comprise the third sefirotic triad. From Yesod proceeds the tenth and last sefirah, Malkhut or Kingdom. Malkhut is the perfection of the sefirotic system, and therefore it is frequently conceived as encircling the other nine. This divine halo, or Shekhinah, is all-encompassing, and therefore the principle that endows the tree of the sefirot with unity.

Often the three sefirotic triads were correlated with the three worlds distinguished by Robert Fludd in figure 52, so that Keter, Binah, and Hokhmah correspond to the empyreal world; Gedullah, Gevurah, and Tiferet to the ethereal world; Nezah, Hod, and Yesod to the elementary world; while Malkhut corresponds to the universe in its entirety. This tripartite system had been presented in the fourteenth century by Menahem ben Benjamin of Recanati, whose work was known to Christians early in the renaissance.[134] Furthermore, the ten sefirot were commonly distributed around a human form, resulting in a microcosmic image of prototypical man known as *Adam kadmon*. The first sefirotic triad furnishes his head, his brains, and his heart; Gedullah and Gevurah serve as arms; Tiferet provides a torso; Nezah and Hod act as legs; Yesod supplies a sexual organ; while Malkhut represents either the self-sufficiency of the archetype, or the female companion who is necessary to the male to make him whole. This configuration of the sefirot was sometimes associated with the *merkabah* chariot described by Ezekiel from his vision (Ezekiel, 1:16-28). Other common configurations for the ten sefirot include the Menorah, and a circle with Tiferet in the center.

In the renaissance the influence of the cabala on Christian thought was both intense and pervasive. Giovanni Pico della Mirandola

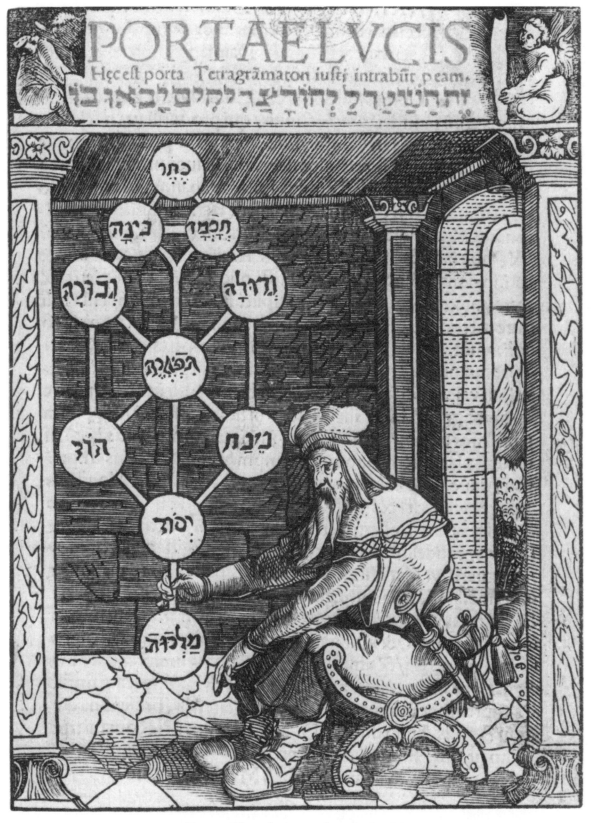

Fig. 54. *The sefirotic tree from Paulus Ricius.*

89

injected the cabala into the mainstream of West European culture with his famous 900 theses to be defended in public debate at Rome in 1486. One of these theses, perhaps the most notorious, maintained that "no science can better convince us of the divinity of Jesus Christ than magic[135] and the cabala." After the untimely death of Pico, his older friend, Johann Reuchlin, continued to expound the cabala with comparable enthusiasm and even greater learning. Reuchlin was the leading Hebraist of his day as well as a recognized master of Greek, and he may rightly be called the architect of the Christian cabala.[136] Because he was a focal figure for German humanism — indeed, the great-uncle and mentor of Melanchthon — he is also sometimes placed in the vanguard of the Reformation. For this highly respected pedagogue, the cabala was the repository of recondite wisdom, an enlargement of the Pentateuch that made the books of Moses at once more extensive and more profound.

With *De occulta philosophia libri tres,* Agrippa further enriched the literature drawing upon cabalistic lore. He meddled the cabala with the teachings of Hermes Trismegistus, Orpheus, Pythagoras, Plato, and the Church Fathers to arrive at a composite doctrine that he called "divine philosophy." Agrippa rapidly assumed the stature of a cult figure preaching a quasi-religion. Soon the most erudite and powerful men of Europe, including several popes, were convinced of the cabala's importance. And as late as John Milton, poets were still sentimentally lauding the syncretist's "divine philosophy" (see *Comus,* lines 476-80).

Pico, Reuchlin, and Agrippa believed, like most of their educated contemporaries, that the doctrine of the cabala stemmed from supernatural knowledge imparted to Adam at the moment of his creation. Thence it passed down to Noah, and eventually to Abraham. When Abraham emigrated to Egypt, it became available to that nation. Moses became acquainted with the cabala there; and during the forty years while the Israelites wandered in the wilderness, he greatly increased his knowledge of it both through private study and through further instruction by an angel of God. The first four books of the Torah, in fact, are his esoteric exposition of this secret doctrine.

During the renaissance the discovery of this ancient and exotic corpus of writings was enormously exciting to those who were attempting to reconstruct a *prisca theologia.* Pico, for example, reports that Pope Sixtus IV arranged for several cabalistic texts to be translated into Latin for public use, and Pico himself avidly sought out and studied what he could find:

> When I had procured myself these books at no small expense and had read them through with the greatest diligence and unwearied labor, I saw in them (God is my witness) a religion not so much Mosaic as Christian. There is the mystery of the Trinity, there the incarnation of the Word, there the divinity of the Messiah; there I read the same things on original sin, on Christ's atonement for it, on the heavenly Jerusalem, on the fall of demons, on the orders of angels, on purgatory, on the punishments of hell, which we daily read in Paul and Dionysius, in Jerome and Augustine. In those matters that regard philosophy, you may really hear Pythagoras and Plato, whose doctrines are so akin to Christian faith that our Augustine gives great thanks to God that the books of the Platonists came into his hands.[137]

With unbridled zeal, therefore, Pico studiously conflated the cabalistic cosmogony with that of platonism and Christianity. Thereafter the cabala, the *Timaeus,* and the Bible were seen as equal authorities, usually as parallel texts professing the same eternal verities even if in different terms.

To demonstrate how readily the Hebraic tradition coalesced with the most conventional of Christian thought, we need only continue with the passage from *The French academie* quoted on page 84, above. La Primaudaye proceeds by comparing the triplex structure of creation (see figure 53) with the tabernacle that Moses built according to God's specifications to provide a suitable place of worship (Exodus, 26:1 ff.). As La Primaudaye formulates this renaissance commonplace, "Our great prophet, of whom we have learnt the creation of heaven and earth [i.e., Moses], hath evidently described these three worlds in the structure of his marvellous tabernacle." And he goes on to note that Moses divided his tabernacle "into three parts, whereof each doth lively represent each world."

In this explication of *creatio triplex*, La Primaudaye is calling upon an ancient rabbinic tradition that similarly explicated the arcane meanings of Moses' curiously detailed tabernacle, a tradition that was made public by Philo Judaeus in the first century and was brought to bear upon Christian thought at least as early as St. Clement of Alexandria in the early third century (*Stromata*, V.vi). More immediately, however, La Primaudaye is calling upon Pico — in fact, his discoure is nothing more than an unacknowledged paraphrase of the "Second Proem to the Whole Work" that Pico placed before the *Heptaplus*. In this sevenfold exegesis of the hexaemeral miracle, Pico sets forth a theosophical cosmology with an evident cabalistic strain.

Pico's Second Proem begins with a clear-cut tripartite scheme for the universe:

> Antiquity imagined three worlds. Highest of all is that ultramundane one which theologians call the angelic and philosophers the intelligible, and of which, Plato says in the *Phaedrus* [247C], no one has worthily sung. Next to this comes the celestial world, and last of all, this sublunary one which we inhabit.

No diagram of the universe could be more precise in the distinction of its several parts. Pico then turns to the rabbinic motif of Moses' tabernacle as an emblem of this tripartite scheme:

> These three worlds were clearly diagrammed by Moses in the construction of his wonderful tabernacle. He divided the tabernacle

into three parts, none of which could more expressly represent the corresponding world of which we have spoken. The first part, not protected by any roof or umbrella, was open and exposed to showers, snow, sun, heat, cold; and, to make it more obviously an image of this sublunary world of ours, there dwelt there not only clean and unclean men, the holy and the profane, but also animals of many kinds; and there was even a continuous alternation of life and death in the offerings and living sacrifices. Both the two remaining parts were protected and free from external harm on all sides, just as the celestial and supercelestial worlds are susceptible of neither injury nor harm.

Pico continues to discuss "the three worlds" in Jewish terms and next touches upon one of his brashest theses. He demonstrates how knowledge of this cosmology, this exercise in magic and the cabala, convinces us of the divinity of Jesus Christ:

> By this we are also reminded of the higher mystery of the Gospel. Since the way to the supercelestial world, to communion with the angels, was opened for us by the cross and blood of Christ, for that reason, at the moment of his death, the veil of the temple was rent asunder, the veil by which the Holy of Holies, which we have said signifies the angelic world, was separated from the other parts. This was a sign that the approach to the kingdom of God now lay open for men, the approach to God Himself, who flies above the cherubim.

Theology, philosophy, and cosmology are inextricable for Pico, a true syncretist who saw man's purpose as the intellectual fusion of all knowledge in an abstract scheme of the divine mind. In Pico's scheme, there is no question of man's place in the universe or of his relationship to God. And man is made aware of these important matters by his microcosmic constitution. He literally incorporates within himself the full range of qualities that comprise the hierarchical structure of our universe:

There is, moreover, besides the three that we have mentioned, a fourth world in which are found all those things that are in the rest. This is man himself. . . . Man is a lesser world, in which are seen a body compounded from the elements, and a heavenly spirit, and the vegetative soul of plants, and the sense of brutes, and reason, and the angelic mind, and the likeness of God.[138]

With Sir Thomas Browne, we might exclaim, "O, altitudo!" How clearly we see the privileged position of man in this extremely complex, but nonetheless benevolent, system.

In the next century the clarity and precision of Pico's scheme impressed men who were more thoughtful than the somewhat pedestrian La Primaudaye. The *Heptaplus*, in fact, was translated into French by Nicolas LeFèvre de la Boderie, who published it at Paris in 1579 along with his brother Guy's translation of Francesco Giorgio's *De harmonia mundi totius cantica tria*. Giorgio was a member of the Franciscan Order of Minor Friars in Venice, and his widely read treatise on the harmony of the universe, first published at Venice in 1525, drew heavily upon cabalistic materials, especially the *Zohar*. Pico's *Heptaplus*, therefore, is an appropriate companion-piece in the large folio published by the LeFèvre *frères*.

By way of introduction to this syncretic volume, Nicolas LeFèvre wrote a prefatory essay entitled "Le coeur . . . , ou les 32. sentiers de sapience." These "32 paths of knowledge" actually amount to a cabalistic methodology for interpreting the Bible as allegory. According to the subtitle, it is a "Discours fort utile pour entendre et exposer les sainctes Escriptures." Illustrating this essay is **Figure 55**, which follows the passage quoted on pages 91-92, above. The caption at the top announces that the intricate scheme displays "what each of the three worlds is provided by its root, its square, and its cube; as well as how the universe is revealed through the numbers outside the circles, by which we may perceive the har-

mony and integrity of the whole system; and how we may take as true the saying of Anaxagoras, who placed 'all things in everything, and each thing in every other thing.'" The diagram itself sets forth creation as a hierarchy comprising twenty-eight items, numbered along the left-hand side. A marginal gloss further explains that "this series of numbers proceeding from 1 to 28 according to the perfect number and the cube of 3 declares the secret and mystery of the soul and of the world described and demonstrated by Plato in the *Timaeus*." In pythagorean mathematics, 28 is a "perfect number"—that is, the sum of its possible factors is equal to the number itself $(14 + 7 + 4 + 2 + 1 = 28)$.[139] Moreover, the world-soul is quantified as "the cube of 3" (see pages 97-98, below), and when this number is augmented by the divine One, the result is 28 $(27 + 1 = 28)$. Such are the numbers, weights, and measures that give structure to our universe.

At the top of this elaborate hierarchy, of course, is "God," "the simple unity," the circle with center everywhere and circumference nowhere. Below Him stretch three clearly delineated large circles, one for each of the three worlds—here labeled "angelic," "celestial," and "corruptible." The angelic world is identified as "the root of unity," the celestial world as "unity squared," and the corruptible world as "unity cubed"—suggesting the dimensional extension of "the simple unity" as it proceeds in stages toward full realization of materiality. Each of these large circles is further articulated into three smaller circles, repeating the pattern of the entire scheme, so that the highest small circle in each instance is "the root," expressed as the divine number 10; the middle is "the square," expressed as 100, the square of 10; and the lowest is "the cube," expressed as 1000, the cube of 10. Dante used a similarly interlaced numerical complex to organize the *Divina commedia*.

To identify details now, in the topmost large circle, the *monde angelique*, we have the nine orders of angels: "Seraphim," "Cheru-

L'introduction

QVANT A CE QVE CHACVN DES TROIS

mondes est pourueu de sa racine, quarré & Cube, tout ainsi que l'Vniuers, comme il apparoist par les nombres qui sont hors les rondeaux, par là peux-tu entendre l'Armonie & conuenance de tout, & comme peut estre vray le dire d'Anaxagore, qui mettoit omnia in omnibus & singula in singulis.

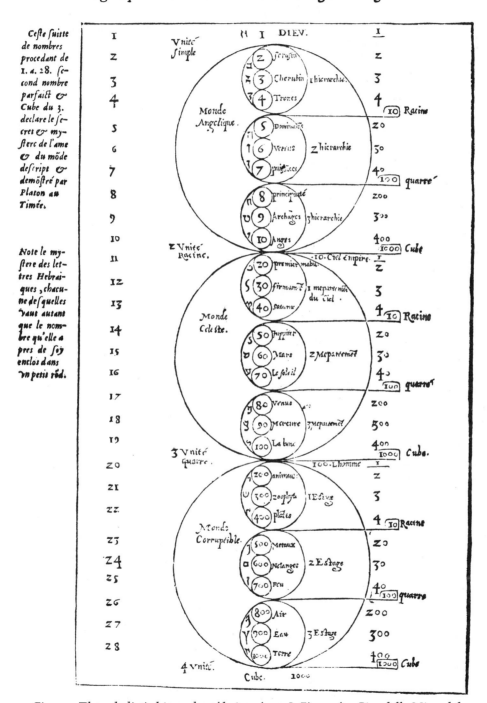

Fig. 55. *The cabalistic hierarchy of beings from LeFèvre after Pico della Mirandola.*

93

bim," and "Thrones" make up "the first hierarchy," which is "the root" of this circle; "Dominations," "Virtues," and "Powers" make up "the second hierarchy," which is "the square"; while "Principalities," "Archangels," and "Angels" make up "the third hierarchy," which is "the cube." We come now to "the empyreal heavens," a label placed appropriately where the two upper circles touch because the angelic orders are reflected in the spheres that comprise the visible heavens below.

In the second large circle, the *monde celeste*, we have the corresponding nine heavenly spheres: "the primum mobile," "the sphere of fixed stars," and "Saturn" make up "the first compartment of heaven," which is "the root" of this circle; "Jupiter," "Mars," and "the Sun" make up "the second compartment," which is "the square"; and "Venus," "Mercury," and "the Moon" make up "the third compartment," which is "the cube." We come now to the human microcosm, "man," who holds the ambiguous position between the celestial world and the physical world below.

In the bottommost large circle, the *monde corruptible*, we have the components of sublunary physics: "animals," "zoophytes," and "plants" make up "the first rank," which is "the root" of this circle; "metals," "mixtures," and elemental "fire" make up "the second rank," which is "the square"; and the other three elements—"air," "water," and "earth"—make up "the third rank," which is "the cube." So much for the mutable world that comprises the lowest third of the hierarchy.

To explain the numbers running down the right-hand margin requires a bit of pythagorean lore, which LeFèvre provides in the accompanying text. According to that doctrine, the numbers 4 and 10 are interchangeable because 4 contains within itself the potential of 10: $1 + 2 + 3 + 4 = 10$. Furthermore, 4 is the limit of physical extension (see page 99, below). Therefore the series of numbers begins with 1 for the deity, and continues with 2 and 3 and 4. But that is a limit, so a new series must start. The second series must be the squares of the

original series, and these squares are obtained by multiplying the original series by 10, the equivalent of 4, thereby producing 20 and 30 and 40. But again 40 is a limit, so once more a new series must start. This third series must be the cubes of the original series, and these cubes are obtained by multiplying the original series by 10 squared (i.e., 100), the equivalent of 4 squared, thereby producing 200 and 300 and 400. By this arithmetic, a special relationship between 1 and 4 and 10 is irrefutably established, a relationship highly meaningful to a pythagorean. This series of numbers demonstrates how the divine monad proliferates to the tetrad, the number of the extended universe, and yet how the tetrad holds latent within its multeity the perfection of the decad, which returns the series to its divine origin.[140] The relation between 1 and 4 and 10 in the pythagorean doctrine was seen as cognate to the relation between the One, the tetragrammaton, and the ten sefirot in the cabala, and therefore corroboration of it.

To conclude with figure 55, the cabalistic alignment of this diagram is obtrusively indicated by the Hebrew letters that appear immediately to the left of "God" and each of the smallest circles. In ancient languages — Greek and Latin, as well as Hebrew — the letters of the alphabet were used also as numbers, so that inside each of these smallest circles is the number equivalent to each of the Hebrew letters. As the marginal gloss instructs us, "Note the mystery of the Hebrew letters, each of which has the value of the number enclosed in the small circle beside it." Elsewhere Agrippa gives additional information on this topic:

> Simple numbers signifie Divine things; numbers of ten, Celestiall [things]; numbers of an hundred, terrestiall [things]; numbers of a thousand, those things that shall be in a future age.[141]

To exploit this equivalency between numbers and letters, a method of literary analysis known at *gematria* was developed. According to this method, the numbers equivalent to the letters of a word are added together, and any other word with the same total may be considered identical and interchanged with it. During the Reformation *gematria* became an important instrument of biblical exegesis, especially for the Book of Revelation, and we are indebted to it for ascertaining the identity of the Beast through his number, 666.

Such a diagram as figure 55 was the paradigm for organizing the multifarious items of creation into a comprehensive, yet knowable, scheme. Pico's syncretism retained its influence until the new astronomy made gravity, not the deity, the controlling force in cosmic mechanics. **Figure 56** is another derivative of Pico's system, although it comes as late as mid-seventeenth century. It appears in Athanasius Kircher's syncretistic compendium, *Musurgia universalis*, published in 1650 at Rome, and it purveys the same information as the preceding figure.

In figure 56 we see the deity represented by an all-encompassing circle (distorted into a form approaching an ellipse), which is labeled "the circle of worlds" and which flames with divine fire. Ranging vertically within this inclusive circle are the three worlds depicted similarly in figure 55. Each is further articulated in the same manner into three smaller circles, and each of them into three yet smaller circles. Therefore each large circle comprises nine small circles, and consequently is called an "ennead." The numbers within the small circles repeat the relationships of root, square, and cube that are indicated along the right-hand margin of figure 55. To give details of these three enneads, then, we have in the topmost circle "the first ennead, or series of the angelical world, displayed in numbers"; and it is articulated as "the triad of the first rank of the angelic choir," "the triad of the second rank of the angelic choir," and "the triad of the third rank of the angelic choir." We have in the middle circle "the second ennead, or series of the starry world expressed in numbers"; and it is articulated into a "first rank,"

"second rank," and "third rank." In the bottommost circle we have "the third ennead, or series of the elementary world"; and it likewise is articulated into three ranks.

To suggest the three-dimensional quality of this structure, Father Kircher has repeated this information in another arrangement of three contiguous circles that stretches horizontally across the diagram and intersects the three circles arranged vertically. The horizontal configuration, however, is identical with the vertical one and represents the same concept, though the various items are labeled in different terms (and somewhat inaccurately?). The topmost circle (on the right) contains the nine angelic orders, the primum mobile, and the sphere of fixed stars. The middle circle contains the seven planetary spheres. The lowest circle contains (from the bottom) the four elements, man, the three qualities of the soul (to sense, to live, and to exist eternally), and mixed things.

As a last bit of information in this diagram we should note the two mirror-image triangles that run the full length of the three horizontal circles. The triangle with its base at the top is labeled "the pyramid of light," and it vanishes to nothingness when its apex touches the lowest level, at elemental earth. The triangle with its base at the bottom is labeled "the pyramid of darkness," and it vanishes to nothingness when its apex touches the highest level, the enclosing circle of the deity. This is another of those arrangements composed of two equal but intersecting triangles so dear to Robert Fludd (see figures 18, 84), an arrangement wherein he demonstrates the inversely proportional relationship between the equivalent halves of a two-phase system.

The basic premise underlying figure 56 is of course a belief in cosmos, a certainty that a creating godhead has produced our universe and has endowed it with his perfection. Since he is both its maker and model, the cosmos reflects his beauty and completeness and unity —though within the finite coordinates of time and space. In classical times this belief was

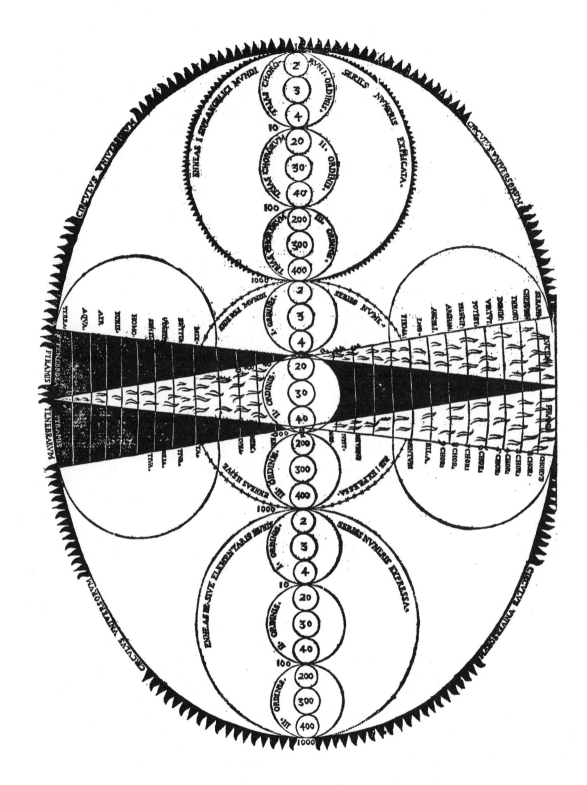

Fig. 56. *The cabalistic hierarchy of beings from Kircher.*

most emphatically enunciated in Plato's *Timaeus*, which assimilated the theology and science of the pythagorean school and made them staples of every subsequent school of thought in Western culture until the new physics of Newton. The *Timaeus*, therefore, describes the primary image in the cosmographical glass.

According to Timaeus, the creating godhead is denominated a poet (ποιητής > ποιεῖν, "to make"), a workman (δημιουργός), or an architect (τεκταινόμενος) — epithets freely employed also in the renaissance. Early in his celebrated essay *De dignitate hominis*, for example, Pico refers to God the Father as *architectus Deus*, and later in the same paragraph as *optimus opifex*.[142] During the act of creation, this "best of workmen" kept his eye on an ideal model (παράδειγμα), his own being, which he proceeded to reproduce in physical terms. The model consists of various perfect proportions based upon mathematical ratios, so the product of creation renders palpable a previously abstract mathematical arrangement. Agrippa cites Boethius' treatise *De arithmetica* (I.ii) to emphasize the importance of numbers in this cosmogony:

> *Severinus Boethius* saith, that all things which were first made by the nature of things in its first Age, seem to be formed by the proportion of numbers, for this was the principall pattern in the mind of the Creator. Hence is borrowed the number of the Elements, hence the courses of times [i.e., the cycle of the seasons], hence the motion of the Stars, and the revolution of the heaven, and the state of all things subsist by the uniting together of numbers.[143]

In this tradition, number and form and idea are synonymous, and the creating deity, as in the Book of Wisdom (11:21), expresses himself in a quantifiable medium. As a consequence, the platonic tradition was distinguished by its use of mathematics. Plato's god was characterized as the archgeometer, and mathematics was the core discipline in the Academy.

In the Timaean cosmogony, the marvel of creation lies precisely in the crucial act of transforming the ideal model into a substantial body. The definition of godhead, in fact, consists in this very ability to cross the discontinuity between intellectual and physical. Starting with no more than an idea, the deity has the will and the power to create an extended time-space continuum. The cosmogonist must therefore explain the miracle of how an extended body can generate from a form without substance. He must explain how the multitudinous items of our environment can generate from the static uniformity of God's idea — not only the wonder of how body can generate from insubstantial form, but also the paradox of how multeity can generate from unity.

The prototype for this explanation is offered by Plato himself in his discussion of the world-soul. After the world-body was created in accordance with the paradigm in God's mind, He next contrived a world-soul to mediate between the two, between the diverse finite and the unified infinite. The creating godhead devised a third entity known as "soul" (ψυχή), which partakes of both the ideal and the physical, and holds the two in liaison. Plato details the process step-by-step as a mathematical progression, describing a scheme whereby unity proliferates into multeity until the limit of physical extension is reached:

> First He took one portion from the whole;
> then He took a portion double of this;
> then a third portion, half as much again
>   as the second portion, that is, three
>   times as much as the first;
> the fourth portion He took was twice as
>   much as the second;
> the fifth three times as much as the third;
> the sixth eight times as much as the first;
>   and
> the seventh twenty-seven times as much
>   as the first.
>
> (*Timaeus*, 35C-36A)

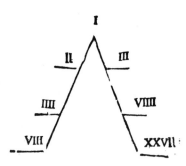

Fig. 57. *The platonic lambda from Macrobius.*

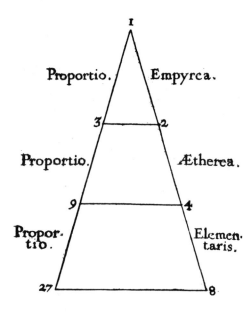

Fig. 58. *The three levels of creation amalgamated with the platonic lambda by Fludd.*

The result can be represented by a mathematical figure (**Figure 57**), known commonly as the platonic lambda because it is shaped like the Greek letter Λ. At the top is the number 1, representing the unity of the original idea. On the left, this unity proceeds to proliferate by a geometrical progression of the archetypal even numbers, reaching 2, then 4, and finally 8. On the right, this unity proceeds to proliferate by a geometrical progression of the archetypal odd numbers, reaching 3, then 9, and finally 27. Since all numbers must be either even or odd, this process exhausts the possibilities for proliferation. Furthermore, since the three stages of this proliferation achieve the limit of extension—that is, no figure can be extended beyond three dimensions, a cube—the proliferation halts at this stage. The limit of extension in the even series is 8, the cube of 2; the limit of extension in the odd series is 27, the cube of 3. The diagram, in fine, is a perfect model of the universe—"perfect" in the sense that it represents the process of creation carried through to completion and comprising all the possibilities. There can be no numbers other than odd and even numbers, and these numbers cannot be given physical extension beyond their cubes. This diagram therefore depicts the *idea* of the universe as it initially resides in the mind of God. In the *Commentarius in somnium Scipionis* Macrobius discusses the relevant passage in Plato at great length, and figure 57 comes from an edi-

tion of that text printed in 1485 at Brescia. The platonic lambda became a renaissance commonplace.[144]

Figure 58 is interesting because it correlates the platonic lambda with the three levels of creation: the empyreal world, the ethereal world, and the elementary world. Pursuing the argument that he demonstrates in figure 52, Robert Fludd shows that the three stages of proliferation between the monad and the cube may be identified with the three stages of substantiality in our created universe. The stage between the monad and the first extended number (3 on the left and 2 on the right) is the *proportio empyrea.* In this "proportion" (or relationship), we cross the dividing line between the dimensionless state and extension. Incorporeality translates to corporeality; infinity and eternity transmute to space and time. The second stage, between the simple number and the square (between 3 and 9 on the left and between 2 and 4 on the right), is the *proportio aetherea.* And the last stage, between the square and the cube (between 9 and 27 on the left and between 4 and 8 on the right), is the *proportio elementaris.* The fact that the cube is the limit of physical extension explains why there are three distinct levels of creation, no more and no less—or rather, the physical fact corroborates the theological premise that the universe is an image projecting the trinal aspect of the deity.

At the same time that the number 3 was seen as the limit of physical extension since a cube exhausts the possibilities of dimension, by another argument as old as Pythagoras the number 4 also was seen as the limit of physical extension. According to this reasoning, the number 1 is a point •, the number 2 produces a line •—•, and the number 3 produces a plane surface △. But the number 4 is required to produce a volume △. Clearly, 4 is the smallest number that can provide an extended body, as opposed to a point, a line, or a plane surface. Moreover, the number 4 disposed as an extended body comprises all of the possible dimensions in which a number might be arranged. Therefore 4 is the limit of physical extension.

This argument becomes central in the explanation of another paradox in the Timaean cosmogony, the paradox of how opposites can be reconciled. First, Plato assumes that there must be only four elements, since the number 4 exhausts the possibility of physical extension. A fifth element would simply have no place in the *schema* for the world's body. Aristotle postulated a fifth element, of course, but his quintessence was excluded from the mundane region and confined to the supralunary. The argument for only four elements is comparable to the one proposing that God created the universe *ex nihilo* since His infinitude precludes the possibility of any pre-existent matter. It is a conclusion arrived at wholly by logic, quite independent of empirical data and divorced from our actual experience. Our senses, in fact, might tell us something quite different. But for Plato—and for almost everyone until well into the seventeenth century—there were four elements because the number

4 delimited the world's substance. Everything in the sublunary region was composed of earth, water, air, and fire.

Therefore when the archgeometer laid out the universe, he perforce faced the task of interrelating these four distinct elements. From them he must devise a continuum. Moreover, two of them, fire and water, are exact contraries. Fire is hot and dry, while water is cold and moist. The apparently impossible task of reconciling these opposites contains another exposition of the miracle of creation and additional proof of God's unique power.

The deity began the physical creation with fire and earth—fire to make the world visible, and earth to give it solidity. Visibility and tangibility are necessary attributes of every palpable body. Then, in order to hold fire and earth together in some sort of binding relationship, he placed a mean between them, because as we know from mathematics, "It is not possible that two things alone should be conjoined without a third" (*Timaeus,* 31B-C). But a problem still lingers; the creation is still deficient. If the creation were meant to be a plane figure only, a single mean between two extremes would be sufficient, because a surface can be defined by three points. But creation must proceed to the figure of an extended body with volume, so a single mean is inadequate. Two means are required to provide four terms. Plato states the case explicitly:

> If the body of the All had had to come into existence as a plane surface, having no depth, one middle term would have sufficed to bind together both itself and its fellow-terms; but now it is otherwise: for it behoved it to be solid of shape, and what brings solids into unison is never one middle term alone but always two. (32B)

The requirement of two means between the extremes of fire and earth justifies the existence of four elements, and also demonstrates that the universe assimilates all of its potential components without excluding anything. The resultant scheme accommodates each of the

Fig. 59. *Christ as Plato's demiurge creating the four elements from Bartholomaeus.*

four elements, as Plato concludes: "Thus it was that in the midst between fire and earth God set water and air."

When Bartholomaeus Anglicus discussed the elements in his *De proprietatibus rerum,* he had this scheme in mind, as **Figure 59** indicates. It comes from John Trevisa's translation of Bartholomaeus printed by Wynken de Worde in 1495 at Westminster. In the diagram we see Christ as creator standing upon an orb of the world to proclaim His earthly supremacy. With His left hand He manipulates fire, while His right hand motions toward earth. These two elements were the starting materials for the heavenly maker. Air in the upper left corner and water in the lower right corner stand in readiness for use between the two extremes of fire and earth.

What Bartholomaeus' diagram leaves unmentioned is the mathematical complexity of cosmos. Plato, however, was insistent that

cosmos depends upon strictly defined mathematical ratios. In fact, the creating godhead arranged his scheme as an arithmetical proportion:

> Having bestowed upon them so far as possible a like ratio one towards another—air being to water as fire to air, and water being to earth as air to water—he joined together and constructed a Heaven visible and tangible. For these reasons and out of these materials, such in kind and four in number, the body of the Cosmos was harmonized by proportion and brought into existence. (32B-C)

The submission of each element in this mutually dependent arrangement is preliminary to cosmos and a prerequisite for the physical manifestation of the elements in a sense-perceptible body. In his "De natura rerum" the Venerable Bede repeats Plato's argument, and the collected edition of Bede's works in 1563 provides a fully explicit diagram.

In Bede's diagram (**Figure 60**), the extremes and the means are openly set forth. Fire and earth, the two elements with which the creating deity began, are the extremes—as they are, incidentally, in the extended universe that we perceive with our senses (earth is the lowest element and fire, visible in the stars, the highest). Their incompatibility is indicated by the word "inmediate," which signifies that they cannot be related by a single mean. But fire and water are "mediate," and so are air and earth— that is, each of these two pairs can be related by a mean. In consequence, the extremes of fire and earth, though themselves "inmediate," can be incorporated into a unified system by these two interlocking progressions. The logic can be represented mathematically by the following proportions:

$$\text{fire} : \text{air} = \text{air} : \text{water}$$
$$\text{air} : \text{water} = \text{water} : \text{earth}$$
$$\therefore \text{fire} : \text{air} = \text{air} : \text{water} = \text{water} : \text{earth}$$

The bonds between the contrary elements (fire and water, and air and earth) are simple arith-

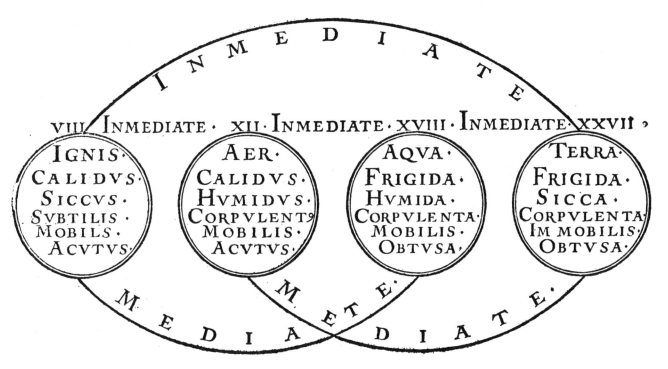

Fig. 60. *The four elements as a mathematical proportion from Bede.*

metical means, and a cosmos of four disparate items ensues.

There is additional information in figure 60 of a corroborative sort, again out of Plato. To emphasize the disparateness of the elements, five qualities are given for each. Fire, for example, is hot, dry, tenuous, mobile, and sharp; while water is cold, moist, heavy, mobile, and blunt. No two elements, of course, exhibit exactly the same qualities.

Finally, we must explain the numbers above each element. These numbers — 8, 12, 18, 27 — represent an attempt to associate this diagram of cosmos as a mathematical proportion with the diagram of cosmos as the platonic lambda (figure 57). Fire is designated as 8, the limit of extension of the even series in the platonic lambda, 2^3. Earth is designated as 27, the limit of extension of the odd series in the platonic lambda, 3^3. Since air and water are means between fire and earth, their numbers must be composite multiples of 2 and 3. Both air and water must represent a number comprised of three digits multiplied together, since they are physically extended (a "cube"),

and these digits must be either 2's or 3's. The number of air, since it is next to fire, has a preponderance of 2's—i.e., $2 \times 2 \times 3 = 12$; while the number of water, since it is next to earth, has a preponderance of 3's—i.e., $3 \times 3 \times 2 = 18$. By such a computation the number of air becomes 12 and the number of water becomes 18. The fact that such a system of arithmetical relationships can be devised corroborates the validity of the platonic lambda.

This sort of quasi-mathematical lore based upon the *Timaeus* was the authoritative cosmology of the middle ages. It was disseminated not only by Macrobius and Bede, but also by Isidore of Seville. In his *Liber de responsione mundi & astrorum ordinatione*, first printed in 1472 at Augsburg, Isidore gives much the same account of cosmos. **Figure 61** is taken from that text, and purveys the same theory as figure 60. Here, however, the arithmetical proportion is expanded from a simple linear arrangement to one with a suggestion of volume. The interlocking rings suggest a dimensional structure for the four elements. Moreover, the positioning of the two means (water and air)

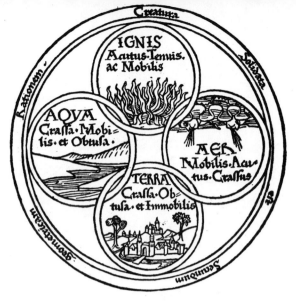

Fig. 61. The four elements as two pairs of opposites reconciled by mathematical means from Isidore.

between the two extremes (fire at the top and earth at the bottom) is more directly apparent here than in figure 60. Water and air are more evidently in mediate positions. Even though it is a *schema* arrived at by logic rather than by observation, the diagram still approximates certain palpable qualities, accentuated by the *visibilia* representing the four elements in the four circles. Nonetheless, to prevent our being misled down the path of empiricism, the inscription around the rim of the diagram firmly reminds us: "A geometrical plan insures the durability of the extended universe." And this *ratio*, of course, resides in the mind of the archgeometer.

It was an easy step from the arrangement of the four elements in this sort of arithmetical proportion to an arrangement of them as two pairs of opposites reconciled in a stable system. In fact, as we noted from the start, the *schema* of figure 60 was devised to explain the paradox of how opposites can be reconciled. But a need was felt to rearrange the arithmetical proportion of Bede in such a way as to display more immediately the intricate interdependency of the four elements.

The pythagorean tradition, which lay squarely behind the *Timaeus*, provided the most concise and satisfying theory. It offered an ingenious though simple arrangement of four terms known as the τετρακτύς, which was reverentially attributed to Pythagoras himself. The tetraktys was the *mysterium mysteriorum* of the pythagorean sect, a sacred symbol associated by later syncretists with the Hebrew tetragrammaton. La Primaudaye cites Hierocles of Alexandria, the fifth-century publicist of Pythagoras' *Golden Verses*, to establish the significance of this version of the number 4:

> *Hierocles* the interpreter of *Pythagoras*, doth so extoll this number of fower, that he affirmeth it to be the cause of all things, and that nothing can be said or done, which proceedeth not from it, as from the roote and foundation of all nature. And therfore did the Pythagorians sweare by this number, as by some holy thing, making (as may be easily conjectured) allusion to that great fower-lettered name of the Hebrues.[145]

As Hierocles declares, with La Primaudaye's endorsement, the pythagoreans viewed the tetraktys as a miraculous tetrad which sprang from the unified infinite of the divine monad and gave it sense-perceptible dimension. In this doctrine, the tetraktys is "the roote and foundation of all nature."

The pythagorean tetrad of elements was based on the premise that there are four basic qualities (hot, cold, moist, dry), and that these qualities determine the four elements. This premise was supported by Aristotle, most notably in the *De generatione et corruptione* and in the *Meteorologica*. It was repeated by every major medieval authority from Macrobius to Vincent de Beauvais, and was accepted by most renaissance scientists until Paracelsus, and perhaps until Robert Boyle. La Primaudaye makes the usual statement:

> [The elements] cannot be in number above fower; that is just so many, and neither more nor lesse then there are first qualities predominant in them, which are heat, moisture, colde and drienes; which neverthelesse alone and by themselves do not constitute an element: for they cannot have the power both to doe and to suffer; as it is needfull

that there should be in the generation and corruption of all things: neither can the foresaid qualities consist above two together, for feare least contrarie things should be found in one selfe same subject.[146]

Carefully echoing Aristotle, La Primaudaye notes that each element must subsume two qualities in order "both to doe and to suffer" — that is, in the cycle of generation and corruption to be both an active agent and a passive sufferer. More of this in a moment. La Primaudaye observes also that no single element can adopt more than two qualities lest an element comprise incompatible qualities — that is, if an element subsumes the two qualities of hot and moist, for example, it cannot adopt an additional quality of cold, because that would be incompatible with hot, nor an additional quality of dry, because that would be incompatible with moist.

Given the four basic qualities, it is obvious that they group themselves into two pairs of contraries: hot–cold and moist–dry. This relationship between the four qualities may be schematized as follows:

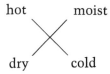

In this arrangement, adjacent qualities are then in a position to interact to produce an element — that is, hot and moist interact to produce air, moist and cold interact to produce water, cold and dry interact to produce earth, and dry and hot interact to produce fire. The result is presented in **Figure 62**, taken from Agostino Nifo's commentary on Aristotle's *Meteorologica* printed in 1531 at Venice. The basic qualities appear in the four corners, marked A, B, C, D. As the woodcut explicitly designates, however, hot and cold are incompatible, as are also moist and dry. The relationship of each pair of contraries *inconstat*. The relationship of adjacent qualities *constat*, though, so that hot and moist produce air, etc.

This in its most rudimentary guise is the tetraktys.

The pythagorean tetrad so devised is one of the most frequent commonplaces in renaissance science. It came out of the middle ages and continued undiminished, at least in popular treatises, right into the seventeenth century. **Figure 63a**, from Charles de Bouelles' *Liber de generatione*, displays the elemental tetrad in its simplest form. The four elements are placed at the corners of a square, and the quality that adjacent elements share is indicated along the side between them. That is, fire and earth share the quality dry, earth and water share the quality cold, water and air share the quality moist, and air and fire share the quality hot. La Primaudaye provides the comprehensive gloss for this diagram:

> [The qualities] being joyned two and two, they are correspondent the one to the other, as the qualities of heat and drines, which are in the fire: the heat & moisture, which are in the aire: cold & moisture, which are in the water: and cold & drines, which are in the earth. But heat & cold which are active

Fig. 62. *The Pythagorean tetrad from Nifo.*

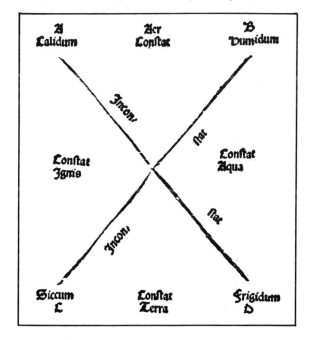

103

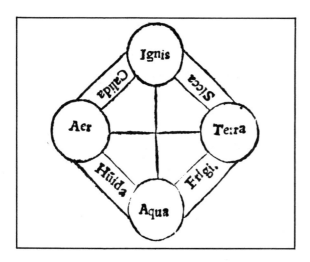

Fig. 63a. *The tetrad of elements from Bouelles.*

qualities, and moisture & drines which are passive qualities, are altogether contrarie. And therefore can they not consist both together in one selfe same element: wherupon it commeth to passe, that the fire & the water, the aire & the earth are cleane contrarie one to another.[147]

La Primaudaye, like Bouelles in figure 63a, concludes that not only the basic qualities, but also the resultant elements may be aligned as two pair of contraries: fire–water and air–earth.

Carrying on from La Primaudaye's final statement, we must note that figure 63a makes another important point about the tetrad: it suggests the dynamics of the four elements. In figure 62 the basic qualities are disposed as two pairs of contraries; but here, the elements themselves are disposed as opposites. Fire is emphatically shown to be the opposite of water, and earth is shown to be the opposite of air. In accord with aristotelian physics, between each pair of contraries there develops an outward thrust, which tends to disrupt the system — what Empedocles described as a primordial hate. This tendency leads toward corruption, toward decay in nature. But since each pair of adjacent elements share a quality, around the sides of the square there develops a concordancy, which tends to keep the system

intact — what Empedocles described as a primordial love. This tendency leads toward generation, toward synthesis in nature. A common metaphor for this amity between the elements was the cosmic dance, as La Primaudaye explains it:

> The elements are agreeable one to another, with their coupled qualities. . . . So that the fower elements are (as if each one of them had two hands, by which they held one another) as in a round daunce.[148]

Figure 63a, then, displays the cosmos in its tetrad form as a dynamic equilibrium. Not only does it demonstrate the paradox of opposites reconciled, but also the paradox of mobile stasis — to use an image from T. S. Eliot, how the wheel may turn, and still be forever still.

The result is a stable system, since the outward disruptive force is balanced by the cohesive force of sharing, but a system that is given to flux. It is dynamic, going through phases where hate and love dominate in turn—where generation evolves into corruption, but the concomitant decay provides the source of a fresh cycle of birth, growth, and death. In this cycle, hate and love are mutually responsive. As hate reaches its maximum strength, love proportionally diminishes; and vice versa. As hate becomes the aggressive agent, love becomes the passive sufferer; and as love becomes the aggressive agent, hate becomes the passive sufferer — so that hate and love produce a self-consistent system of acting and suffering, rather like the Chinese symbol of yin and yang. In this system, hate and love are exact counterparts, mirror-images — so that, as Eliot expresses it, "Acting is suffering / And suffering is action" *(Murder in the Cathedral)*.

In other terms equally important, the tetrad explains the perpetual transmutation of the elements among themselves. It provides a mechanism whereby one element can change by definable degrees into another element. This is the reason for Aristotle's interest in the pythagorean tetrad. As an example of this process of transmutation, fire can change to air by suppressing the quality of dry and accentuating the quality of hot, which it shares with air. Thereby fire exercises its affinity with air and becomes most like it. As a second step of transmutation, the newly formed fire/air can further change to water by suppressing the quality of hot and accentuating the quality of moist. In this fashion, an element can transmute even into its contrary. But because the tetrad is a self-contained system governed by a dynamic equilibrium, the amount of each element remains constant despite the continual flux, and therefore equal to the amount of every other element. This is another statement of the paradox of stasis despite mutability.

Perhaps most important, the pythagorean tetrad presents a system wherein each element can relate to every other element simultaneously, thereby demonstrating the paradox of four-in-one. Each element relates to its two adjacent elements by sharing a quality, and it relates to its contrary by being its opposite, its exact counterpart. In this fashion, each element inheres in each of the others at all times. The resultant system can be described mathematically, as it was in platonic academies, as a series of interlocking progressions where two extremes are conjoined by an arithmetical mean (see figure 60). The contraries fire and water, for example, are linked by a mean, earth. Moreover, air is also an arithmetical mean between fire and water, so there are two means between these two extremes. There are in fact two means between every pair of extremes, however the arrangement might be turned, so the requirement for an extended body, as Plato had prescribed in the *Timaeus*, is invariably met (see the quotation on page 99, above). The elemental tetrad is a mathematical exposition of cosmos, a *ratio geometrica* in the mind of God.

It may be wise at this point to reiterate that the tetrad is a conceptual diagram of the universe without reference to any physicality. That is, although elements are displayed as opposites and as neighbors, this presentation has nothing to do with their arrangement in the world we perceive with our senses. These are not spatial relationships. The physical dimension of the diagram, in fact, is apparent only, not real, an inevitable deception tolerated to render the concept knowable. Bouelles, in fact, offers an alternate version of the tetrad which at first glance obscures its quadripartite form and its system of opposites conjoined by means. **Figure 63b**, however, so far as information is concerned, is identical with figure 63a. Each element is shown as the product of two qualities—fire at the top, for example, is the product of dryness and heat. Moving down the ladder, we see that each quality in its criss-crossing alternately remains the same and becomes its opposite—heat at the top left, for example, remains the same when it is a component of air; becomes its contrary, cold, when it is a component of water; remains cold when it is a component of earth; but returns to heat, the contrary of cold,

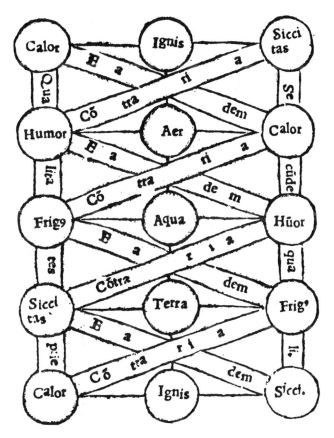

Fig. 63b. *A rearrangement of the tetrad by Bouelles.*

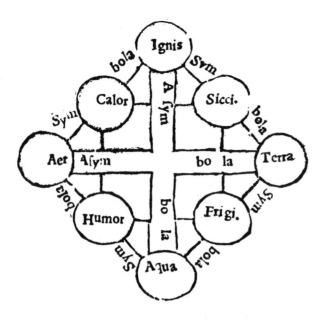

Fig. 63c. *A fully articulated tetrad of elements and qualities from Bouelles.*

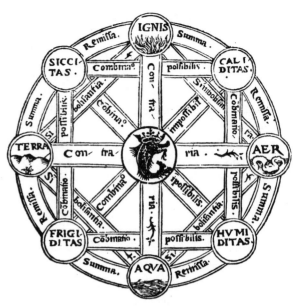

Fig. 64. *The Pythagorean tetrad from Finé.*

when it is a component of fire at the bottom.

We must note also another category of information in this diagram: it distinguishes between "primary qualities" and "secondary qualities," what we might better call dominant and recessive qualities. The qualities on the left are dominant; those on the right, recessive. In practice, this means that each element, though composed of two qualities, has a dominant quality and a recessive quality. Fire, for example, has heat for a primary quality and dryness for a secondary quality. Therefore in its transmutation, the quality of dryness recedes while the quality of hotness increases, until fire acquires an affinity with air. The transmutation then proceeds as the primary quality of moistness in the newly formed fire/air becomes dominant.

What this arrangement of the pythagorean tetrad in figure 63b emphasizes is the mediate position of air and earth between the extremes, fire and water. Figure 63b should be compared with figure 61, and the distinct difference between the two should be noted. Figure 61 shows how two means are placed between fire and earth, two extremes in the sense that they

are the two elements with which the godhead began creation, and the highest and the lowest elements in the physical stratification of the elements (see figures 15, 21). Figure 63b, in contrast, shows how two means are placed between each pair of qualitative contraries in the universe. Each pair of contraries are conjoined by two means, thereby producing an extended body, so that a comprehensive system results. Moreover, this system is based on the concept of qualities alone without reference to palpability, so that the pythagorean tetrad is an insubstantial form, a divine idea.

Bouelles returns the tetrad to its usual quadripartite form in **Figure 63c**. There the affinities (symbola) and the contrarieties (asymbola) are immediately evident in the tetrad of qualities imposed at right angles upon the tetrad of elements.

The classic statement of the pythagorean tetrad appears in **Figure 64**, taken from Oronce Finé's *Protomathesis*. The four basic qualities are in place at the corners of a square, each diagonally across from its opposite. Dryness is diagonally across from moistness, and heat diagonally across from cold. Opposites cannot combine, and consequently these diagonals are labeled *combinatio impossibilis.* Adjacent qualities, however, may combine, and the *combinationes possibiles* are also labeled. Each adjacent pair of qualities combines to produce an element—dryness and heat at the top, for example, combine to produce fire. In this combination, heat is *summa* and dryness is *remissa*—that is, heat is the dominant quality in fire, and dryness the recessive quality. And so on around the circle of elements: for air, heat is recessive and moistness dominant; for water, moistness is recessive and coldness dominant; for earth, coldness is recessive and dryness dominant. Transmutation among the elements takes place along this line. Furthermore, adjacent elements are compatible because they share a common quality—fire and air, for example, share the quality of heat; and this compatibility is indicated by the label *simbolisantia.* Elements opposite one another, however, are contraries, and the lines between them are so labeled. To end on an extraneous note, the crowned dolphin in the center of the figure is a proud declaration by Finé (who probably drew this diagram himself) that he was regius professor of mathematics in the Collège de France, as well as a tribute to his birthplace, Le Dauphiné.

This tetrad pattern was the archetypal idea in the mind of the creating deity, and it precisely informs the universe. Not only does it provide the pattern for cosmos as a whole, but it imprints its form upon every level of creation. The tetrad is the abstract *schema* for the macrocosm, and also for the multitudinous microcosms that reproduce in small its exhaustive fullness. As a consequence, an elaborate network of correspondences exists between the various levels of creation. Put another way, each microcosm, through sharing the tetrad pattern, is correspondent to each and every other microcosm. The universe, in fact, is one immense collage of interlocking tetrads, repeating one another by shadow or reflection.

The doctrine of cosmic correspondence is confidently expressed by Bartholomaeus Anglicus in his thirteenth-century encyclopedia, *De proprietatibus rerum,* which Stephen Batman translated in 1582. In a chapter entitled "What is the world?" Bartholomaeus answers this rhetorical question by offering three alternative but complementary definitions, which Batman glosses in the margin as "the Celestiall world, the Elementall world, the lesser world."[149] The text itself carefully distinguishes between these three conceptions. The first is a non-corporeal world, an idea in the mind of God, recognizable despite its Christian coloration as the archetypal idea in the mind of the demiurge in Plato's *Timaeus:*

> For Divine understanding is called the world, that is to wit *Mundus Archetipus,* and is bodilesse, unseene, and everlasting. . . . And so the first world is everlasting & during in thought and minde of God.

The second is the sense-perceptible world composed of the quintessential ether and the four elements, as Aristotle had described it:

> In the seconde manner, the world is called all things that is contained in the roundnesse of heaven. As heaven, in the which the starres shine: and fire in which all things heate: aire, by the which all things that hath lyfe breedeth & proveth: & water that beclippeth the sides of the earth: earth, that sustaineth and holdeth up, and feedeth all these lowe things of this worlde.

Finally, there is the lesser world of the human microcosm, which literally incorporates the characteristics of both the conceptual and the physical worlds:

> In the third manner, man is called, the lesse world, for he sheweth in himselfe likenesse of all the world.

The theory of cosmos emphasizes the orderliness and the unity of our environment, evident no matter where or when we look. In spatial terms, our world is a beautifully articulated complex, integrated vertically as well as

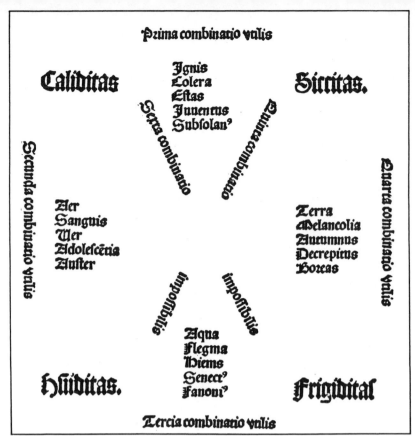

Fig. 65. *Various correspondences implied in the tetrad according to Peyligk.*

horizontally. In temporal terms, the seasons hold their beneficent cycle, recurring in predictable sequence and running the full gamut of possible circumstances. Moreover, we as lesser worlds share this order and variety, and have a natural place in it.

Fig. 66. *The expanded tetrad according to Isidore.*

The pythagorean tetrad expanded into a system of cosmic correspondences was a cliché of renaissance science, philosophy, and religion. **Figure 65**, taken from Johann Peyligk's *Philosophiae naturalis compendium* (Leipzig, 1499), is a concise example of it. Here the macrocosm of the four elements is further adumbrated by microcosms of the four bodily humours, the four seasons, the four ages of man, and the four cardinal winds. To deal with particulars in the diagram, the four basic qualities, as in figure 64, are situated at the corners of a square. Along the top, heat and dryness provide "the first fruitful combination" and produce the element fire. Correspondent to fire (and listed below it) are cholera (or yellow bile) in the microcosm of the bodily humours, summer in the microcosm of the annual seasons, childhood in the microcosm of man's ages, and Subsolanus, the East Wind, in the microcosm of cardinal winds. Along the left of the square, heat and moistness provide "the second fruitful combination" and produce the element air. Correspondent to air are blood, spring, adolescence, and Auster, the South Wind. Along the bottom, moistness and cold provide "the third fruitful combination" and produce the element water. Correspondent to water are phlegm, winter, old age, and Favonius, the West Wind. Along the right side of the square, cold and dryness provide "the fourth fruitful combination" and produce the element earth. Correspondent to earth are melancholy (or black bile), autumn, middle-age, and Boreas, the North Wind. Dryness and moistness, however, cannot combine, and so the diagonal between them, which is labeled "the fifth combination," is "impossible." Similarly, the diagonal between heat and coldness, which is labeled "the sixth combination," is also impossible.

This lore, as we might expect, had come intact from the middle ages.[150] Quite early Isidore of Seville had summarized it in his *De natura rerum*, and the result is depicted in **Figure 66**, taken from the *editio princeps* of that

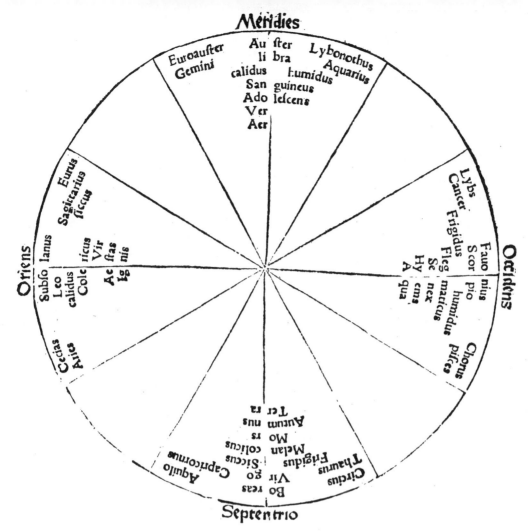

Fig. 67. *The tetrad as wind-rose from Eck after Aristotle.*

text printed in 1472 at Augsburg. As the caption in the center of the diagram clearly states, this beautifully stylized woodcut interrelates the cosmoi of the physical world, the year, and man. At the top is fire, flanked by its two basic qualities, dry and hot, and correspondent to summer and yellow bile. At the right is air, flanked by hot and moist, and correspondent to spring and blood. At the bottom is water, flanked by moist and cold, and correspondent to winter and phlegm. At the left is earth, flanked by cold and dry, and correspondent to autumn and black bile. No representation of infinite variety could be simpler. The interlacing is continuous, suggesting the integrity of this scheme and approaching the perfection of the circle at eight symmetrical points.

As we shall see, the pythagorean tetrad often underwent strange metamorphoses not always immediately recognizable. **Figure 67**, taken from Johann Eck's commentary on Aristotle's *Meteorologica* printed at Augsburg in 1519, is a case in point. Actually, it purveys the same information as figure 66, but with additional microcosms included. First, around the outside of the circle appear the four cardinal points of the compass: according to the prevalent convention, south is at the top, west on the right, north at the bottom, and east on the left. Just inside the circle are the twelve major winds, divided into four groups of three each. Inside the winds come the twelve signs of the zodiac, similarly divided into four groups of three each. Next come the basic qualities, two designated for each element. Then the four

Fig. 68. *The expanded tetrad according to Walkington.*

complexions are given: sanguine, phlegmatic, melancholy, and choleric. Finally, the three innermost circles contain the ages of man, the seasons of the year, and the four elements. Ostensibly, however, this tetrad is a wind-rose, and therefore it appears as a circle with twelve divisions.[151]

Figure 68 demonstrates the persistence of the expanded tetrad into the seventeenth century. In his *Optick glasse of humors* (London, 1607), a medical text of a bookish sort, Thomas Walkington recounts the entire concept and offers this diagram by way of illustration. Even the details by now are familiar. Starting at the center and ranging outwards, we have correspondences between the complexions, the ages of man, the seasons, the cardinal winds, and the elements. For good measure, Walkington next arranges the seven signs of the planets around his circle and names four of them: Mars, Jupiter, the Moon, and Saturn. Finally, he includes the twelve signs of the zodiac around the outside of the circle, dividing them as in figure 67 into four groups of three each. There are discrepancies, however, between the correspon-

dences designated in figure 68 and those in figure 67. In its latter-day incarnations the tradition was allowed to degenerate.

Picking up the signs of the zodiac around the outside of Walkington's diagram, we can turn to another metamorphosis of the expanded tetrad: man's life as a twelve-part cosmos accommodated to the components of time. This emblem was omnipresent in the middle ages,[152] and **Figure 69** is perhaps the most explicit example of it to survive into the renaissance. Figure 69 appears in an early edition of Bartholomaeus Anglicus' *De proprietatibus rerum* printed at Lyons in 1485, where it illustrates the chapter "On Time." In essence, the diagram consists of three concentric circles, each of which exhausts the possibilities for variety in its particular system and thereby achieves the perfection of a unified infinite. In the outer circle appear the twelve signs of the zodiac, exhausting the possibilities for variety in the moving of the heavens and thereby achieving the perfection of a year, the annual unit of time.

In the middle circle appear twelve vignettes, each representing an activity appropriate to one of the twelve months, a commonplace in medieval literature and art. In its totality, this circle exhausts the possibilities of human experience and thereby achieves the perfection of a good, full life. To interpret this motif we should begin in the lower right portion of the circle where a two-headed Janus sits before a festive board and represents January. But no account of this motif can improve upon Bartholomaeus' own commentary (as John Trevisa translated it):

> Januari . . . hath that name of a god feyned that hyghte Janus, for to hym that month was halowed. . . . And he is paynted wyth two frontes, to shewe and to teche the begynnynge and ende of the yere. . . . And he is paynted etynge and drynkynge of a cuppe, for that tyme beestes nede grete plente of mete. . . .

Frebruari is paynted as an olde man sittynge by the fyre heetinge & warmynge his fete and hondes, for that tyme is stronge colde for the sonne is ferre and hath be for so longe tyme. . . .

Marche is paynted as it were a gardyner, for that tyme superfluytees of vynes and of other trees ben shredde & paryd. . . .

Apryll is paynted berynge a floure, for in that monthe the erthe hath that begynninge to be clothed and arayed wyth floures. . . .

May is a tyme of myrthe, of love, of gladnesse, and of lykynge. For moost in May byrdes synge & make Joye. . . . For May is a tyme of solace and of likynge, therfore is it paynted lyke a yonge man rydyng & berynge a foule on his honde.

The month of June is ende of spryngynge tyme, and begynnynge of Somer. . . . And thenne the heete of the sonne dryeth humoures in mores & rotes, & all thynge drawyth to rypenesse, & therfore he is paynted as mowynge haye. . . .

Julius is paynted wyth an hoke repynge corne, for thenne is covenable repynge tyme. . . .

In this month [August] corn is gaderyd in to bernes. And therfore he is payntyd wyth a flaylle thresshynge corn and makyth the erthe bare. . . .

Fig. 69. *The tetrad as an explanation of time according to Bartholomaeus.*

This month [September] is the ende of Somer & bigynnyng of Harveste. In this month grapes ben rype, & therfore he is paynted in a vynyerde, as a gardyner gad-crynge grapes in a baskette. . . .

This month [October] is kyndly colde & drye. . . . And therfore this month is paynted in the lyknesse of a sower that sowyth his sede.

This monthe [November] with his dry-nesse and colde constreynyth and byndyth and dryeth, and makyth leves of trees falle. . . . And therfor this month is paynted as a chorle betyng okes and fedynge his swyne with maste and hockornes.

In that monthe [December] for sharpe-nesse of colde foules & beestes that ben fedde in house ben quyete & of lytell mev-yng. And therfore thei wexe fatte, and therfore that tyme they ben slayne. And of thyse monthes a yere is made, as well of the sonne as of the mone.[153]

Despite some inconsistencies between the text, and the illustration, we can see the precise detail that rendered this motif a staple of the medieval scene. The manifold activities of

Fig. 70. *Bartholomaeus' diagram in* The kalender of shepardes.

man, especially as he tilled his soil and fol-lowed the natural cycle of the seasons, pro-vided a paradigm of human experience.

The inner circle of figure 69 is the most dif-ficult to interpret, particularly for modern eyes; but obviously it is composed of two half-circles, careful counterparts of one another. In the top half-circle, a young woman holds a bouquet of flowers and kneels in a grassy mea-dow beneath leafy trees. The season is unmis-takably summer—in fact, the young woman here looks very much like the female figure representing Virgo among the zodiacal signs in the outer circle. That woman also holds a flower. In the bottom half-circle, a mature man warms his hands before a fire and sits in a barren field beneath leafless trees. The season is unmistakably winter—in fact, this man is identical with the male figure representing February in the monthly occupations of the middle circle. The man is clearly associated with February, the last month in the year ac-cording to the pagan calendar when the sun runs through the sign Pisces to complete his annual cycle. The woman is associated with Virgo, the sign exactly opposite Pisces in the zodiac when the sun is strongest. The two half-circles depict counterparts, then, which op-pose one another in every detail. And yet the two half-circles taken together form a circle, a self-sufficient system that is perfect, both in the sense of being complete and of being ideal. Thereby the opposites of man-woman, sum-mer-winter, youth-age are embodied in a perfect scheme. The inner circle—like the middle circle, though in a more rudimentary and concise form—similarly exhausts the pos-sibilities of human experience and achieves perfection.

Finally, in figure 69 each of the three circles is correspondent to the other two; and the tet-rad pattern, though it is elaborated to a twelve-part system in the two outer circles and re-duced to a two-part system in the inner circle, underlies the whole. The paradoxes of the tetrad—substantiality from insubstantiality, multeity in unity, reconciliation of opposites, mobile stasis — all the paradoxes of the tetrad inhere in this diagram. In sum, it represents that orderly moving of the heavens known since the *Timaeus* as "time."

A version of the figure we have been studying appears in each of the numerous editions of Bartholomaeus in the renaissance, including the momentous English translation of John Trevisa printed by Wynken de Worde in 1495 (y1ᵛ). The diagram received even wider dis-

semination in England through its inclusion in the immensely popular *Kalender of shepardes*, first translated in 1503 from a French original and kept in print throughout the sixteenth century. **Figure 70**, taken from an edition published about 1518, shows how closely the perennial almanac reproduced the familiar diagram from Bartholomaeus' text.

By the time Bartholomaeus' encyclopedia was again translated into English by Stephen

Fig. 71. *Bartholomaeus' diagram in a degenerated form as occupations for the months.*

113

Fig. 72.
*Occupations for
the months from
Bede.*

Ianuarius.
Poto.

1

7

Iulius.
Spicas declino.

Februarius.
Ligna cremo.

2

8

Augustus.
Messes meto.

Martius.
De uite superflua demo.

3

9

September.
Vina propino.

Aprilis.
Do germen gratum.

4

10

October.
Semen humi iacto.

Maius.
Mihi flos seruit.

5

11

Nouember.
Mihi pasco sues.

Iunius.
Mihi pratum.

6

12

December.
Mihi macto.

Batman in 1582, the diagram that correlated the moving of the heavens and man's life had degenerated considerably. It appears in a suitable place to illustrate the chapter "Of Time," but in a simplistic form of nothing more than twelve circular vignettes representing the various activities appropriate to each month (**Figure 71**). And the vignettes are arranged in four rows of three rather than in a circle. The cosmic significance of this illustration, however, should not be forgotten. It is an icon of man, the microcosm, and therefore of the universe in its ample plenitude.

The information contained in figure 71 and in the middle circles of figures 69 and 70 — that is, the occupations associated with each of the twelve months — was an accessible motif that had been widely used in the middle ages.[154] It appeared everywhere and retained its popularity for centuries. **Figure 72** is a particularly handsome and informative example printed in 1563. It adorns a text of Bede's "Libellus de tonitruis" published in his complete works, presumably for no reason other than that Bede gives the significance of thunder in each month of the year. In any case, this depiction of the monthly occupations of man is notable because the zodiacal signs are incorporated directly into the vignettes, and because each vignette bears a descriptive caption. For January, the caption announces, "I am drinking"; for February, "I am burning logs"; for March, "I am draining sap from my trees"; for April, "I am putting in my tender plants"; for May, "A flower has bound me to my love"; for June, "I am mowing and raking the meadow"; for July, "I am cutting my grain"; for August, "I am gathering my harvest"; for September, "I am drinking my wine"; for October, "I am planting seed"; for November, "I am fattening my hogs"; for December, "I am slaughtering one of my cattle." Although each of the vignettes is distinct, a discrete entity, together the twelve of them comprise an all-inclusive totality that is comparable in its completeness to the six days' work of the hexaemeron. Fig-

ure 72 may be profitably compared to figures 10 and 11. It is the same sort of self-consistent and all-inclusive system. It may be profitably compared also to the woodcuts that stand before each of Spenser's twelve eclogues in *The Shepheardes Calender*. In each instance, the twelve occupations taken together run through the varieties of human experience and represent the interminable fullness of God's creation.

In figures 65-70 we discern a complexity and density that accrue from the amalgamation of several microcosms into a single scheme. Each of these figures is an expanded tetrad that interconnects several different levels of creation and exemplifies the correspondences between them. Even figures 71 and 72 display the microcosm of man as a synthesis of twelve typical activities and relate him to the cosmos as imaged in the zodiac, thereby placing him in the context of time.

Often the complexity and density of the expanded tetrad was presented more obviously, without the decorative or pictorial trappings, simply as a table of correspondences. **Figure 73** is a clear-cut example of this sort of exposition. It comes from the *De occulta philosophia libri tres*, masterwork of the colorful polymath, Agrippa, written by 1510 though not printed in a complete text until 1533 at Cologne.[155] Agrippa was one of the more restive sixteenth-century occultists, moving from one royal court to another throughout Europe. He came to London in 1510 on a diplomatic mission for Maximilian I of Germany and stayed with John Colet, dean of St. Paul's. Thomas Nashe records the surely apocryphal tale of how the earl of Surrey while visiting Italy importuned Agrippa to show him the fair Geraldine back in England, and how Agrippa used his magic mirror to do so. In the discipline of cosmography, Agrippa was best known for his division of the universe into three worlds: the elementary, the celestial, and the intellectual (see pages 85-86, above) — an adaptation of the scheme that Pico had taken from Recanati (see

Fig. 73. The universe as a table of correspondences based on the number 4 according to Agrippa.

Nomen dei quadrili terum.	יהוה				In mundo Arche typo unde lex prouidentiæ
Quatuor triplicita tes siue hierar chie intelligibiles	Seraphim Cherubim Throni	Dominationes Potestates Virtutes	Principatus Archangeli Angeli	Innocentes Martyres Confeßores	In mundo intelle- ctuali, unde lex fatalis
Quatuor angeli præsidentes cardinibus cœli	מיכאל Mihaël	רפאל Raphaël	גבריאל Gabriel	אוריאל Vriel	
Quatuor præfecti elementorum.	שרף Seraph	כרוב Cherub	תרשיש Tharsis	אריאל Ariel	
Quatuor animalia sanctitatis	Leo	Aquila	Homo	Vitulus	
Quatuor triplicita tes tribuum Iraël	Dan Aßer Nephtalim	Iehuda Isachar Zabulon	Manaße Beniamin Ephraim	Ruben Simehon Gad	
Quatuor triplicita tes apostolicæ	Mathias Petrus Iacobus Maior	Symon Barptolomæus Matthæus	Iohannes Philippus Iacobus Minor	Thadæus Andreas Thomas	
Quatuor euangeli stæ	Marcus	Iohannes	Matthæus	Lucas	
Quatuor triplicita tes signorum	Aries Leo Sagittarius	Gemini Libra Aquarius	Cancer Scorpius Pisces	Taurus Virgo Capricornus	In mundo cœlesti à quo lex naturæ
Stellæ & planetæ ad elementa relati	Mars & Sol	Iupiter & Venus	Saturnus & Mercurius	Stellæ fixæ & Luna	
Quatuor qualita tes cœlestium ele mentorum	Lumen	Diaphanum	Agilitas	Soliditas	
Quatuor elemen ta	אש Ignis	רוח Aër	מים Aqua	עפר Terra	In mundo elemen tali ubi lex gene rationis & cor ruptionis
Quatuor qualita tes	Calidum	Humidum	Frigidum	Siccum	
Quatuor tempora	Aestas	Ver	Hyems	Autumnus	
Quatuor cardines orbis	Oriens	Occidens	Septentrio	Meridies	
Quatuor mixtorū genera perfecta	Animalia	Plantæ	Metalla	Lapides	
Quadruplicita ani malia	Progreßiua	Volatilia	Natantia	Reptilia	

pages 91-92, above). Agrippa, in fact, adapted this three-part scheme as the organizing principle for the *De occulta philosophia*, and figure 73 appears in this compendium of theoretical and practical sorcery, which continued as an unassailable authority for well over a century.

Agrippa's table is exactly translated by **Figure 74a**, taken from an English rendition published as *Three books of occult philosophy* in 1651 at London. This table of correspondences is presented as "The Scale of the Number four, answering the four Elements" (page 186), and is one in a series of such tables devised for each of the first ten numbers and the number 12.[156] At the top of figure 74a, prominently placed, is the tetragrammaton in Hebrew, "The name of God with four letters." In the column at the far right, the several levels of creation are indicated. At the top of the column, coexistent

116

Quæ respondēt elementis in plātis.	Semina	Flores	Folia	Radices	
Quæ in metallis.	Aurum & ferrum	Cuprū & stannū	Argentumuiuum	Plumbū et argentū	
Quæ in lapidibus.	Lucētes & ardētes	Leues & trāspētes	Clari & cōgelati	Graues & opaci	
Quatuor hominis elementa.	Mens	Spiritus	Anima	Corpus	In minore mundo scilicet homine à quo lex prudentiæ.
Quatuor potentiæ animæ.	Intellectus	Ratio	Phantasia	Sensus	
Quatuor iudiciariæ potestates.	Fides	Scientia	Opinio	Experimentum	
Quatuor uirtutes morales.	Iustitia	Temperātia	Prudentia	Fortitudo	
Sensus respondētes elementis.	Visus	Auditus	Gustus & olfactus	Tactus	
Quatuor humani corporis elemēta.	Spiritus	Caro	Humores	Ossa	
Quadruplex spūs.	Animalis	Vitalis	Gignitiuus	Naturalis	
Quatuor humores.	Cholera	Sanguis	Pituita	Melancholia	
Quatuor complexionum mores.	Impetus	Alacritas	Inertia	Tarditas	
Quatuor principes dæmoniorum nocētes in elemētis.	סמאל Samael	עזאזל Azazel	עזאל Azael	מהזאל Mahazael	In mūdo infernali ubi lex iræ & punitionis.
Quatuor flumina inferna.	Phlegethon	Cocytus	Styx	Acheron	
Quatuor principes dæmonioru super quatuor angelos orbis.	Oriens	Paymon	Egyn	Amaymon	

with the tetragrammaton, is "the Originall world" (the *mundus archetypus* in the Latin version, figure 73). Beneath "the Originall world," and flowing from it, comes the hierarchy of "the Intellectual world," "the Celestiall world," "the Elementary" world, "the lesser world, *viz.* man," and "the infernall world."

In the column at the far left, the several systems which exist at each of these levels of creation are indicated. To begin at the top, for example, in "the Intellectual world" there are seven systems to be displayed: "Four Triplicities or intelligible Hierarchies" (i.e., the nine orders of angels augmented with three orders of saints, grouped in four categories of three each), "Four Angels ruling over the corners of the world," "Four rulers of the Elements," "Four consecrated Animals," "Four Triplicities of the tribes of Israel" (again, a system of twelve items, grouped in four categories of three each), "Four Triplicities of Apostles" (once more, a system of twelve items), and "Four Evangelists." At the next level of creation, in "the Celestiall world," there are three systems to be displayed: "Four Triplicities of [zodiacal] Signs" (yet once more, a system of twelve items), "the Stars and Planets" (the seven planetary spheres augmented with the sphere of fixed stars, grouped in four categories of two each), and the "Four qualities of the Celestiall Elements." At the next level of creation, in "the Elementary" world, there are nine systems to be displayed: "Four Elements," "Four qualities," "Four seasons," "Four corners of the World," "Four perfect kinds of mixt

117

186 Of *Occult Philoſophy.* Book II.

The Scale.

The name of God with four letters.	יהוה				In the Originall world, whence the Law of providence.
Four Triplicities or intelligible Hierarchies.	Seraphim. Cherubin. Thrones.	Dominations. Powers. Vertues.	Principalities. Archangels. Angels.	Innocents. Martyrs. Confeſſors.	In the Intellectual world, whence the fatall Law.
Four Angels ruling over the corners of the world.	מיכאל Michael.	רפאל Raphael.	גבריאל Gabriel.	אוריאל Uriel.	
Four rulers of the Elements.	שרפ Seraph.	כרוב Cherub.	תרשיש Tharſis.	אריאל Ariel.	
Four conſecrated Animals.	The Lion.	The Eagle.	Man.	A Calf.	
Four Triplicities of the tribes of Iſrael.	Dan. Aſſer. Nephtalin.	Jehuda. Iſſachar. Zabulun.	Manaſſe. Benjamin. Ephraim.	Reuben Simeon. Gad.	
Four Triplicities of Apoſtles.	Mathias. Peter. Jacob the elder.	Simon. Bartholemew. Mathew.	John. Phillip. James the younger.	Thaddeus. Andrew. Thomas.	
Four Evangeliſts.	Mark.	John.	Mathew.	Luke.	
Four Triplicities of Signs.	Aries. Leo. Sagittarius.	Gemini. Libra. Aquarius.	Cancer. Scorpius. Piſces.	Taurus. Virgo. Capricornus.	In the Celeſtiall world, where is the law of nature
The Stars, and Planets, related to the Elements.	Mars, and the Sun.	Jupiter, and Venus.	Saturn, and Mercury.	The fixt Stars, and the Moon.	
Four qualities of the Celeſtiall Elements.	Light.	Diaphanouſneſs.	Agility.	Solidity.	
Four Elements.	אש Fire.	רוח Ayre.	מים Water.	עפר Earth.	In the Elementary, where the Law of generation and corruption is.
Four qualities.	Heat.	Moyſture.	Cold.	Dryneſs.	
Four ſeaſons.	Summer.	Spring.	Winter.	Autumne.	
Four corners of the World.	The Eaſt.	The Weſt.	The North.	The South.	
Four perfect kinds of mixt bodies.	Animals.	Plants.	Metals.	Stones.	
Four kinds of Animals.	Walking.	Flying.	Swimming.	Creeping.	

Book II. Of *Occult Philoſophy.* 187

What anſwer the Elements, in Plants.	Seeds.	Flowers.	Leaves.	Roots.	
What in Metals.	Gold, and Iron.	Copper, and Tin.	Quickſilver.	Lead, & Silver.	
What in ſtones.	Bright, and burning.	Light, and tranſparent.	Clear, and congealed.	Heavy, & dark.	
Four Elements of man.	The Mind.	The Spirit.	The Soul.	The body.	In the le[ſſer] world, *viz.* man, from wh[ence] is the Law [of] prudence.
Four powers of the Soul.	The Intellect.	Reaſon.	Phantaſy.	Senſe.	
Four Judiciary powers.	Faith.	Science.	Opinion.	Experience.	
Four morall vertues.	Juſtice.	Temperance.	Prudence.	Fortitude.	
The ſenſes anſwering to the Elements.	Sight.	Hearing.	Taſt, and ſmel.	Touch.	
Four Elements of mans body.	Spirit.	Fleſh.	Humours.	Bones.	
A four-fold ſpirit.	Animall.	Vitall.	Generative.	Naturall.	
Four humours.	Choller.	Blood.	Flegme.	Melancholly.	
Four Manners of complexion.	Violence.	Nimbleneſs.	Dulneſs.	Slowneſs.	
Four Princes of divels, offenſive in the Elements.	סמאל Samael.	עזאזל Azazel.	עזאל Azael.	מהזאל Mahazael.	In the infern[all] world, where the Law of wrath, and [pu]niſhment.
Four infernal Rivers.	Phlegeton.	Cocytus.	Styx.	Acheron.	
Four Princes of ſpirits, upon the the four angels of the world.	Oriens.	Paymon.	Egyn.	Amaymon.	

CHAP.

Fig. 74a. *An English version of Plate 73.*

bodies," "Four kinds of Animals," "What answer the Elements, in Plants" (i.e., the parts of a plant correspondent to each of the four elements), "What in Metals" are correspondent to the elements, and "What in stones" are correspondent to the elements. And so on for the other two levels of creation, the microcosm of man and the infernal world.

Read horizontally, this table sets forth all of the items in any given system, and consequently represents the system in its completeness. A horizontal line is a total unit. Furthermore, since each system is comprised of four parts, the number 4 can be abstracted from the table as its essential form. The number 4 literally informs every system, is the common denominator for every level of creation. This truth is self-evident to the adept, since creation emanates from the tetragrammaton.

So there is horizontal dimension in this table: each unit is extended into four parts. But also there is vertical dimension. Not only does the table provide all the items in any given system when read across, but also when read up-and-down the table provides an elaborate network of correspondences that embraces all of the systems. The items in each of the four vertical columns under the tetragrammaton are correspondent to one another — that is, an item that fills a certain position in a system is correspondent to every other item that fills an analogous position in its system. For example, to read the left-hand column of the four columns under the tetragrammaton — and to start with fire, because we are already aware of these correspondences — fire (reading downward) is correspondent with the basic quality of heat, with the season of summer, with the direction of East, with animals among physical creatures ("mixt bodies"), especially walking animals, with seeds in plants, with gold and iron among the metals, and with the qualities bright and burning in stones. At the next level, in the microcosm of man, fire is correspondent with the mind, with the intellect among the powers of the soul, with faith among man's powers to learn, with justice among the moral virtues, with sight among the senses, and so forth. Reading upward in the other direction from fire, we see that fire in the celestial world is also correspondent with the celestial quality of light, with the planets Mars and the Sun, and with the zodiacal signs Aries, Leo, and Sagittarius. Continuing into the intellectual world, fire is correspondent with the Evangelist Mark, with the Apostles Mathias, Peter, and Jacob the Elder, with the tribes of Israel named Dan, Asser, and Nephtalin, with the lion among sacred animals, and so forth. When we turn to the other elements, we see that air partakes in a comparable range of correspondences, and water and earth similarly inhere in a vertical series of correspondent items.

Moreover, just as any item implies the other three items in its system on a horizontal level — as we have seen in the pythagorean tetrad for example, fire literally implies air, water, and earth — so also any item implies the other

numerous items that are correspondent to it in a vertical column. Fire *is* heat, summer, the East, a walking animal, seeds, etc. In a real sense, therefore, though not necessarily in a physical sense, St. Mark can be represented by a lion. They are correspondent and accordingly interchangeable. In consequence, this network of correspondences provides a rich store of metaphors. A correspondence allows the transfer of meaning from one level to another — the literal definition of "metaphor," as its etymology tells us. Be it noted, though, that these metaphors are predetermined. They are givens, data of a scientific sort in this ontology. They are not devices arbitrarily contrived by a poet.

Fig. 74b. *The universe as a table of correspondences based on the number 1.*

The Scale of Unity.

In the exemplary world.	ʼIod	One Divine eſſence, the fountain of all vertues, and power, whoſe name is expreſſed with one moſt ſimple Letter.
In the intellectuall world.	The ſoul of the world.	One ſupreme Intelligence, the firſt Creature, The fountain of lives.
In the Celeſtial world.	The Sun.	One King of Stars, fountain of life.
In the Elementall world.	The Philoſophers Stone.	One ſubject, and inſtrument of all vertues, naturall, and ſupernaturall.
In the leſſer world.	The Heart.	One firſt living, and laſt dying.
In the Infernall world.	Lucifer.	One Prince of Rebellion, of Angels, and darkneſs.

Notice also that these metaphors are valid in the intelligible realm only, and do not submit to sense perception. This entire scheme, actually, is a mental construct—a *concept*, not a *percept*. For example, summer is correspondent to, and therefore a metaphor for, not the signs of the zodiac that dominate during the summer months—that is, Cancer, Leo, and Virgo. But rather summer is correspondent to three zodiacal signs placed symmetrically around the circle: Aries, Leo, and Sagittarius, only one of which really falls within the summer season. Obviously some principal other than physicality is operative. And that principle is based upon the efficacy of an innate and insubstantial, though perfect, form—upon a network of ideal relationships that extends both horizontally and vertically throughout our three-dimensional universe. Figure 74a, then, is a diagram of that network, based upon the form inherent in the number 4.

A comparable diagram can be prepared where the inherent form is the number 2 or 3 or 6 or 8—any number, in fact, up to and including 10. Agrippa works in the strait tradition of pythagoreanism which saw numbers as forms—triangles and squares and cubes—forms that exist in abstraction and that may (or may not) be imposed upon matter. In consequence, Agrippa's text is fully implemented by tables for each of the first ten numbers.

Figure 74b, for example, is a table for the number 1, "The Scale of Unity." In the commentary, Agrippa makes clear that 1 is in truth a unity, and cannot be divided into parts; yet, since this unity is evident everywhere in the universe, the number 1 manifests itself at every level of creation. At the top of figure 74b is the abode of deity, that which exists outside the confines of our created universe. Agrippa calls it "the exemplary world," what he calls elsewhere "the originall world." It is inhabited by "One Divine essence . . . whose name is expressed with one most simple Letter." This letter, given in the middle column, is the Hebrew *Yod* (which is also in He-

The Scale of the Number

In the originall	יהוהיהויהי The name Jehova of ten letters collected.				או הא The Name Jehova letters.
	אהיה Eheie. כתר Kether.	יהוה Iod Jehovah. חכמה Hochmah.	יה האלהים Jehova Elohim. בינה Binah.	אל El. הסד Hesed.	מניבר Elohim גורה Geburah
In the intelligible world.	Seraphim. Haioth ha-kados. Metattron.	Cherubim. Ophanim. Jophiel.	Thrones. Aralim. Zaphkiel.	Dominations. Hasmallim. Zadkiel.	Powers. Seraphin Camael.
In the Celestiall world.	Reschith ha-gallalim. The Primum Mobile.	Masloth. The sphere of the Zodiake.	Sabbathi. The Sphere of Saturn.	Zedeck. The sphere of Jupiter.	Madim. The Sph. Mars.
In the Elementary world.	A Dove.	A Libard.	A Dragon.	An Eagle.	A Horse.
In the lesser world.	Spirit.	Brain.	Spleen.	Liver.	Gall.
In the infernall world.	False Gods.	Lying spirits.	Vessels of iniquity.	Revengers of wickednes.	Juglers.

brew the divine number 10). The remainder of the table is then devoted to the created universe itself. In the column at the left, ranging beneath "the exemplary world," are the five levels of creation as Agrippa defined them: "the intellectuall world," "the Celestial world," "the Elementall world," "the lesser world" (i.e., the microcosm of man), and "the infernall world." In the middle column, ranging beneath *Yod*, are the primate items at each of these levels of creation. In the column at the right, we see the epithets appropriate to each item in the middle column. According to this scheme, the items in the middle column are clearly correspondents, one with each and all of the others.

Ten.

יוד הא Extended.		אלהים צבאות The name Elohim Sabaoth.			The name of God with ten letters.
אליה Eloha. תפארת Tiphereth.	יהוה צבאות Jehovah Sabaoth נצה Nezah.	אלהימצבאות Elohim Sabaoth. הוד Hod.	שדי Sadai. יסוד Iesod.	ארני Adonai melech. מלכות Malchuth.	Ten names of God. Ten Sephiroth.
Vertues. Malachim Raphel.	Principalities. Elohim. Haniel.	Archangels. Ben Elohim. Michael.	Angels. Cherubim Gabriel.	Blessed souls. Issim. The soul of Messiah.	Ten orders of the blessed according to Dionysius. Ten orders of the blessed according to the traditions of men. Ten Angels ruling.
Schemes. The sphere of the Sun.	Noga. The sphere of Venus.	Cochab. The sphere of Mercury.	Levanah. The sphere of the Moon.	Holom. Jesodoth. The sphere of the Elements.	Ten spheres of the world.
Lion.	Man.	Genitals.	Bull.	Lamb.	Ten Animals consecrated to the Gods.
Heart.	Kidnyes.	Lungs.	Genitals.	Matrix.	Ten parts intrinsecall of man.
Aery powers.	Furies the seminaries of evil.	Sifters or tryers.	Tempters or ensnarers.	Wicked souls bearing rule.	Ten orders of the damned.

Fig. 74c. *The universe as a table of correspondences based on the number 10.*

Figure 74c in similar fashion sets forth "The Scale of the Number Ten." In the left-hand column, again, we have "the originall" world and the five levels of creation that extend vertitcally in order from it. In the right-hand column we have labels for the various systems that extend horizontally across the table at each level of creation. At the top is "The name of God with ten letters," which in its full form is *Elohim Sabaoth*. Occupying an unlabeled intermediate region between Jehovah and His creation, we have, in accord with the cabala, the "Ten names of God" mentioned in the Talmud and the "Ten Sephiroth" (see pages 87-88, above).[157] Occupying "the intelligible world," we have the ten orders of angels according to Dionysius the Areopagite, the ten orders of angels according to the cabala, and the ten archangels of the cabala. Occupying "the Celestiall world," we have the "Ten spheres of the world," in both Hebrew and Latin (here translated into English). Occupying "the Elementary world," we have "Ten Animals consecrated to the Gods." Occupying "the lesser world" of man, we have the ten parts of his body. And at the bottom, occupying "the infernall world," we have the "Ten orders of the damned." Again, the items in any vertical column are correspondent to one another.

121

The Scale of the Number twelve.

	הוא Holy	ברוך B'lessed	הקרש He			אב בנזרוח הקרש Father, Son, Holy Ghost.						
The names of God with twelve letters.												In the originall world.
The great name returned back into twelve banners. יהוה	יהוו	יוהה	הוהי	הויה	ההיו	ויההי	יוהה	והיה	היהו	היוה	ההיו	
Twelve orders of the blessed Spirits.	Seraphim.	Cherubim.	Thrones.	Dominations.	Powers.	Vertues.	Principalities.	Archangels.	Angels.	Innocents	Martyrs.	Confessors.	In the Intelligible world.
Twelve Angels ruling over the signs.	Malchidiel.	Asmodel.	Ambriel	Muriel.	Verchiel.	Hamaliel.	Zuriel.	Barbiel.	Adnachiel	Hanael.	Gabiel.	Barchiel.	
Twelve Tribes:	Dan.	Ruben.	Judah.	Manasseh.	Asher.	Simeon.	Issachar.	Benjamin.	Napthalin	Gad.	Zabulon.	Ephraim.	
Twelve Prophets.	Malachi.	Haggai.	Zachary.	Amos.	Hosea.	Micha.	Jonah.	Obadiah.	Zephaniah	Nahum.	Habakuk	Joel.	
Twelve Apostles.	Mathias.	Thadeus.	Simon.	John.	Peter.	Andrew.	Bartholemew.	Philip.	James the elder.	Thomas.	Matthew.	James the yonger.	In the Celestiall world.
Twelve signs of the Zodiack.	Aries.	Taurus.	Gemini.	Cancer.	Leo.	Virgo.	Libra.	Scorpius.	Sagittarius	Capricorn	Aquarius.	Pisces.	In the Elementall world.
Twelve Moneths.	March.	April.	May.	June.	July.	August.	September	October.	Novemb.	December	January.	February.	
Twelve Plants.	Sang.	Upright Vervain.	Bending Vervain.	Comfrey.	Lady's Seal.	Calamint.	Scorpiongrass.	Mugwort.	Pimpernel.	Dock.	Dragonwort.	Aristolochy.	
Twelve stones.	Sardonius.	A Carneol	Topaze	Calcedony.	Jasper.	Emrald.	Berill.	Amethyst.	Hyacinth.	Chrysoprasus.	Crystall.	Saphir.	In the Elementary world.
Twelve principall members.	The head.	The neck.	The arms.	The brest.	The heart.	The belly.	The kidnies.	Genitals.	The hams.	Knees.	Legs.	Feet.	
Twelve degrees of the damned, and of Divels.	False gods	Lying spirits.	Vessels of iniquity.	Revengers of wickedness.	Juglers.	Aery powers.	Furies the sowers of evils.	Sifters or Tryers.	Tempters or ensnarers.	Witches.	Apostates.	Infidels.	In the infernall world.

Fig. 74d.　The universe as a table of correspondences based on the number 12.

Three books of occult philosophy provides such a table also for the number 12 (**Figure 74d**), an unusually adaptable number in cosmic speculation—as Agrippa says, "that whereby the Celestials are measured."[158] At the top of this table is the name of God expressed in twelve letters. In the column at the far right are the same levels of creation as in the other tables from this text, starting with "the originall world" at the top (though the lesser world of man is mislabeled "Elementary.") In the column at the far left, several systems at each level of creation are indicated, starting with "the great name returned back into twelve banners" at the top, and continuing with "Twelve orders of the blessed Spirits." Significantly, there are exactly twelve of these systems, so that this table is a square of twelve items across and twelve items down. The items in the twelve vertical columns, of course, are

	Lux perspicua cum humore æquabili.	Lux perspicua cum humore inæquabili.	Lux opaca in humore inæquabili.	Lux opaca in humore æquabili.
	Calidum Humidum.	Calidum Siccum.	Frigidum Siccum.	Frigidum Humidum.
ELEMENTA COMMVNIA.	AER	IGNIS	TERRA	AQVA
ELEMENTA CÆLESTIA.	Lux qualis in ♃ ♀	Lux qualis in ♂ ☉	Lux qualis in ♄ ☿	Lux qualis in ☾
ELEMENTA ÆTHEREA.	Splendor aut vehiculum aëreum.	Splendor aut vehiculum igneum.	Splendor aut vehiculum terreum.	Splendor aut vehiculum aqueum.
ELEMENTA SVBLVNARIA.	Lumen aëreum ex perspicuo & æquabili.	Lumen aut subiectum igneum ex perspicuo & inæquabili.	Lumé terreum ex opaco & inæquabili.	Lumen aqueú ex opaco & æquabili.
HVMORES ET TEMPERAMENTA	Sanguis & sanguineú temperamentum.	Cholera & biliosa crasis.	Atra bilis & crasis melancholica.	Pituita & crasis phlegmatica.
AETATES.	Pueritia. Pubertas. Adolescentia.	Iuuentus. Aetatis virilis exordia.	Senectus & ætas decrepita.	Virilis ætas. Senium.
ANNI TEMPORA.	Ver Galeno temperatum.	Aestas.	Autumnus Galeno inæqualis.	Hyems.
CARDINES MVNDI.	Meridies.	Ortus.	Septentrio.	Occasus.
VENTI.	Auster cum collateralibus.	Eurus.	Aquilo.	Zephyrus.
PARTES ANIMALIVM.	Caro, pulmones, medullæ.	Parenchymata, vt hepar, splen, cor.	Solidæ partes, vt ossa, nerui, cartilag. venæ, arteriæ.	Cerebrum, adeps, stomachus, intestina.
PARTES VINI, OLEI ET SIMILIVM.	Flos { Vini. Olei.	Vinum feruentius aut oleum.	Fex { Vini. Olei.	Mustum aut oleum quod iam concoqui pridem cæpit.
ANALOGIA accidentiú cæterorú præsentiú sensibilium. { Visu Auditu Gustu Olfactu Tactu.	Aërea. Aequabilia tenuia.	Ignea Tenuia leuia, sed inæquabilia.	Terrea Crassa & inæquabilia.	Aquea Crassa, sed æquabilia quævis.

Fig. 75. *The universe as a table of correspondences based on the four elements according to Cornelius Gemma.*

correspondent to one another, and consequently serve as a compilation of metaphors that are absolute, not partial or doubtful.

This mode of diagraming the universe as a table of correspondences continued to be popular in the renaissance. **Figure 75** is an example taken from Cornelius Gemma, *De arte* *cyclognomica, tomi III* (Antwerp, 1569), which contains several such tables based upon different numbers. In this diagram, which should be compared with figures 73 and 74a, the pythagorean tetrad is obviously the organizing principle. The four elements, set near the top in large type, distinguish four columns of correspondent items. In the box above each element, its two basic qualities are given—for example, above air is "hot" and "moist." In the column at the far left, there are listed the various systems organized by the tetrad of elements: reading downward, "the common elements," "the celestial elements," "the atmospheric elements," "the sublunary elements," "humours and temperaments," "the ages of man," "the seasons of the year," "the cardinal directions," "the winds," "the parts of the body," "the parts of wine, oil and similar things," and "the correspondence of other qualities according to sense perception." This table unmistakably represents a three-dimensional scheme, a type of the extended universe. It is an abstract of our time-space continuum based upon the number 4.

Figure 76 is a similar scheme, though based upon the number 9. It appears in Athanasius Kircher's *Musurgia universalis,* and documents the persistence of this tradition at least until the mid-point of the seventeenth century. As usual, Father Kircher brings the tradition to its fullest fruition and compiles a comprehensive range of correspondences. He thinks of the creation as a grand symphony (see also figure 13), a notion we shall find diagrammed in figures 79-83; and here he explicates the universal harmony as ten "enneachords"— that is, a chord of nine notes. The caption at the top explains the principle: "The wholesome harmony of the world, manifesting the symphony of all nature in ten enneachords."

In effect, figure 76 sets forth the nine-fold correspondences between ten distinct categories of existence, which are denominated by italicized labels across the top of the table: the *mundus archetypus* or God, the starry region or *coelum empireum,* the mineral region, stones, plants, trees, swimming creatures, flying creatures, four-legged creatures, and various colors. Reading downward under each of these labels, we have a hierarchy for that category. For example, under God in the *mundus archetypus,* we have the nine orders of angels; under *coelum empireum,* we have the sphere of fixed stars and the seven planetary spheres (each indicated by a symbol and by the note it plays in the music of the spheres), with earth making up the ninth item in the enneachord and "playing the lowest note among the elements" (terra cum elementis proslambanomenos; see figure 83); under the *mundus mineralis,* we have a variety of metals, starting at the top with "salts, stars, and minerals," and including quicksilver (argentum vivum); and so forth.

When we read across this table horizontally, what we have is a series of correspondences between these ten categories of existence. The third line from the bottom, for example, indicates a correspondence between the order of Princes among the angels, the planet Mercury (which plays the note *parhypate*), the mineral quicksilver, the semiprecious stones agate and jasper, the peony in the plant world, the rosy-apple tree, the beaver among swimming creatures, the parrot among winged creatures, the dog among four-legged creatures, and the color deep blue. The fourth line from the bottom indicates a correspondence between Powers, Venus, tin, the beryl, ragwort, myrtle, the trout, the swan and the dove, the deer, and bright green.

At the far left in figure 76 is a musical scale revealing the note each category plays in the universal symphony. Between the lowest and the next category, there is a "tone," a whole note. Between the lowest and the third category from the bottom, there are two tones. Between the lowest and the fourth category, there is a *diatesseron,* "a fourth"; and then a *diapente,* "a fifth"; six notes; seven notes; and next a *diapason,* a full scale of eight notes that we call an "octave." Between the lowest and

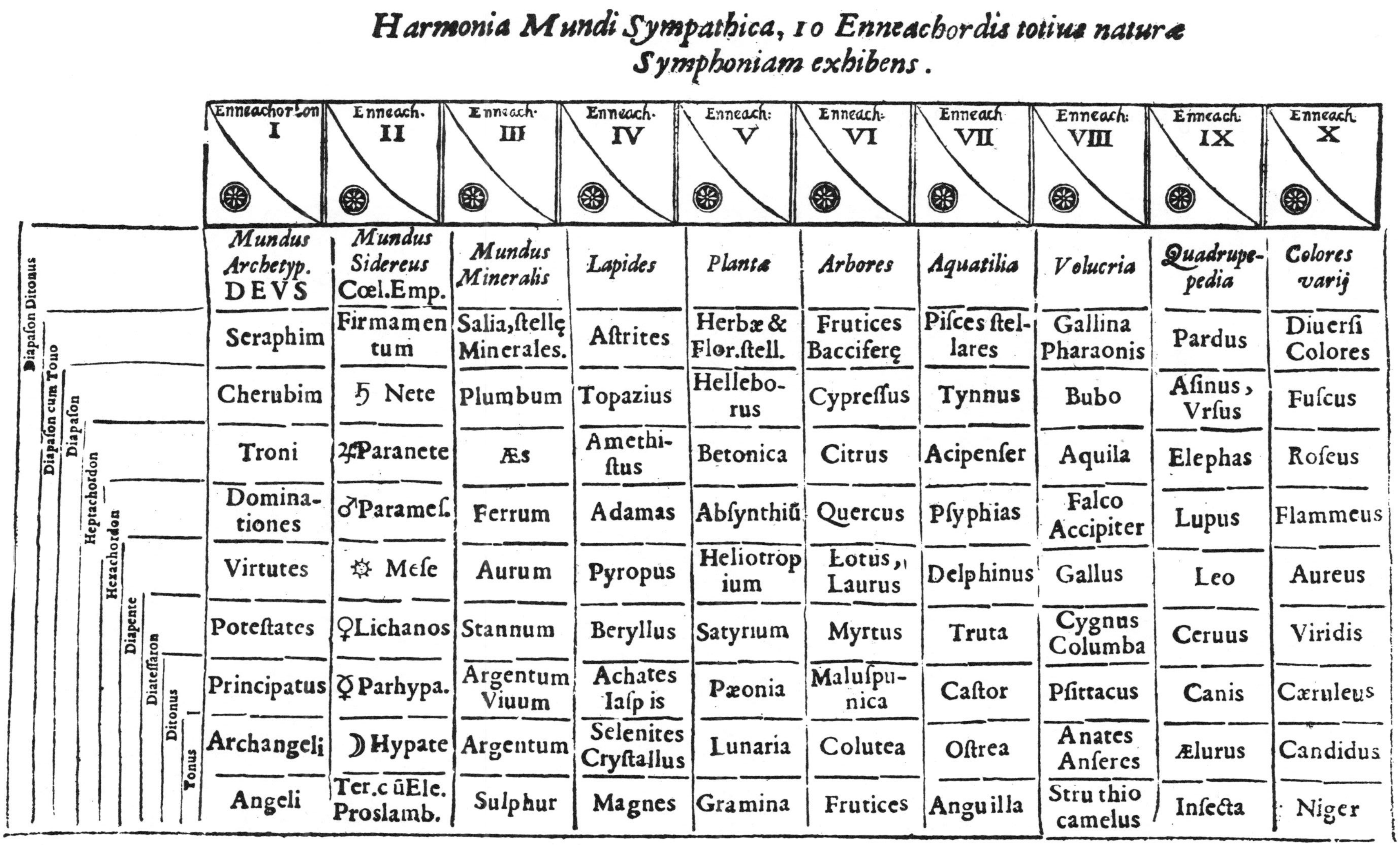

Harmonia Mundi Sympathica, 10 Enneachordis totius naturæ Symphoniam exhibens.

Enneachordon I	Enneach. II	Enneach. III	Enneach. IV	Enneach. V	Enneach. VI	Enneach. VII	Enneach. VIII	Enneach. IX	Enneach. X
Mundus Archetyp. DEVS	*Mundus Sidereus* Cœl.Emp.	*Mundus Mineralis*	*Lapides*	*Plantæ*	*Arbores*	*Aquatilia*	*Volucria*	*Quadrupe-pedia*	*Colores varij*
Seraphim	Firmamen tum	Salia, stellę Minerales.	Astrites	Herbæ & Flor. stell.	Frutices Bacciferę	Pisces stel-lares	Gallina Pharaonis	Pardus	Diuersi Colores
Cherubim	♄ Nete	Plumbum	Topazius	Hellebo-rus	Cypressus	Tynnus	Bubo	Asinus, Vrsus	Fuscus
Troni	♃ Paranete	Æs	Amethi-stus	Betonica	Citrus	Acipenser	Aquila	Elephas	Roseus
Domina-tiones	♂ Parames.	Ferrum	Adamas	Absynthiũ	Quercus	Psyphias	Falco Accipiter	Lupus	Flammeus
Virtutes	☉ Mese	Aurum	Pyropus	Heliotrop ium	Lotus, Laurus	Delphinus	Gallus	Leo	Aureus
Potestates	♀ Lichanos	Stannum	Beryllus	Satyrium	Myrtus	Truta	Cygnus Columba	Ceruus	Viridis
Principatus	☿ Parhypa.	Argentum Viuum	Achates Iaspis	Pæonia	Maluspu-nica	Castor	Psittacus	Canis	Cæruleus
Archangeli	☽ Hypate	Argentum	Selenites Crystallus	Lunaria	Colutea	Ostrea	Anates Anseres	Ælurus	Candidus
Angeli	Ter. cũ Ele. Proslamb.	Sulphur	Magnes	Gramina	Frutices	Anguilla	Struthio camelus	Insecta	Niger

Diapason Ditonus
Diapason cum Tono
Diapason
Heptachordon
Hexachordon
Diapente
Diatessaron
Ditonus
Tonus

Fig. 76. *The universe as a harmonious arrangement based on the number 9 according to Kircher.*

the highest category there is a diapason plus a tone. And finally, between the lowest category and the inclusive label at the top there is a double diapason. But more of this shortly. Suffice it to say here that this scheme with its vertical and horizontal extension is a verbalized representation of our dimensional universe correlated with its representation as a musical opus.

The tetrads and the tables of correspondences that we have looked at are what we might call arithmetical representations of the universe, because they are based upon particular numbers: 4 or 12 or 9. But in addition to arithmetic, other disciplines in the Boethian quadrivium were also called upon to organize the diversity of creation into a comprehensive scheme. According to Boethius (and the generations of those who followed him), arithmetic is the science that deals with numbers as aggregates of discrete units unrelated to anything else—that is, as autonomous multitudes. Music, in contrast, is the science that deals with numbers in relation to one another—that is, as ratios between multitudes so that harmonious proportions can be devised. In this doctrine music is not the aural perception of vibrations in the air, but rather the contemplation of ratios that reveal special relationships between numbers—an intellectual appreciation of proportion and symmetry comparable to the unheard melodies that emanate from Keats' Grecian urn. Geometry, similar to arithmetic, is the science that deals with numbers unrelated to anything else, but as continuous quantities rather than aggregates of units—that is, as magnitudes. And astronomy is the science that deals with magnitudes in motion, so that the factor of time is introduced as the body moves from one point in space to another. As long as the quadrivium prevailed, then, the creating deity expressed himself not only arithmetically through the tetrad and similar schemes based upon multitude, but also in terms of music and geometry, and of course, astronomy.

A noteworthy example of a geometric diagram of the universe is **Figure 77**, a conglomerate of several continuous quantities depicted as simple forms such as the circle, the triangle, and the rectangle.[159] This figure serves as frontispiece for Helisaeus Röslin's *De opere dei creationis seu de mundo hypothesis*, a vol-

SIGNACVLVM MVNDI PITHAGORICVM.

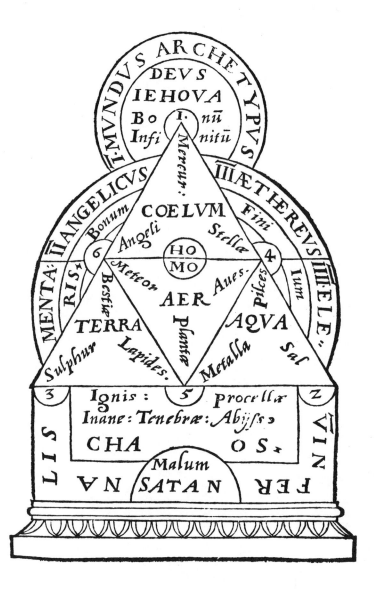

Fig. 77. *A geometrical configuration of the universe according to Röslin.*

ume that we have considered earlier because it concludes with figure 44. Röslin labels his diagram "A pythagorean representation of the universe," though in actual fact the association with Pythagoras or his school is tenuous —no more than that Pythagoras had posited numbers to be first principles in physics. Here we see various items delineated as appropriate geometrical forms, and the coalition of these forms results in an exhaustive image of our universe in its totality.

At the top in figure 77 a circle (I) represents "the archetypal idea of the world" in the mind of "Jehovah," Who is "infinite" and absolutely "good." This *mundus archetypus* is mirrored in a lower and larger circle where, as in figure 52, it is projected into a hierarchy of three lower regions: the "angelical" (II), the "ethereal" (III), and the "elementary" (IV). This inferior circle is "good," like its superior model, but "finite." The elementary region is farthest from the perfection of its creator, and therefore it is further reduced to a triangle in the middle of the diagram, with its corners filled by "1. mercury," "2. salt," and "3. sulphur" (the three elements in the Paracelsan scheme). But this large triangle is itself further articulated into four smaller triangles, and each of these is identified with one of the four elements of classical cosmology (fire is indicated by *coelum*, the traditional location of elemental, as opposed to physical, fire). In the triangle of fire, in addition to mercury, there are angels and stars, the proper residents of heaven. In the triangle of earth, in addition to sulphur, there are animals and stones, creatures associated with land. In the triangle of water, in addition to salt, there are fish and metals, creatures associated with water (metals, unlike stones, are malleable—that is, they flow because of a liquid component). In the triangle of air, determined by the other three triangles, there are weather phenomena (meteora), birds, and plants, creatures that reside in the atmosphere. Finally, in a small circle occupying the center of the large triangle, reproducing the circular perfection of the macrocosm, rests

"man." Half of his being inhabits the divine region of heavenly fire, but the other half inheres in the gross region composed of the base elements: earth, air, and water. He is a creature at once central to the scheme, and yet he plays no clearly defined part in it.

At the very bottom of figure 77 a rectangle represents the infernal region, which comprises two main items, "Chaos" and "Satan." Chaos is a rectangle, suggesting the permanence of its existence, since it rests upon a stable base; but unlike the square of the tetrad, it is uneven in its dimensions, and consequently imperfect and unjust. It contains "fire, storms, the void, darkness, and the abyss." Satan is a half-circle, suggesting his affinity to divine perfection, at least before his fall from heaven, but also measuring his enormous deviation from the circular deity at the top. He is "evil," in contrast to the goodness of Jehovah. In sum, this diagram is a collage of geometrical forms, each with its particular symbolic significance; and when conjoined, the forms cumulatively produce an emblem of the universe in its entirety, synthesizing its disparate parts and reconciling (or at least relating) the opposites of good and evil.

Cosmic speculation of this geometrical sort, though at a much more sophisticated level, obsessed Johann Kepler, and he devoted his most serious thought to it. Kepler, in fact, culminated the tradition of pythagorean-platonic cosmology, and only incidentally formulated what we now blithely call "the laws of planetary motion." The famous three laws are imbedded in arguments scattered in Kepler's writings,[160] and it was Newton who gathered them together and presented them as a coherent theory. This is not to impugn Kepler's importance, but rather to align him properly with his Timaean antecedents.

What makes Kepler so interesting, and what guaranteed his repeated frustration, was an allegiance to both the old ontology and the new. While he was an orthodox cosmologist expecting to find perfect circles and harmonious proportions in the universe, he was also a modern empiricist, using data gathered by new and improved instruments. Kepler was at the fork where the paths of religion and science diverged. He epitomizes — along with Descartes and Thomas Browne — the dilemma of the man who finds cherished orthodox beliefs refuted by what his senses report.

To deal with this dilemma, Kepler attempted to manipulate the theories arrived at by pure speculation so that they would accord with his observational data. A case in point is his determination of the orbit of Mars, which proved to be a crux in his career.[161] It had been a self-evident truth, accepted since the *Timaeus* and confirmed by Aristotle, that the planets perform perfect circles as they move around their courses. This was true, Kepler assumed, whether the earth were placed at the center of the universe, as the followers of Ptolemy and Tycho insisted, or whether the sun were placed in the fixed position, as Kepler himself believed following Copernicus. But by 1600 there were sufficiently accurate observational data to plot the orbit of Mars; and to his consternation, Kepler found that the orbit of Mars when plotted from observations, both his own and Tycho's, was *not* a circle. What a quandary! The new truth was in direct conflict with the old. Empirical science was refuting a basic principle of the most revered theory.

To resolve this quandary took several years of intense effort. In the end, after considerable anguish and sometimes despair, Kepler put forward his most consequential hypothesis: that planetary orbits are ellipses with the sun at one focus. This has become known as the first planetary law.

But before forsaking the circle as the paradigm for celestial motion, Kepler felt compelled to show that the ellipse also possesses certain virtues that permit its use in cosmos. Although the ellipse does not exhibit the same perfection as a circle, nonetheless it incorporates certain proportions that reveal a mathematical design and result in harmony. The ellipse has two foci, admittedly, rather than a single center; but these two foci and the circumference are in a mutual and predictable relationship. Moreover, if a planet performs an elliptical orbit, the speed at which the planet travels at any given moment varies in relation to its distance from a focus, so that a continuous ratio exists between two quantities (the speed of the planet and its distance from the sun). The velocity of the planet is inversely proportional to its distance from the sun. In that way Kepler detected a harmonious proportion in the universe and a musical plan. Furthermore, though the speed of the planet varies, a line drawn between it and the sun (what we would call the "radius vector") sweeps out the same area for any given period of time. This is the so-called second planetary law. For example, in any thirty days a line drawn between Mars and the sun sweeps out a constant area no matter where Mars might be in its orbit. So although there is constant motion (the wheel turning), there is also a constant fixity (the wheel is forever still). Before Kepler could accept the physics of his hypothesis, he had to demonstrate by such evidence that inviolable cosmic harmonies are operative in his proposed geometric scheme.

An even more interesting example of Kepler's cosmic geometry occurs as an effort to determine the distances between planets in our solar system. How far the planets are from the center of the universe and from one another had been a perennial concern of cosmologists from the beginning, because it has to do with the proper limits of our finite universe and the placement of the primum mobile. In his first publication, the *Mysterium cosmographicum* (Tübingen, 1596), Kepler at the early age of twenty-five set out to explain these distances. He excitedly announced that the planetary intervals are determined by a relationship between the five regular figures of solid geometry. A quarter-century later, at the height of a busy career, Kepler returned to his wholly deductive argument and made it the unifying thesis of his major work, the *Harmonices mundi libri V* (Linz, 1619). **Figures**

78a-c come from that extensive treatise on the harmony of the universe.

Since Kepler's theory about the planetary intervals depends upon the shape of the regular solids and the virtues that Timaean cosmology had assigned to each of them, we must reconstruct this topos of ancient geometry, although today it may be no more than a quaint curiosity. Nonetheless, for most mathematicians from Pythagoras to Kepler, the regular solids held a special, almost a sacred, significance. First, then, a definition: a regular solid is a three-dimensional form with all its faces equal and all its angles equal. The regular solid most familiar to us is the cube, with square faces and right angles. But, as the Greeks knew, there are four more: the tetrahedron, the octohedron, and the icosahedron, all of which have trianglar faces and angles smaller than a right angle; and the dodecahedron, which has pentagonal faces and angles wider than a right angle. This makes a total of five regular solids, no more and no less. Because of the symmetry of the regular solids—each has all its faces equal and all its angles—they were considered the most nearly perfect of all polyhedra, approaching the sphere in its perfection.

Much lore had accrued to these figures as mathematicians had pondered their special qualities over the centuries.[162] Of particular interest to Kepler, though, was their association with the four elements. Each of the elements had been identified with one of the regular solids: fire with the tetrahedron, air with the octohedron, earth with the cube, and water with the icosahedron, while the heavens in their entirety were identified with the dodecahedron. In this way, the fact that there are exactly five regular solids is made to accord with the fact that there are exactly four elements in the sublunary region plus quintessential ether for the celestial spheres. Unmistakably, the intention is to demonstrate that these geometrical forms are the building blocks in creation. Often they were seen as the original ideas in the mind of the Timaean godhead, the forms that he used as models in the fabrication of our time-space continuum.

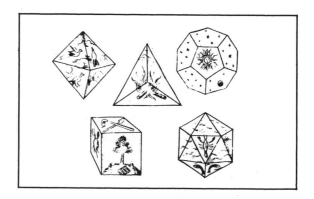

Fig. 78a. *The correspondence between the five regular solids and the four elements plus the heavens.*

Kepler accepted this belief without reservation, as **Figure 78a** shows. There we see each of the elements appropriately inhering within its assigned regular solid: winged creatures indicate that air inheres in the octohedron; burning logs indicate that fire inheres in the tetrahedron; a tree, a root vegetable, and two digging tools indicate that earth inheres in the cube; and various creatures from the sea indicate that water inheres in the icosahedron. In addition, to make up the necessary number 5, the sun, the moon, and numerous stars indicate that the quintessence of the ethereal region inheres in the dodecahedron.

While adopting this correspondence between the regular solids and the elements as an indisputable fact, Kepler strove to produce empirical evidence to support it. He methodically correlated the physical properties of each element with the properties of its correspondent regular solid. The cube is assigned to earth, Kepler tells us, because "in the case of the cube its uprightness on a quadrate base conveys a certain impression of stability, which property also belongs to terrestrial matter."[163] The octohedron can be suspended by two opposite corners and spun as in a lathe, so that it represents "a certain image of mobility" suitable to air, the most mobile element. "The sharpness and thinness of the tetrahedron" suggest the complexion of fire; while "the globular form

129

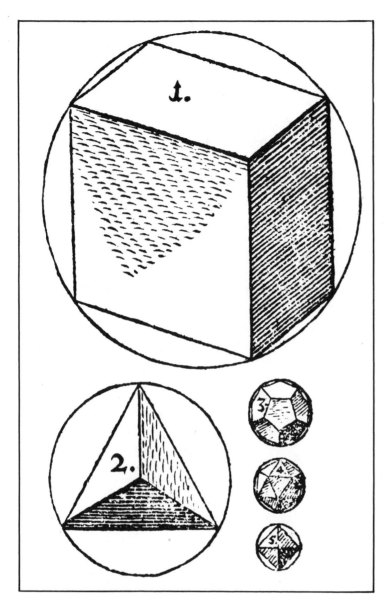

Fig. 78b. *The regular solids circumscribed by spheres.*

upon which the heavenly maker modeled his creation, Kepler set about to discover how these modules were arranged in the universal scheme. Already in the *Mysterium cosmographicum* Kepler had opened his "Preface to the Reader" with a statement of purpose:

> It is my intention, Reader, in this book to demonstrate that the Highest and Most Good Creator in the creation of this mobile world and the arrangement of the heavens had his eye on those five regular bodies, which have been most celebrated from the time of Pythagoras and Plato right down to our own day, and that to their nature He accommodated the number of heavenly spheres, their proportions, and the system of their motions.[164]

Not only must the regular solids inform the elements that make up the various parts of the cosmos, but they must inform also the cosmos at large, the macrocosm. It was but a short step from this assumption to Kepler's hypothesis that the intervals between the planets are determined by the distances between spheres circumscribing the regular solids as they are placed concentrically.

In the *Harmonice mundi* Kepler fulfilled the intention he had brashly announced twenty-four years earlier. The closeness of the argument and the minuteness of the detail reveal Kepler's seriousness as he sets about propounding the hypothesis that he took to be his most important achievement. He begins by inscribing the regular solids in spheres (**Figure 78b**). This operation had been familiar to mathematicians at least since the time of Euclid, who in the last book of his *Elements* had shown how to construct the regular solids and had proved that each can be inscribed in a sphere. This step prepares for Kepler's conclusion, the revelation that he exultantly offers as the organizing principle in the arrangement of planets.

The fully worked out scheme appears in **Figure 78c**.[165] From the fact that there are only five regular solids, Kepler concludes that there can be only five planetary intervals—that is,

of the icosahedron," a figure with the largest number of faces, suggests "a water-drop." Finally, "the dodecahedron is left for the celestial form, having the same number of faces as the celestial zodiac has of signs; and it is shown to be the most capacious of all the figures, and accordingly the heavens embrace all things."

With this conviction that the regular solids are correspondent to the physical components of the universe and that they are the forms that there are six planets circling the sun fixed in the center. This scheme exhausts the available modules for the cosmic structure and explains why there are only six planetary orbits in the Copernican system. Then from the diagram we see how the intervals between planetary orbits are determined by the five regular solids circumscribed successively around the planetary spheres in a heliocentric universe. The orbit of Venus is determined by a sphere circumscribing an octohedron, which in turn circumscribes the sphere of Mercury. The orbit of the earth and its attendant moon is determined by a sphere circumscribing an icosahedron, which in turn circumscribes the sphere of Venus. The orbit of Mars is determined by a sphere circumscribing a dodecahedron, which in turn circumscribes the sphere of the earth. The orbit of Jupiter is determined by a sphere circumscribing a tetrahedron, which in turn circumscribes the sphere of Mars. Finally, the orbit of Saturn is determined by a sphere circumscribing a cube, which in turn circumscribes the sphere of Jupiter. For each planet, Kepler calculates the distance for its "median orbit," although its "aphelion" and its "perihelion" are shown as well.[166] "The path of the sun according to Tycho Brahe" is also indicated.

As coincidence would have it, the intervals between the planets as calculated by Copernicus were quite close to the intervals determined by this geometric construction. Therefore it was not unreasonable for Kepler to think he had at long last discovered the key to planetary arrangement in the divine plan. From our vantage point, we may view this construction as a sterile essay that merely clutters the history of astronomy and leads nowhere. We may impatiently dismiss it as a whimsical fantasy based upon false premises. But Kepler and his contemporaries viewed it otherwise. He was jubilant because his empirical observations confirmed the hypothesis he had arrived at deductively by theoretic speculation. And in the midst of this arcane speculation lies the third planetary law: as stated in modern terms, that

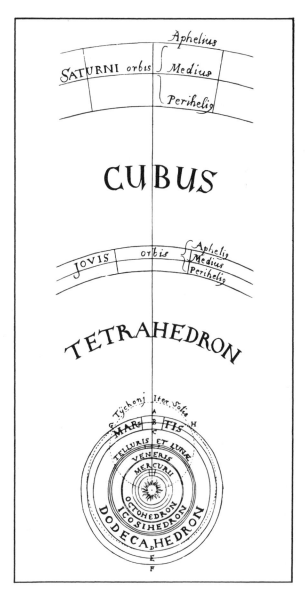

Fig. 78c. *The world-system determined by geometry of the regular solids according to Kepler.*

the squares of the periods of revolution for the planets are to each other as the cubes of their mean distances from the sun. For Kepler, this formulation meant that once again he had uncovered harmonious proportion in our world, and had further revealed the hand of the Highest and Most Good Creator. By the same token, he would have been horrified to know that his research led to a theory reducing his Creator to a clockmaker who wound his mechanism once, and then with a yawn of indifference or laziness turned his attention to other matters.

When Kepler expressed himself in terms of ratios and proportions, he was thinking not merely of numbers; and when he dealt with regular solids and symmetries, he was concerned not solely with geometrical forms. He was instead searching for relationships between quantities, an activity that the quadrivium placed in the discipline of music. He was exercising a reverential esthetics that assumed God to be good and beautiful, and our world to be created in His image. Kepler was seeking to discover the divinely instituted harmony that pervades the universe and binds its diverse parts into a concordant whole. Consequently, he called his work the *harmonice mundi*.[167]

According to legend, Pythagoras first proposed universal harmony in the sixth century B.C.—as Yeats says, "World-famous golden-thighed Pythagoras / Fingered upon a fiddle-stick or strings / What a star sang and careless Muses heard." Plato took it over from the pythagoreans and accorded it a place of prominence in the last book of the *Republic*, one of his most popular works during the renaissance. In the memorable conclusion to Book X when Er trips out of time and space and describes his vision of the eight celestial spheres wheeling about the spindle of Necessity, he populates each sphere with a siren who sings one note of the diapason (616C-617B). Aristotle snidely repudiated this music of the spheres (*De caelo*, 290b12-291a27), but other authorities solemnly transmitted the theory and embellished it with precise detail. Pliny, Plutarch, Censorinus, and especially Macrobius were eager proponents of universal harmony.[168]

The literalness with which this concept was translated into visual image is illustrated in **Figure 79**, taken from Robert Fludd's *Utriusque cosmi . . . historia*.[169] There we see the entire universe depicted as a musical instrument with a single string that stretches from the highest item in creation to the lowest, from angelic choirs to silent stones. Along this monochord two octaves of notes are marked, and also co-

ordinately the familiar hierarchy of three worlds: the angelical, the ethereal, and the elemental. Harmonies exist within each of these worlds, as well as harmonies between them. At the top, a divine hand reaches from a cloud to tune this *fides mundana*. Fludd himself explains his intention in a caption above the figure: "We set forth here quite precisely the monochord of the universe with its proportions, consonances, and intervals; and we show that its motive force is extra-mundane [i.e., the hand of God]."

In this diagram we observe that the string is apportioned among fifteen musical notes, going from low G at the bottom through middle G at the position of the Sun to high G at the very top. These fifteen notes mark the intervals between adjacent items in the hierarchy, and may be a full tone or a half tone, as the right side of the instrument indicates in its shadowed area. In effect, then, we have two octaves—or *disdiapason*, two "diapasons," to use Fludd's term.[170] The lower diapason, which stretches from earth at the bottom to the sphere of the Sun, is the "material diapason"— that is, composed of matter. The upper diapason, which stretches from the sphere of the Sun to the top of the monochord, is the "formal diapason"—that is, composed of form only, devoid of matter. Within these two diapasons exist also the harmonic proportions that are conventional in the pythagorean tuning system: the *diatesseron*, or "fourth," and the *diapente*, or "fifth." All of these harmonic proportions are labeled on the right, while the proportions expressed as numerical ratios are labeled on the left.

So much for the musical notes. Now we must turn our attention to the hierarchy of items in the three worlds that constitute creation. Starting from the bottom, we have first the elemental world comprising the four elements: earth, water, air, fire. Stretching above the elemental world, we have the ethereal world comprising the spheres of the seven planets with the Sun placed appropriately in their midst and terminated by the sphere of

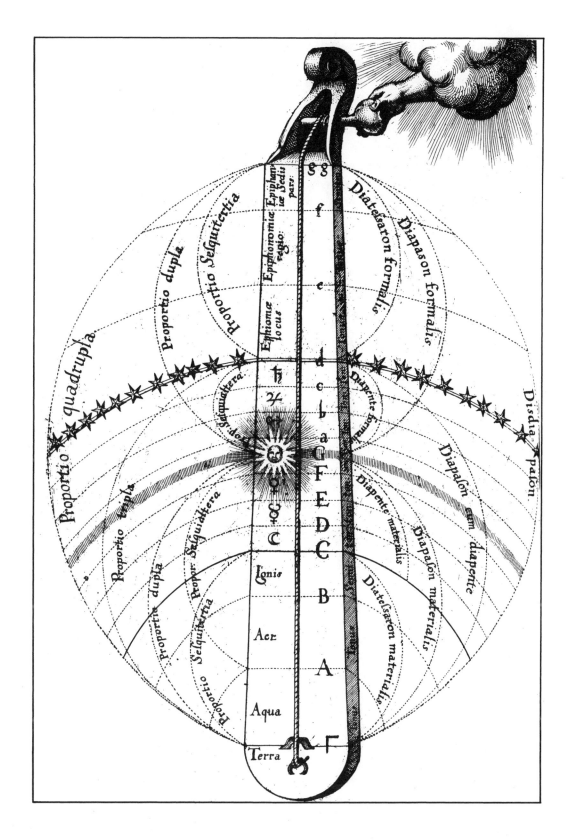

Fig. 79. *The universe as a monochord from Fludd.*

fixed stars. Completing the continuum at the top, we discover three orders of angels: "the place of the ephioma," "the region of the epiphonomia," and "part of the seat of the epiphania." Suggestively, the uppermost item shades off into what is not clearly visible — it is *part* of the seat of the epiphania.

With the musical notes and the items of hierarchical creation in mind, we are now ready to discern the several harmonies in our universe. Again starting at the bottom, we see that the four elements taken together make up the "material fourth" (diatesseron materialis), which expresses the ratio 4/3 (proportio sesquitertia, 1⅓). Those items from air to the Sun, inclusively, make up the "material fifth" (diapente materialis [note the error in the engraving: the arc of the *diapente materialis* and the corresponding arc of the *proportio sesquialtera* should terminate at the note C]), and a fifth expresses the ratio 3/2 (proportio sesquialtera, 1½). The octave from low G to middle G is the "material diapason," as we have noted, and of course it expresses the ratio 2/1 (proportio dupla).

Moving now to the "formal diapason," we see at once that it displays the same harmonies as the "material diapason" — in fact, they are mirror images of one another. The angelical world at the top is the "formal fourth" just as the elemental world at the bottom is the "material fourth," and both express the sesquitertial ratio of 4/3. Coming down the string, we see next that the celestial spheres from the sphere of fixed stars to the sphere of the Sun make up the "formal diapente," which expresses the ratio 3/2, echoing the harmony of the "material diapente," the interval from the sphere of the Sun to the sphere of the Moon. The symmetry of the diagram is exact.

To conclude, the items stretching down from the sphere of fixed stars to the bottom — that is, the ethereal and the elemental worlds taken together — produce an octave plus a fifth, a 3/1 ratio (proportio tripla); and the sum total of all items stretching from the empyrean at the top to earth — that is, the angeli-

cal, the ethereal, and the elemental worlds taken together—produce two octaves, a 4/1 ratio (proportio quadrupla). Every category in creation therefore has a place in this scheme. Each item participates in the universal harmony—indeed, is essential to the perfection of that harmony.

The musical theory behind figure 79 is the well-known tuning system ascribed to Pythagoras, the harmonics that had dominated the discipline of music, both speculative and practical, since the earliest classical times. In this tuning system, the intervals that produce distinct notes are determined by ratios between the first four integers: 1, 2, 3, 4 (4, we must recall, is the limit of physical extension, and consequently all musical notes must be contained within that limit; see page 99, above). The resultant ratios are then found to be 2/1, 3/1, 4/1, 3/2, and 4/3 — a range that exhausts the possibilities. Hence, the possible harmonies are 2/1, the *proportio dupla* (the diapason, or octave); 3/1, the *proportio tripla* (the diapason plus a fifth); 4/1, the *proportio quadrupla* (the double diapason, or two octaves); 3/2, the *diapente* (the fifth); and 4/3, the *diatesseron* (the fourth). These harmonies are standard in classical, medieval, and renaissance treatises on music. **Figure 80**, which sets them forth, is notable only for the thoroughness and lucidity with which it displays the theory.[171]

Figure 80 comes from Giorgio Valla's *De expetendis, et fugiendis rebus opus* (Venice, 1501), a large two-volume omnibus of knowledge that does indeed expound recherché topics. It is an early contribution to humanistic science, and predictably relies heavily upon the middle ages, especially Boethius. Valla's discussion of music is wholly traditional, and therefore congenial to our purpose. To use it as a gloss on figure 79, turn his diagram on its left side, so that the lowest note (proslambanomenos) is at the bottom.

In Valla's diagram we see "the immutable system of the double diapason," as the caption states at the top; and an inclusive arc stretches

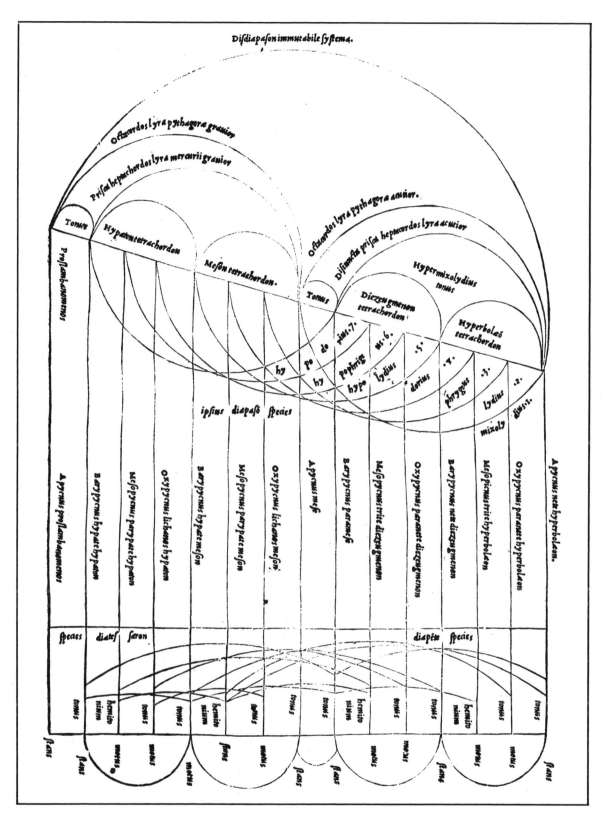

Fig. 80. *The Pythagorean tuning system from Valla.*

all the way across the fourteen intervals, which produce fifteen notes. Next the large arc is divided into two equal smaller arcs, each comprising seven intervals and eight notes — that is, two octaves. Each of these is labeled "the eight-chorded lyre of Pythagoras" to identify it as the pythagorean tuning system. The octave at the left is the "heavier" (i.e., lower) one, and that at the right the "lighter" (i.e., higher). Each of these octaves is in turn divided into two parts: a full tone and a unit of six intervals producing seven notes. The top seven notes of the octave on the left are designated "the original seven-chorded lyre of Mercury," which is "heavier." The top seven notes of the octave on the right are designated "the original lyre with seven distinct chords," which is "lighter." These heptachords in their turn are then broken down into two tetrachords each. What we have, in sum, are harmonic systems that inhere in larger and larger harmonic systems until we reach the all-inclusive system of the double diapason, which is delimited by the 4/1 ratio.

The next feature to notice in the diagram is the exposition of "the sorts of diapasons" — what is usually called the "modes" in classical music. The possibilities allow eight modes: the mixolydian, the lydian, the phrygian, the dorian, the hypolydian, the hypophrygian, the hypodorian, and the hypermixolydian. The intervals wherein each of these modes consists are indicated by seven numbered arcs, with the interval for the hypermixolydian mode being congruent with "the original lyre with seven distinct chords."

Next in the diagram comes a list of the names for the fifteen notes, and each is described at the bottom as a full tone or a half tone. The remaining feature of the diagram is an intricate series of arcs near the bottom which arranges the notes into various fourths and various fifths. Despite its jumbled appearance, the system is a model of intricate organization.

We have not, however, depleted the rich associations of universal harmony. The comprehensiveness of the concept is perhaps even better demonstrated in **Figure 81**, which appears prominently as a frontispiece before Franchino Gafori's *Practica musicae* (Milan, 1496).[172] There also we have a continuum, though in this instance in the form of a three-headed dragon dangling sinuously from the throne of Apollo down through the celestial spheres to elemental earth. The planets plus the sphere of fixed stars are represented one above the other on the right in a series of circular vignettes which depict each planet as a mythological deity riding in a triumph, a frequent convention in astronomical writings. Each of the celestial spheres produces a musical note, as in figure 79, so that the diapason of eight notes is achieved. The notes are labeled just to the left of the dragon. Moreover, each celestial sphere is identified with one of the classical modes of music, labeled just to the right of the dragon. The sphere of fixed stars, for example, plays the note *mese* and follows the hypermixolydian mode; while Saturn just below it plays the note *lychanos meson* and follows the mixolydian mode. The intervals between the planets, also as in figure 79, are indicated to be full tones or half tones. Unlike figure 79, however, Gafori's diagram does not assign notes to the four elements, although they appear as hemispheres at the bottom. This is a single octave — "the eight-chorded lyre of Pythagoras," the lower diapason of the double diapason displayed in figure 80.

In addition to the pythagorean tuning system, Gafori's diagram incorporates an ancient mythological motif that had come to full development in Martianus Capella.[173] Gafori identifies each of the celestial spheres with one of the Muses, and that gracious host inspires the music of the spheres. Michael Drayton turns the motif into didactic poetry:

And unto these as by a sweet consent,
The sphery circles are equivalent,
From the first moover, and the starry
 heaven,

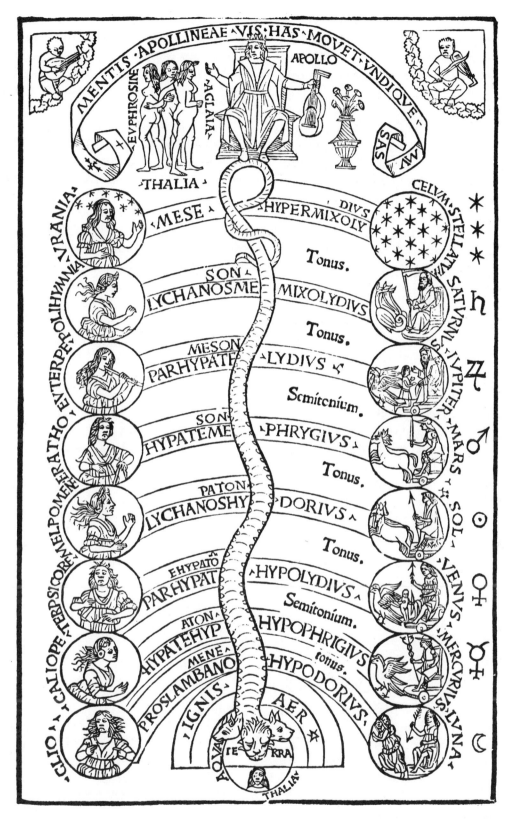

Fig. 81. *The frontispiece of Gafori's* Practica musicae.

To glorious Phoebe lowest of the seaven,
Which Jove in tunefull diapazons fram'd,
Of heavenly musick of the Muses nam'd.
(*Endimion and Phoebe*, lines 915-20)

In their guise as authors of "heavenly musick," the Muses appear in Gafori's frontispiece within circular vignettes on the left. The sphere of fixed stars, for example, is correspondent to Urania; while Saturn is correspondent to Polyhymnia. Since there are nine Muses and only eight celestial spheres, however, some provision must be made for the extra Muse. Accordingly, Thalia is assigned to Earth at the bottom (and in the center of this universe). The symphony of the Muses—each playing her distinctive instrument, and yet all joining in perfect consonance—is of course another traditional icon used to express universal harmony (see figure 106). Consequently, presiding over this scene is Apollo, whose eminence is enhanced by a line from Ausonius which flutters above his head: "The power of the Apollonian mind completely controls these Muses."[174] Beside Apollo on the left stand the three Graces in their customary posture of intertwined arms, and in each upper corner a little putto plays a musical instrument.

Figure 81 renders visible a scheme for universal harmony. This concept is given a temporal as well as a spatial dimension, moreover, by the three-headed dragon that hangs from Apollo's throne and threads his way down the length of the continuum. Gafori is drawing upon a well-known passage in the *Saturnalia* (I.xx.13), where Macrobius discusses various statues used in sun worship. When we bring this passage to bear upon Gafori's diagram, we learn that the head of this dragon on the left is that of a wolf representing the past, the head in the middle is that of a lion representing the present, and the head on the right is that of a dog representing the future. Past, present, and future incorporated in a single system—like the eight notes of the diapason and the nine muses in Apollo's symphony—produce a whole that is greater than the sum of its parts. By integrating the full range of components, the whole exhausts the possibilities and achieves the infinitude of unity. In this case, the three-headed dragon intimates time under the aspect of eternity. Because of its perfection, Gafori is saying, this scheme will last forever.

As a particular instance of universal harmony, the music of the spheres had been singled out for special attention, witness Gafori; and the doctrine was applied with single-minded precision. As far back as Plato's vision of Er in the *Republic*, a siren had sat upon each planetary sphere and had sung her assigned note in the heavenly diapason. It was Pliny, however, who called upon the authority of Pythagoras to specify the musical intervals between the celestial spheres:

> *Pythagoras* otherwiles using the tearmes of musicke, calleth the space betweene the earth and the Moone a Tonus, saying, that from her to *Mercurie* is halfe a tone: and from him to *Venus* in manner the same space. But from her to the Sunne as much and halfe againe: but from the Sunne to *Mars* a Tonus, that is to say, as much as from the earth to the *Moone*. From him to *Jupiter* halfe a Tonus: likewise from him to *Saturne* halfe a Tonus: and so from thence to the Signifer Sphaere or Zodiake [i.e., sphere of fixed stars] so much, and halfe again. Thus are composed seven tones, which harmonie they cal Diapason, that is to say, the Generalitie or whole state of concent and accord, which is perfect musicke.[175]

It was then left to Plutarch to give the name of the note that each planet plays in its heavenly circuit:

> Some attribute to the earth, the place of the musicall note Proslambanomenos: unto the moone Hypate: unto *Mercurie* and *Lucifer* [i.e., Venus] Diatonos and Lichanos: the sunne they set upon Mese (they say) containing Diapason in the middes, distant from the earth one fifth or Diapente, and from the sphaere of the fixed starres a fourth, or Diatesseron.[176]

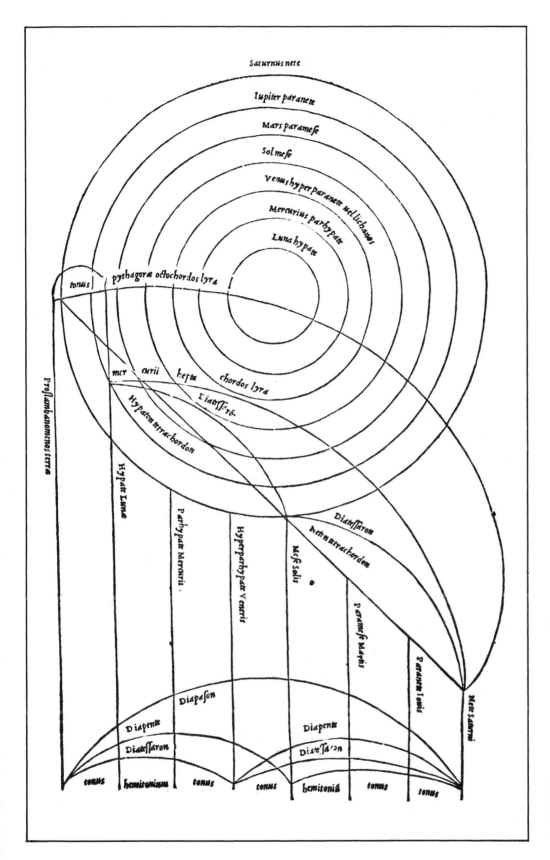

Fig. 82. The Pythagorean tuning system amalgamated with the planetary spheres from Valla.

139

Figure 82, also from Valla's learned omnibus, correlates this information with the pythagorean tuning system and provides a neat diagram of just how the celestial spheres produce their music.[177]

As in figure 81, in figure 82 each of the planetary spheres plays a single note in the diapason — though each planet is lowered one note in the scale. In Gafori's diagram, for example, the Moon plays *proslambanomenos*, the lowest note; while in Valla's diagram that note is played by Earth. Valla's arrangement is the more usual.

In any case, at the bottom of figure 82 the pythagorean tuning system is displayed, with its full tones and half tones, its fourths and its fifths, and ultimately its diapason. The notes in this scale are extended upward as parallel lines and are projected onto a diagonal, which represents "the eight-chorded lyre of Pythagoras." Along this diagonal projection of the diapason, the musical intervals that Valla designated on the lower octave in figure 80 are again marked: a full tone and "the seven-chorded lyre of Mercury," which in turn is articulated into two "fourths," the "*hypate* tetrachord" and the "*nete* tetrachord." This scheme is next placed over a scheme · of concentric circles representing the celestial spheres to suggest a correlation, so that the Moon plays the note *hypate*, Mercury plays the note *parhypate*, Venus plays the note *hyperparhypate* (incorrectly *hyperparanete* in the diagram) or *lichanos*, and so forth. Then cosmic harmonies similar to those that Fludd disclosed in figure 79 become apparent. The interval between the Earth and the Moon is a full tone. The interval between the Moon and the Sun, comprising also Mercury and Venus, is the *hypate* tetrachord, a fourth. Therefore the interval between the Earth and the Sun can be seen as a diapente, or fifth. Furthermore, the interval between the Sun and Saturn, comprising also Mars and Jupiter, is the *nete* tetrachord, another fourth. In consequence, the diapente from Earth to the Sun and the diatesseron from the Sun to Saturn make up a complete diapason. Thus the music of the spheres is explicated in precise detail, with each planet having its particular note to play, with each planet participating in a diatesseron, and of course with each planet participating in the diapason.

A comprehensive scheme that interrelates the music of the spheres with Ptolemaic cosmology is offered in **Figure 83**. This wide-ranging diagram comes from Johann Eck's edition of Aristotle's *De caelo* (Augsburg, 1519), a text that he prepared with several other of Aristotle's physical treatises for use by students in the university of Ingolstadt. This is pretty much the last word in representations of the macrocosm, the composite picture, the synthesis of models that the four disciplines of the quadrivium could devise.

In figure 83, south is at the top, north at the bottom, west on the right, and east on the left — the usual orientation for maps in this period. Since this world-system is geocentric, the four elements are situated in the center and are shown as four concentric spheres. Each is distinguished by an appropriate visibilium as well as by a label. Earth, the heaviest, fills the central position, with water and air following in succession, while fire, the lightest element, holds the outermost of the sublunary spheres. These four spheres, of course, are stationary and do not revolve.

Next come the seven celestial spheres, one for each of the planets, and the sphere of fixed stars (firmamentum stellatum). There is also the cristalline sphere, the sphere that is invisible to us, but nonetheless necessary to produce the precessional motion and to bring the total of celestial spheres to the divine number 10. Each of the planets is labeled by its astronomical symbol and also by its name (in the genitive case, because *orbis* or *sphaera* or *coelum* is understood). To the right of its name, the period of revolution for each planet is given. For example, the Moon goes around in twenty-eight days, Mercury goes around in one year, and so forth up to Saturn, the slowest of the planets, which

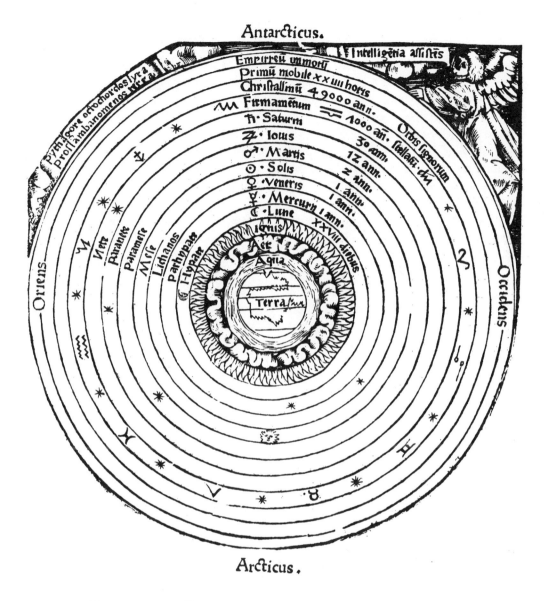

Fig. 83. *Universal harmony from Eck after Pythagoras and Ptolemy.*

requires thirty years to complete its orbit. In the *firmamentum stellatum*, stars are symmetrically placed around the circle; and interspersed among these stars are the signs of the zodiac, which are conventionally represented by suitable constellations. The period of revolution for the sphere of fixed stars is one thousand years. The cristalline sphere contains the caption *orbis signorum*, though actually this caption pertains to the sphere of fixed stars just below, because it is the "sphere of zodiacal signs." The artisan who cut this woodblock, however, had no room in the sphere of fixed stars to include such a caption, so he located it immediately above its proper place. The period of revolution for the cristalline sphere is 49,000 years, the Great Year of the platonists.[178]

As the outermost celestial sphere, rounding out the divine number 10 and acting as a boundary for the finite universe, the primum mobile performs its revolution in twenty-four hours. Obviously, there is a large discrepancy between the period of revolution for the primum mobile and that for the cristalline sphere (and adjacent spheres), and we must take care to explain it. To do so, we must begin to visualize this model as a three-dimensional machine in motion. Practically speaking, each of the spheres beneath the primum mobile has two motions that are contradictory, a faster motion that results directly from the daily rotation of the primum mobile and a slower motion that accumulates into a contrary period of revolution as the planet lags behind the primum mobile in its turning.

To understand this, we must remember that the Earth is stationary, and the entire celestial apparatus, from the sphere of the Moon through the primum mobile, circles about it each twenty-four hours. This circling is from east to west, as we know, because the Sun rises in the east and sets in the west. Therefore with respect to this diagram, the celestial spheres come out from the plane of the page on the left and move in a circular arc toward the right. The primum mobile does indeed complete its circle from east to west in the assigned time, so its period of revolution is exactly twenty-four hours from point of origin back to point of origin. The other celestial spheres, however, do not move with the full force of the primum mobile, and therefore do not complete an entire revolution in twenty-four hours. The force that turns the other celestial spheres is transmitted by friction from the primum mobile to the cristalline sphere, and thence by friction down through the sphere of fixed stars and each of the planetary spheres. Consequently, those spheres near the primum mobile are carried the greatest distance by it, and those spheres farther away receive less motion from it. In the case of the Moon, for example, the force from primum mobile is diminished to such an extent that the Moon goes only 27/28 of a total circle in twenty-four hours. Each day the Moon lags behind 1/28 of its orbit. Therefore in twenty-eight days it in effect performs a complete revolution *in the opposite direction*, from west to

east. As another example, Mercury completes only 364/365 of its orbit in twenty-four hours, and consequently performs a revolution in the opposite direction in a year's time. In contrast, Saturn moves so rapidly along with the primum mobile that it lags behind very little. In fact, it takes thirty years for Saturn to accumulate a complete period of revolution in the opposite direction. And the cristalline sphere requires the enormous number of 49,000 years to perform an orbit from west to east. What we have for periods of revolution in figure 83, then, are twenty-four hours for the primum mobile, moving from east to west (out of the page on the left hand toward the right), but for the other nine celestial spheres, much greater periods—shortest for the Moon and longest for the cristalline sphere—moving in the opposite direction, from west to east (out of the page on the right hand and toward the left).

Beyond the ten celestial spheres lies the "immutable empyrean" (empirreum immotum), the infinite and eternal region that serves as the abode of God and His attendants. It is of course boundless, though here seemingly confined within a sphere because of the difficulty of representing unlimited space within the borders of a woodblock. In the upper right corner an assisting angel (intelligentia assistens) places his hand on the outer rim of this model and pursuant to God's behest applies that force which makes it move. Thereby the divine will is executed as physical event.

In the upper left corner a label proclaims that this is "the eight-chorded lyre of Pythagoras" (Pythagorae octochordos lyra) as in figures 80 and 82, and naturally "Earth plays the lowest note" (proslambanomenos terra). In addition, the note that each of the seven planets plays is indicated in its sphere to the left of its symbol. The total number of notes properly comes to eight, so that the diapason is fulfilled.

This eight-chorded lyre of Pythagoras, like the assisting angel that translates God's idea into nature's fact, demonstrates that this model bridges, or rather encompasses, both the conceptual and the physical. It represents a perfect scheme in the conceptual world of essences, but also serves as the paradigm for the actual operation of our universe — for the "grateful vicissitude, like day and night," in the words of Milton (*Paradise Lost*, VI.8), for the orderly sequence of the seasons — for all those generations and corruptions that constantly invigorate our world with ongoing vitality:

The Sunne . . . rising and setting maketh the day and the night, by comming towards us, and going from us, causeth the yeres continually to be renewed, and by the obliquity or crookednes of the Zodiacke with the helpe of the twelve signes which are in it, doth distinguishe by his Solstices and Equinoxes, the fower seasons of the sommer and winter, of the spring and harvest: In the which consisteth the vicissitude of life and death, and the change of all thinges: by the mediation of the first qualities, hot and cold, drie and moist, being duely tempered for generation, and unproportionably distempered for corruption.[179]

When the French humanist Louis LeRoy looked into the cosmographical glass, this is the composite and all-inclusive image that he saw.

The macrocosm, then, could be disclosed in many different models based upon the several disciplines of the quadrivium. It could be an arithmetical variation of a single number, such as the tetrad, or an amplification of a single number into a network of correspondences, such as the table for the number 12. It could be a geometrical configuration, plane or solid, that interrelates a group of symbolic forms. It could be a visual depiction of ratios between numbers, a configuration that exhibits proportions and symmetries — what later ages, following the Greeks, called harmony. It could be an elaborate *machina mundi* of spheres turning at varying speeds — what the renaissance classified as astronomy because it dealt with bodies in motion. Whatever the projected image of the macrocosm, however, it was informed by the idea of cosmos, the first principle that antedated and controlled the process of creation. In consequence, the order and beauty of cosmos is evident on every hand throughout our universe.

V The Human Microcosm

PARTICULARLY in the lesser world, the microcosm of man, we see the attributes of cosmic perfection. Because Adam, like the creation which he closed, was modeled directly in the image of the divine source, and because we share in this heritage of our first parent, the human body reflects the variety of our universe. Its parts quite literally correspond to the several items of nature: our flesh is like dirt, our veins like rivers, our bones like rocks, our hair like grass. But like the universe, the human body is also ordered and unified—a system of many parts, though subject to the authority of a single will. In concise terms, we incorporate in small the divine principle of cosmos. Agrippa states the humanists' position with unequivocal certainty:

> Seeing man is the most beautifull and perfectest work of God, and his Image, and also the lesser world; therefore he by a more perfect composition, and sweet Harmony, and more sublime dignity doth contain and maintain in himself all numbers, measures, weights, motions, Elements, and all other things which are of his composition; and in him as it were in the supreme workmanship, all things obtain a certain high condition, beyond the ordinary consonancy which they have in other compounds.[180]

When Hamlet exclaims, "O what a piece of work is a man!" (II.ii.315), he is voicing this conviction. And in the background a chorus of hexaemeralists join in rapturous confirmation of it.

Figure 84 illustrates just how exactly the human microcosm incorporated the structures of the universe at large. It comes from Fludd's *Utriusque cosmi . . . historia*, and serves as a companion piece for figure 18. In that diagram, the pyramid of pure form reaches down from the Holy Trinity until it diminishes to nothingness at the surface of the earth, while the pyramid of material substance reaches upward from our planet until it disappears at a point where the empyrean begins. The purpose of the diagram is to visualize the reciprocal relationship between conceptuality and materiality throughout the three levels of our universe —at any level in creation, the greater the conceptuality, the less the materiality; and vice versa.

So also in figure 84 this principle is visualized for the microcosm. Man is divided into three regions: "the intellectual region," comparable to the angelic world in the macrocosm; the middle region, through which runs "the sphere of the sun or of the heart," comparable to the celestial world in the macrocosm; and "the elementary region," comparable to the sublunary world of four elements in the macrocosm. Continuing the analogy, a refulgent equilateral triangle at the top represents "the mind, the light of godliness"; and reaching down from this facsimile of the uniquely di-

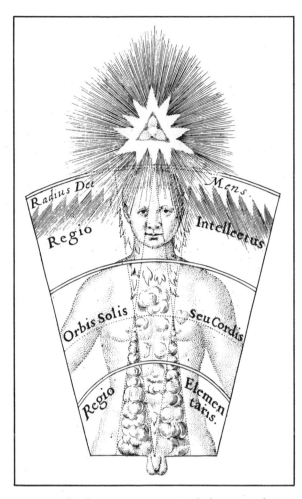

Fig. 84. *The human microcosm dichotomized into material and non-material components.*

Since the macrocosm visibly displays a multeity in its parts, we reasonably expect the body of man to reflect a correspondent diversity. The cabala had actively taught such a doctrine, and astrology assumed it to be a self-evident truth. Agrippa formulates the tenet in exact terms:

> The measures of all the members [of man's body] are proportionate, and consonant both to the parts of the world, and measures of the Archetype, and so agreeing, that there is no member in man which hath not correspondence with some other sign, Star, intelligence, divine name, sometimes in God himself the Archetype.[181]

In consequence, a distinct discipline of human geometry evolved. The body of man was inscribed within circles and squares, with arms raised above his head, extended straight from his shoulders, lowered to his sides — all to demonstrate various principles of symmetry and harmony in God's masterwork. And human geometry became an esthetic criterion, the object of imitation not only in painting and sculpture, but also in architecture and even music.

In his *Three books of occult philosophy*, Agrippa produces a series of illustrations that shows the human body in various significant attitudes. **Figure 85a** presents man in his most

vine faculty is an elongated triangle representing the power of intellectuality. Conversely, intersecting this triangle is an exactly equal triangle that reaches up from the genitals of the body and represents the power of sensuality. Like the macrocosm with its celestial/terrestrial dichotomy, man has a dual nature. Translated into ethics, this means that we have a capacity for good and for evil, and consequently we face a constant moral choice to act in the higher region of the intellect or to descend to the lower region of physical passion. The mid-point where intellectuality and sensuality are in equal measure is "the sphere of the sun or of the heart." At that point, mind and body are in equilibrium, coordinately functioning to produce a well-balanced man.

Fig. 85a. *The human body apportioned within a square.*

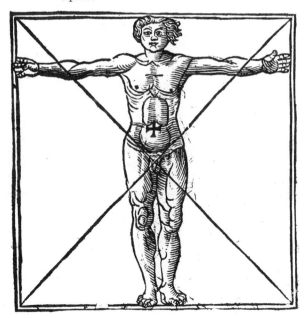

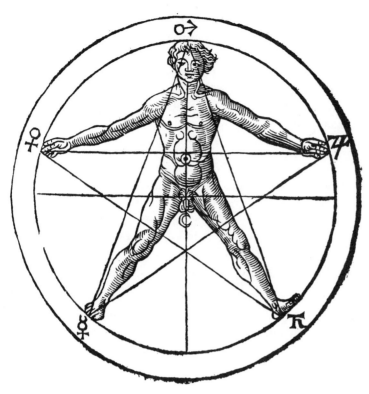

Fig. 85b. *The human body apportioned within a circle.*

Fig. 85c. *The human body distributed within the signs of the zodiac.*

natural position, inscribed within a square and therefore approximated to the tetrad. As Agrippa says:

> The four square measure is the most proportionated body; for, if a man be placed upright with his feet together, and his arms stretched forth, he will make a quadrature equilateral, whose center is in the bottom of his belly. (page 265)

In figure 85a, a symbolic cross marks the navel, the reminder that man fits into a sequence of generations and consequently into the cycles of time. The two diagonals from the corners of the diagram, however, intersect at the genitals of the body. In this position reminiscent of the tetrad, and therefore of the elementary world of physical nature, man has sexual organs as the center of his being.

In **Figure 85b**, as contrast, the human form is inscribed within a circle. The genitals are still the center of man's being, though other significant patterns emerge:

> But if on the same center a circle be made by the crown of the head, the arms being let fall so far till the end of the fingers touch the circumference of that circle, and the feet spread abroad in the same circumference, as much as the fingers ends are distant from the top of the head; Then they divide that circle, which was drawn from the center of the lower belly, into five equale parts, and do constitute a perfect Pentagon; and the Heels of the feet, having reference to the navile, make a triangle of equal sides. (page 266)

In this position, approximating the perfection of the circle, the planets are assigned to various parts of the body: Mars appears at the head, Jupiter at the left hand, Venus at the right hand, Saturn at the left foot, and Mercury at the right foot. Moreover, the Moon, that most changeable of planets, is assigned to the sexual organs, while the Sun, the most noble of the planets, is assigned to the navel.

Continuing in **Figure 85c**, we observe the human form in yet another posture. Now the navel is the center of man's being, and respectability is at last achieved:

> But if the Heels being unmoved, the feet be stretched forth on both sides to the right and left, and the hands lifted up to the line of the head, then the ends of the fingers and Toes do make a square of equall sides, whose center is on the navile, in the girdling of the body. (page 267)

The signs of the zodiac are arranged counterclockwise around the sides of the square, with Aries at the head. In this diagram, man is directly correlated with the annual unit of time, repeating the perfection of the macrocosm in its temporal aspect. By such synchronization man fulfills his dual purpose in the eternal scheme: each of us alone is the creature of a day; but considered *en masse,* numberless generations march forward to eternity.

It was commonplace to depict the microcosm of man in the context of the macrocosm as in figures 85b-c, so that the members of his body correspond to the signs of the zodiac or to the planets. A typical result is **Figure 86**, which comes from an early edition of the perennially popular *Kalendar of shepardes.* One purpose of this diagram is to provide a chart of all the bones in the body, as the caption along the left of the figure discloses, and therefore we have a human skeleton. But more immediate to our purpose, each of the seven planets is assigned to a distinct part of the anatomy. The Sun rules the heart, Venus rules the ears (though her arrow is misdirected), the Moon rules the head, Mercury rules the "lights" (that is, the lungs), Mars rules the gall bladder, Jupiter rules the liver, and Saturn rules "the milt" (that is, the spleen). There may be some rationale to these assignments: for example, the Sun is in the midst of the planets just as the heart is in the midst of the body, and the spleen is the appropriate seat for man's saturnine disposition. The obvious reason for this scheme, however, is a need to

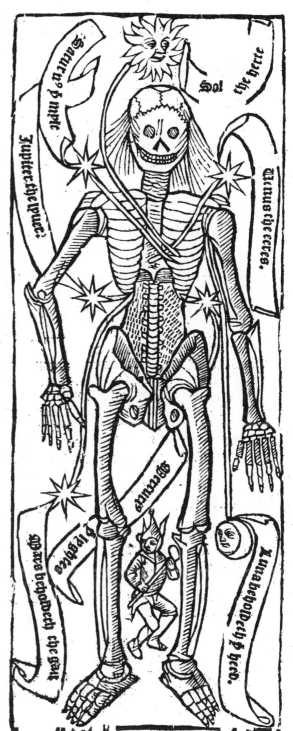

Fig. 86. *The human body distributed among the planets.*

147

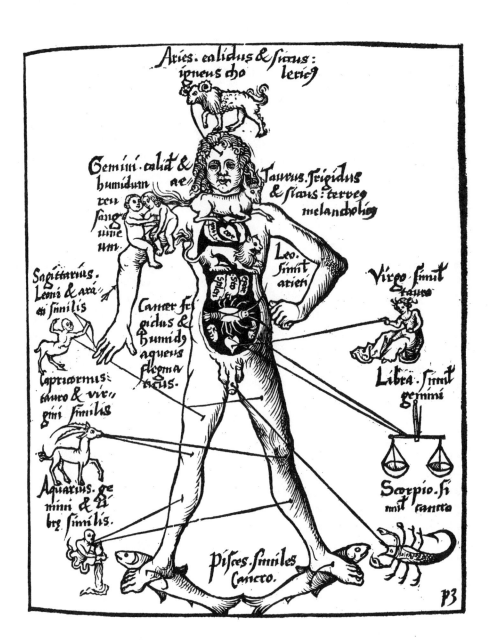

Fig. 87. *The human body distributed among the signs of the zodiac.*

correlate the planets with the human body, and this need is met in a fairly lax manner — that is to say, why is the head assigned a planet, but not the feet? Why the lungs and even the gall bladder, but not the kidneys? The most puzzling omission of all is the genitals. But now we are being refractory, willfully ignoring the intent of this diagram. Since the macrocosm-microcosm analogy was the basis for astrology, the clear purpose of this chart is to help the kitchen astrologer in making decisions about two important medical treatments: when to conduct surgery and when to bleed a patient. The caption along the right side of the figure gives the necessary instructions.

The most common depiction of man as microcosm distributed the parts of his body among the signs of the zodiac — in actuality, a variant of the pythagorean tetrad articulated as a twelve-phase cosmos (see figures 67-69, though the cabala also had posited this thesis). Almost any almanac — and certainly any mul-

148

ti-annual almanac — carried such a diagram.[182]
Figure 87, which comes from the first edition of
Gregor Reisch's late medieval encyclopedia,
Margarita philosophica, is representative of
the type. Each of the twelve zodiacal signs is
given control of a particular organ, limb, or
joint; and since according to the tetrad each
sign partakes of two basic qualities and is correspondent to an element and to a bodily humour, so also each part of the body has the
same associations. Aries, for example, rules the
head; and since it is hot and dry, fiery and
choleric, it imparts these associations to the
head. Its opposite, Cancer, rules the chest,
lungs, and stomach; and since Cancer is cold
and moist, watery, and phlegmatic, so also are
these organs. Gemini rules the arms; and therefore they, like Gemini, are hot and moist, airy,
and sanguine. Taurus, in contrast, is cold and
dry, earthy, and melancholy; and therefore the
neck, which is ruled by Taurus, similarly possesses these characteristics. The other eight zodiacal signs are grouped behind these four pro-
totypes. In consequence, like Aries are Leo,
which rules the heart and liver, and Sagittarius, which rules the pelvis. Like Taurus are
Virgo, which rules the intestines and the rec-
tum, and Capricornus, which rules the knees.
Like Gemini are Libra, which rules the kidneys
and buttocks, and Aquarius, which rules the
lower legs. Like Cancer are Scorpio, which
rules the genitals, and Pisces, which rules the
feet. In some puerile sense, zodiacal man does
indeed follow the temporal pattern of the
macrocosm: his head corresponds to Aries, the
sign that starts with the vernal equinox and
therefore inaugurates a new year according
to the pagan calendar, and his feet correspond
to Pisces, the sign that concludes the yearly
journey of the sun. From head to foot zodiacal
man is a similar unit, a composite of discrete
parts that nonetheless reflects the unifying
principle of cosmos.

In a more sophisticated manner, also **Figure
88** represents man as a temporal microcosm.
In this instance, however, the annual cycle of

Fig. 88. *The human condition as a cycle of the
seasons.*

four seasons rather than the zodiac provides
the pattern. Figure 88 comes from an emblem
book by Barthélemy Aneau, a learned and talented poet, historian, and jurist, who spent his
mature years as principal of the Collège de la
Trinité in Lyons. Aneau had translated the
celebrated emblem book of Alciato into
French, and in his own beautifully printed emblem book he offered a wealth of humanistic
topics. The title of the volume is *Picta poesis:
ut pictura poesis erit* (Lyons, 1552) — recalling
the famous dictum of Horace, *ut pictura poesis,*
and postulating a close relationship, even an
interchangeableness, between visual image
and verbal image. Following the custom of
emblem books, Aneau devotes one page in his
book to each emblem; and in every instance,
he gives at the top of the page a concise caption, then a woodcut vignette, and finally some
verses. The intention, clearly, is to present the
same idea through three distinct, but coordi-
nate and supplementary, means: through
direct statement, through visual image, and
through verbal image. Aneau's is one of the
earlier, as well as more handsome and interesting, of the renaissance emblem books.

149

Figure 88 considers the life of a man in the conventional formula of four ages, and it distributes them among the four seasons of the year. Aneau announces his meaning in the caption at the top, which may be translated somewhat freely: "The condition of mankind is everlasting." The hexastich of verses elaborates this theme:

Spring, summer, autumn, winter—these are the four seasons as the years roll by in a cycle. Likewise man in his lifetime has four ages; he is first a child, then a youth, next an adult, and finally an old man—so that the cycle of human life, like the everlasting world, reveals to us that men are everlasting.

The same statement is repeated in the woodcut between the two verbal presentations. The visual image consists of a circle, symbolizing time in its eternal aspect, divided into four quarters depicting the seasons, the measurable parts of durational time. Taken together, the four quarters comprise a full year, a basic unit of time. Conceptually, as well as visually, this emblem recalls the tetrad of Isidore and its derivatives (figures 66-70), which interrelate the three cosmoi of *mundus*, *annus*, and *homo*. The sun is rising in the quarter for spring, at zenith in the quarter for summer, setting in the quarter for autumn, and below the horizon in the quarter for winter. In each quarter there is vegetation appropriate to the season: ripening grain in spring, grain being harvested in summer, a tree with falling leaves in autumn, a bare tree in winter. In each quarter also a man pursues a suitable occupation: cultivating his grain, cutting his grain, picking fruit, retiring into a cave for the winter. Furthermore, into each quarter a wind god blows, distributing flowers or leaves or hail or cold blasts.

At the bottom of figure 88 a corpse rests in a grave, denoting that the end of man's cycle is death. But at the top, in the opposite position within the diagram, a resplendent Jove with thunderbolt and scepter presides over the entire scene, indicating not only that His providence is continual, but also that He is coexistent with eternity. This is a fulsome statement of the renaissance theme of mutability. Recognition that each human life ends in death induces melancholy. But overcoming the incipient despair in this mood, the macrocosm-microcosm analogy results in optimism, because by completing the finite pattern of his four ages each man perfects the basic unit of cosmos. Thereby he participates in eternity. *Aeterna hominum natura.*

Fig. 89. *The human condition as a microcosm of day and night from Albertus Magnus.*

As figures 87 and 88 exemplify, the little world of man could be depicted as the annual unit of time, either a twelve-phase system of the zodiacal signs or a four-phase system of the seasonal cycle. The human microcosm could also be depicted as the diurnal unit of time, as a two-phase system of day and night (which of course concealed the twenty-four-phase system of twenty-four hours from dawn to dawn). **Figure 89** is a representation of the microcosm within the coordinates of day and night. It serves as title page to Albertus Magnus' *Opus philosophiae naturalis* (Brescia, 1493), a vestige from the middle ages that the renaissance endowed with the permanence of several successive editions.

In figure 89 we see in the center a Christ-like figure with arms extended, a type of everyman. He is circumscribed by a circle, half of which is shaded and carries the moon, indicating that portion of the diurnal unit of time known as night; while the other half of the circle is unshaded and carries the sun, indicating that portion of the diurnal unit of time known as day. Just within the circle twenty-four dots mark the hours within this basic unit of time. The day half-circle and the night half-circle are exact counterparts — that is, paradoxically opposite and yet the same. And taken together, they perfect a circle, a whole which, as the emblem of eternity, is greater than the sum of its two parts. This symbolism shows, like figure 88, that the individual will die, but that human nature in the abstract is everlasting. Reiterating this theme are the four elements forming another circle in the exact center of the diagram. The anthropomorphic figure incorporates these elements, representing the four bodily humours, and thereby partakes of the mobile stasis of the pythagorean tetrad. The pythagorean bias of this diagram is emphasized by the series of digits at the top, the first ten whole numbers which underlie the multitudinous items of creation; while the mathematical instruments in the corners — a scale, a compass, a square, and a ruler — recall that God created the universe according to number, weight, and measure.

There is nothing in the text of Albertus' work to explain this woodcut, which fills the first page of his volume, although there are chapters on time and eternity, and on the human soul. Nonetheless, figure 89 unmistakably purveys one of the salient commonplaces that the middle ages bequeathed to the renaissance. It is an astrological commonplace, and *The kalender of shepardes* gives a concise statement of it:

Here after foloweth the .iiii. elementes, and the .iiii. complexiones of man, and how & in what tyme they reygne in man. Cap. xxix.

Ayre, Fyre, Erthe, and Water. the .xxiiii. houres of the daye and the nyght ruleth Sanguyne, Coleryke, Melancolyke, and Flumatỹke. Syxe houres after mydnyght blode hath the maystry, & in the .vi. houres afore noone coloure [i.e., choler] reygneth, and .vi. houres after none reygneth melancoly, and .vi. houres afore mydnyght reygneth the flumatyke. (I3ᵛ)

In this fashion the lesser world of man, like the macrocosm itself, conforms to predetermined patterns of space and time. Such lore underlies the structure of Milton's earliest masterpiece, *L'Allegro* and *Il Penseroso*. There also we have the passage of twenty-four hours from one sunrise to the next, and human nature is dichotomized into two contrasting halves, one operative during the daylight hours and the other operative during the hours of darkness. Milton, of course, has transformed the crude didacticism of the commonplace, and has produced poetry of a high order. But without question his companion poems are likewise intended to be an icon of human nature as a two-phase cosmos of day and night.

Milton could have found his inspiration in **Figure 90**, from Fludd's *Utriusque cosmi . . . historia*, which offers the same bipartite image of man that figure 89 sets forth. There also we see "microcosmic night" in the shaded bottom half of the engraving, and "microcosmic day" in the unshaded upper half. The commonplace of diurnal man was still current in the early seventeenth century. What Fludd has added is the double diapason of the pythagorean tuning system, so that the human microcosm expresses the musical harmonies of the macrocosm (see figures 79-82).

Another example of diurnal man in the seventeenth century appears in **Figure 91**, taken

from Henry Peacham's emblem book, *Minerva britanna, or a garden of heroical devises* (London, 1612). Peacham was a versatile man-about-London who qualifies as the exemplar of his best-known work, *The compleat gentleman*. He was schoolmaster, traveler, linguist, poet, musician, mathematician, and artist. Peacham prepared both the drawings and the verses for the *Minerva britanna;* and since it contains 204 emblems, he had considerable

Fig. 90. *The human condition as a microcosm of day and night from Fludd.*

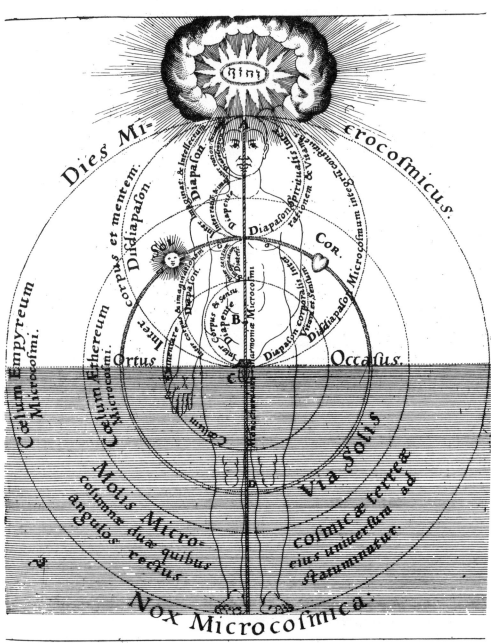

HEARE what's the reason why a man we call
A little world? and what the wiser ment
By this new name? two lights Cœleſtiall
Are in his head, as in the Element:
Eke as the wearied Sunne at night is ſpent,
 So ſeemeth but the life of man a day,
 At morne hee's borne, at night he flits away.

Of heate and cold as is the Aire compoſed,
So likewiſe man we ſee breath's whot and cold,
His bodie's earthy: in his lunges incloſed,
Remaines the Aire: his braine doth moiſture hold,
His heart and liver, doe the heate infold:
 Of Earth, Fire, Water, Man thus framed is,
 Of Elements the threefold Qualities.

Dd1.   And

Fig. 91. *Day and night as an emblem of the human microcosm.*

153

latitude to expatiate upon a wide range of topics. Figure 91 is a typical page from that volume, with its Latin tag at the top, its woodcut of *homo microcosmus* as a sphere comprising sun and moon, and the rhymed verses. Peacham's treatment of the commonplace comes rather late, although he is contemporary with John Donne, who often worked the topos into his witty conceits, as in "A nocturnall upon S. Lucies day." Nevertheless, both poets are employing the same tradition as figure 89, even if the clichés were becoming worn and had lost much of their meaning. Indeed, the last line of Peacham's verse defies interpretation.

Just as the microcosm of man was apportioned according to the "grateful vicissitude, like day and night," again to use Milton's phrase, so also the lesser world could be coordinated with the incessant changes of the weather. One of the incontrovertible proofs of time's passage was the continual succession of weather phenomena — what the renaissance, following Aristotle, called "meteors." The heavens gave insistent evidence of mutability, not only in the daily cycle of sun and moon or the annual cycle of the seasons, but also in the ceaseless formation and disappearance of clouds and snow and lightning and rainbows and a wondrous assortment of related occurrences visible from our lowly habitat. Man was a microcosm, whatever the temporal cycle used to measure the macrocosm, and consequently his parts were correlated with the almost endless variety of atmospheric events.

Figure 92 shows just how various such a correlation between microcosmic man and meteors could be. It is Fludd's "meteorographical precious stone," as the caption across the top indicates.[183] It appears as a foldout in his *Philosophia sacra & vere Christiana seu meteorologia cosmica* (Frankfurt, 1626), a meticulously illustrated folio that completes Fludd's synthesis of science and religion. That passions and other diseases are the meteors of man's body had long been a commonplace, and here we see the topos worked out in exhaustive de-

tail. Donne uses the correspondence to good effect in "A feaver," when he reassures his mistress that she is not seriously ill:

> These burning fits but meteors bee,
> Whose matter in thee is soone spent.
> (lines 21-22)

But this topos was not simply a poetic device, an empty metaphor. Rather it was a scientific fact, acted upon confidently in medical practice. A thorough discussion of the subject is provided by Stefano Roderigo de Castro, professor of medicine in the university of Pisa. He published a large folio intended as a reference work for the treatment of diseases and entitled *De meteoris microcosmi libri quatuor* (Florence, 1621). As late as the middle of the seventeenth century, Athanasius Kircher was still expounding the thesis: Morbi sunt meteora microcosmi.[184]

Returning to figure 92, we may well feel bewildered by the welter of information in the diagram. The general intention is clear, however, and the major features are evident. The tetragrammaton appears in the central panel at the top, the innermost of several refulgent ellipses. Beneath Him flies the archangel Michael, carrying out a divine mission as the "guardian of Beauty" (custos Tiphereth), the central sefirah of the cabala (see figure 54). The path of Michael's flight terminates with the sun, which is in the position of its zenith and whose path marks the boundary of the physical world. It is graced with a biblical quotation: "He placed His tabernacle in the sun" (Psalms, xix.5). In the opposite position within the diagram — that is, in the central panel at the bottom — a human being reclines. This is mortal man, as in figure 88. But to counter pessimism, a banner protrudes from his mouth reiterating the message of the hexaemeron, especially as the cabala had interpreted it: "Man is the perfection and end of all creatures in the universe."

The area between the human figure at the bottom and the empyrean indicated by the tetragrammaton at the top is filled by four nearly concentric half-circle arcs. The outermost arc represents the sphere of elemental fire. It contains the sun at the top, as we have noted. To the left of the sun, it contains in addition the Milky Way, which Galileo had reported to be a congeries of individual stars. Also distributed around this fiery arc are several images of the sun, the moon, and a star as they participate in various meteors resulting from their reflection or refraction. The next three arcs represent the three distinct regions of elemental air (see pages 32-33, above). The uppermost of these is very hot because of its proximity to the sphere of fire, and consequently it is filled with burning meteors. The lowest of these is likewise hot because it absorbs the sunbeams reflected from the earth's surface. The mid-most of these, in reaction against its hot neighbors, is very cold, and therefore it is filled with watery meteors produced by a process of condensation. Finally, at the bottom of this area between mortal and divine, a short arc indicates the surface of the earth, from which the observation of these phenomena is made.

Fludd takes considerable pains to run through the entire repertory of meteorological phenomena that derived ultimately from Aristotle and Pliny, and it may be of some interest to follow him in this determined effort to be exhaustive. In the outermost arc representing the region of elemental fire, we have (starting at the far left) a sun, which, as the lines of perspective indicate, is instrumental in producing a rainbow (arcus or Iris). Three colors of the rainbow are specified — red, green, and purple — and also its center. It is a reflection of beams from the sun, of course, and therefore perspective lines are drawn to where it will be seen on the surface of the earth. During this process, "The sky is serene, which is why it is blue" (Coelum serenum cur sit caeruleum). This sun produces not only a rainbow, but also another phenomenon of reflection known as "double suns" (parelii); and the moon beside it similarly produces double moons. These double suns and double moons are visible

from the surface of the earth, as perspective lines indicate. Next, a star shines through a cloud to produce a phenomenon in the lowest region of air known as a "halo" (halo circa stellam), likewise visible from earth. Similarly, a moon shines through a cloud to produce a halo (halo circa lunam). On the other side of the large sun at the top, a smaller sun shines through a cloud to produce a phenomenon like a rainbow, though this is a complete, unbroken circle (Arcus integer circulus factus quomodo videtur); and this rarity can be seen only from above (by whom?). From the center of this circular rainbow issues a warm "vapour" into the lowest region of air. Next, a sun shines its rays through a cloud to produce "perpendicular lines" of light, which are visible from below. Then, a moon shines through "thin air like an exhalation" (aer tenuis halituolus) to produce a "colored moon, without any other agent in the air," which is visible from the surface of the earth. Finally, a sun shines through "air like a vapour" (aer vaporolus) to produce "an image of the setting sun" (solis imago in occasu), which is also visible from the surface of the earth.

Just beneath the region of elemental fire, the uppermost region of the air contains a number of different burning meteors. Starting from the left side of this arc, we see "a burning plank" (trabs) and "a burning spear" (lancea), several sorts of comets (xiphiae, Mercurialis, miles, tenacula, niger, ceratias), two phenomena involving a star and the sun which occur at dawn (aurora and rosa), a phenomenon where burning seems to appear between chinks in the clouds (chasma), and "flying sparks" (scintillae volantes). The middle region of air, cold and wet, contains a number of different meteors resulting from the condensation of vapours. Starting from the left side of this arc, we see several sorts of "sudden blasts" (flatus repentini) issuing from a cloud, including "a hurricane" (ecnephias), "a cyclone" (turbo), and "a whirlwind" (prester); several sorts of "portentous rains" (pluviae portentosae), including "drops of blood" (guttae sanguiniae), a rain of "stones" (lapides), and a rain of "frogs" (ranae); two sorts of lightning, including the destructive "lightning-bolt" (fulmen) with its "thunder-stone"(lapis ceraunius) and the mere "flash" of lightning (coruscatio); several sorts of precipitation, including "hail" (grando), "rain" (pluvia), and "snow" (nix); and a late afternoon phenomenon called "the redness of sunset" (rubedo vespertina). The lowest region of air contains a miscellaneous assortment of meteors. Starting from the left side of this arc, we see the mirage of "a temple in the air" (templum in aere), a fiery meteor resembling a pair of prancing "goats" (caprae), "a falling spark" (scintilla cadens), "flying stars" (stellae volantes), "frost" (pruina), and "dew" (ros). Also from the periphery of this region blow twelve wind-heads, corresponding to the twelve points of the conventional wind-rose (see figure 67). The West Wind (*Favonius* in Latin, *Zephirus* in Greek) puffs from the right, and the East Wind *(Subsolanus* in Latin, *Apheliotes* in Greek) puffs from the left. Winds were considered in the category of meteors because they are air in motion. Finally, on the surface of the earth there is the temple that produced the mirage, and a cyclone turning in the opposite direction (ex contraria motione) from the one in the middle region of air.

Another prominent feature of figure 92 germane to our purpose is exhibited in the two equal panels that flank the panel of the tetragrammaton at the top. These two panels considered as a unit display an elaborate system of correspondences based upon the number 10, the divine number. In fact, Fludd took this information from Agrippa's "Scale of the Number Ten" (see figure 74c).[185] The categories that are correlated include the ten sacred names of God in the cabalistic tradition,[186] the nine orders of angels plus human souls, the ten sefirot of the cabala (see pages 87-88, above), nine archangels from the cabalistic tradition plus the soul of the Messiah, and nine celestial spheres plus the elementary world. For example, on the far left in the first box, there is a correspondence between the

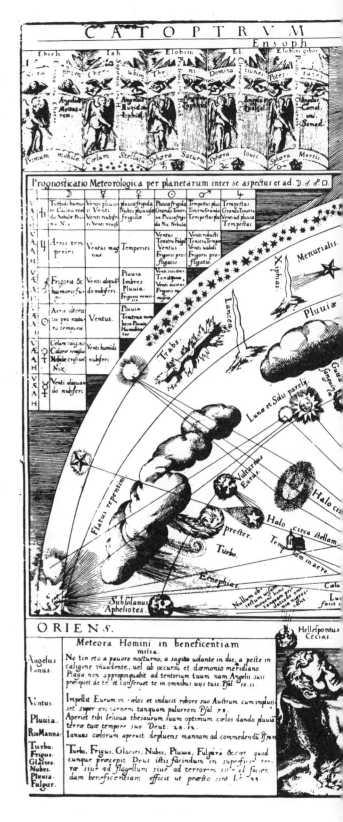

157

Fig. 92. *The human body as a microcosm of atmospheric phenomena.*

Hebrew word *Ehieh,* a name for God meaning "I am"; and the angelic order of the Seraphim; the sefirah "Crown" (*Corona* in Latin, *Cheter* in Hebrew); the archangel Mettatron;[187] and the primum mobile. In the next box, there is a correspondence between the Hebrew word *Jah,* a name for God because it is the first syllable of the tetragrammaton; the angelic order of the Cherubim; the sefirah "Wisdom" (*Sapientia* in Latin, *Hochma* in Hebrew); the archangel Ruziel or Jophiel; and the sphere of fixed stars. In the third box, there is a correspondence between the Hebrew word *Elohim,* a reverential plural form of "God"; the angelic order of Thrones; the sefirah "Prudence" (*Prudentia* in Latin, *Binah* in Hebrew); the archangel Zapthiel; and the sphere of Saturn. We can move successively from box to box across the diagram in similar fashion, until we arrive at the last box on the far right, where there is correspondence between the Hebrew word *Adonai,* meaning "Lord"; souls (note the two human figures praying, where angels have flown in the other boxes); the sefirah "Kingdom" (*Regnum* in Latin, *Malchut* in Hebrew); "the soul of the Messiah," instead of an archangel; and the sublunary world of the elements. Across the top of this long row, including the panel of the tetragrammaton, runs a caption in Hebrew and Latin: "Ensoph or the infinitude of deity." Ten is of course the appropriate number to demonstrate this perfection.

There is a great deal of additional information in figure 92, some of which is pertinent to our theme, but much of which is incidental. In any case, we should take note of the remaining major features of the engraving. In the spandrel on the left above the arc delineating the region of elemental fire, there is a table for prognosticating the weather based on the astrological positions of the six lower planets. In the complementary spandrel on the right, there is an astrological chart offering "an explanation for the large values of the heavens." At the bottom of the diagram flanking the reclining figure to the left, there is a list of "the meteors sent to benefit man," documented by suitable quotations from the Bible. And in the complementary place to the right, there is a list of "the meteors sent as a scourge or punishment for man," again documented by appropriate biblical passages.

Fludd's *catoptrum meteorographicum* is so full of information that a prose transcription of the data extends to several pages. And even then it is doubtful that the verbal paraphrase achieves either the intensity or the fullness of the visual image. The prose statement must necessarily proceed discursively through the body of information, so that its unity is destroyed and many of its intrarelationships are unrecorded. The picture is worth more than any number of words. In the final analysis, the human microcosm was an icon for man more than a description of him.

VI Contingent Systems

ANY COMPONENTS had coalesced to form a well-stocked image of the universe which the renaissance inherited. From the classical tradition came the dogmas of Pythagoras, Plato, Aristotle, Ovid, Ptolemy, and several more. From the Hebraic tradition came the book of Genesis with its extensive commentary and the Psalms. Christianity had assimilated these diverse pieces and had produced a comforting picture of an ordered world, created and maintained by divine providence. Whatever faults appeared were temporary disruptions due to capricious fortune or to the wickedness of men, not to any deficiency in the design. When fifteenth-century cosmographers looked into their books, they found this view supported by Boethius, Isidore, Bede, Bartholomaeus Anglicus, even Sacrobosco. Not surprisingly, therefore, they brought cabalism and other mystical and occult doctrines into the scene. At the same time, however, explorers were providing a clearer description of the earth's geography, and astronomers with increasingly effective measuring instruments were delineating new charts for the heavens. A revision of the established synthesis was called for, and the old order was eventually changed by Copernicans. They modified the center of the orthodox picture and destroyed its frame. But well into the seventeenth century, the image revealed in the familiar cosmographical glass satisfied all but the most restive. In this chapter we shall look at some of the contingent diagrams that reflect the donnés of renaissance cosmography. To our way of thinking, many seem fantastic; but all follow logically from the assumption that our universe is a complex, yet unified, cosmic system.

The human microcosm, as we have seen, was frequently deployed as a convenient guide to the mysteries of time and space. By knowing ourselves we gain some knowledge of the universal plan. Equally commonplace was another cosmic metaphor, the great chain of being, with its graduated degrees leading from the natural world we perceive around us to the most high that at best we conceive with divine aid. Modern scholars after A. O. Lovejoy and E. M. W. Tillyard have made us very much aware of the prevalence and importance of this time-honored motif. It derived from the same impetus as cosmos — an imperative to discern a structural design in our environment. And it was easy to translate the multi-level hierarchy of creation, such as that described in figure 53b, to the more sophisticated image of a multi-linked chain that stretches from the highest of God's creatures to the lowest. Rank and order are rendered manifest by either hierarchy or chain.

In a hierarchy like figure 53b where each level is contiguous with its neighbors, the various components are discrete. In such a system, the salient relationship is likely to be that of the part to the whole, rather than that of the part to its adjacent parts. The prototype of such a system is the diapason, and the result of such a relationship is harmony. But in a chain, the various components are interjoined, and therefore more intimately interrelated each to the next. In such a system, interdependency and continuity are stressed, and Aristotle's concept of the plenum dominates. Furthermore, a chain has a beginning and an end; each link joins to its predecessor and provides anchorage for its successor. The result is a sequence, one link following another, from a *terminus a quo* to a *terminus ad quem*. There is not the network of correspondences, the inner resonance of one component perfecting the pattern shared by all components, so that the proliferation of microcosms is unified by the common principle of cosmos. The chain of being is linear, wholly measurable. We can see it from end to end. Unlike the concept of cosmos, it is not an image of an otherwise inexpressible concept. It is wholly conscious. The chain of being is an idea we can perceive.

But interestingly enough, I have been unable to find a visual representation of the chain in any of the several hundred renaissance books on cosmography that I have searched.[188] Nor is the topos discussed in any medieval or renaissance encyclopedia that I know. It is not a motif that was given concrete expression—an image used by poets, perhaps, but not by natural scientists. The image was unquestionably viable, even commonplace; but I suggest that until the eighteenth century it was considered an archetype only, and not a physical fact.

The closest I have come to a picture of the universal chain is **Figure 93**, which uses the categories of the great chain but arranges them as a stair with eight steps. This woodcut serves as frontispiece to the *De ascensu & descensu intellectus,* a treatise by Ramon Lull. According to learned opinion in the renaissance, this notorious Catalan mystic was the first Christian to assimilate the cabala. After a profligate youth, Lull devoted the mature years of his long life to the promulgation of Christianity among the infidels and to a profitable service at the courts of European kings, including Edward I of England. His dedication to private study led to a reputation as a magician and an alchemist. More rightly, however, he is seen as a theosophist whose method of disclosing reality through logic, the *ars Lulliana*, sustained adherents until the eighteenth century, when Swift could make them the butt of topical jokes in *Gulliver's Travels*. The corpus of Lull's writings is as large as it is obscure, and since his own times has been chaotic. Figure 93 comes from a text that Lull wrote at Montpellier in 1304. The renaissance reverentially preserved it and printed it with two other of his treatises in 1512 at Valencia.[189]

A set of steps, like a chain, is a hierarchical arrangement of items. Actually, figure 93 contains three "intellectual stairways," and an early reader of the British Library copy of Lull's volume has numbered them in ink at the appropriate places. The prominent set of stairs is one *scala intellectualis*—the "first," according to our unknown annotator—but there are two more depicted as concentric circles in a wheel to the left of the main stairway. It will be this *prima scala,* however, that focuses our attention, because there we see the various categories of existence identified by both a label and a type. At the bottom as the lowest step are "a stone" (*lap*[is]), followed by "a flame," next "a plant," and then "an animal," with a lion as the type of this category. These lower steps comprise the palpable world of physical nature. The next step is assigned to "man," who inhabits the world of nature, but who also through his God-given reason participates in the higher ranks. The next step up is "heaven," a different order of existence than the five lower steps, and it provides a domicile, as its type shows, for "an angel" and for "God." The final step at the top serves as entranceway to a magnificent structure that represents

Fig. 93. *The Lullian stairway by which an adept may ascend to knowledge.*

the reward of ascending and thereby assimilating the preparatory steps toward perfection. Lull explains in the text: "We begin at the imperfect, so that we might ascend to the perfect; and conversely, we may descend from the perfect to the imperfect"[190]—hence the title of this treatise. For Boethius, the top of the stair would be the *summum bonum*; for alchemists, the stable completeness of the philosophers' stone that culminated the seven stages of the opus (see figure 109). The neophyte who stands at the bottom of these stairs

161

holds a banner that reads *Intellectus conjunctus,* suggesting the "integrated understanding" that he seeks. This "castle of knowledge," to recall the title page of Robert Recorde's textbook (figure 4), represents that ultimate knowledge which only the dedicated can achieve. As the banner over it proclaims, "Wisdom has built for herself a home," and a beatifying sun beams down upon it from above.

The second *scala intellectualis* is presented as contiguous segments around the outer circle of the wheel that the aspiring neophyte holds in his left hand. In the words of Lull, "It is composed of twelve terms by which the understanding crosses over to the sense-perception of things and of their hidden qualities."[191] These terms are difficult to translate into English because their meanings shade into one another; but reading counterclockwise from the neophyte's hand, in Latin they are *actus, passio, actio, natura, substantia, accidens, simplex, compositum, individuum, species, genus,* and *ens.* As the text explains, "With these twelve terms the understanding ascends and descends along the first *scala,* so that it understands and knows those things which are contained in that scale."[192]

The third *scala intellectualis* in figure 93 is also presented as contiguous segments around a circle, the inner circle within the second *scala.* It comprises five steps, again difficult to translate into English with the proper nuances of meaning: *sensibile, imaginabile, dubitabile, credibile,* and *intelligibile.* According to the text, "By these steps the understanding ascends from the sensible to the intelligible; and conversely, it descends from the intelligible to the sensible"[193] — where "sensible" and "intelligible," of course, have their platonic meanings. By traversing these three *scalae intellectuales,* then, the human understanding bestrides the extended continuum from imperfect to perfect, from object to subject, from the sense-perceptible to that which can be known by mind alone. In that way, it ranges the full extent of God's creation from lowest to highest, and knows by direct apprehension each link in the cosmic chain.

In Lull's scheme there is a clear moral intention as the understanding ascends or descends the *scalae intellectuales.* Up is good; down is bad. According to Pico della Mirandola, at the moment of his creation God instructed Adam: "Thou canst grow downward into the lower natures which are brutes; thou canst again grow upward from thy soul's reason into the higher natures which are divine."[194] The ethics of this circumstance is made explicit by Charles de Bouelles in his *Liber de sapiente,* published in a collection of his treatises at Paris in 1510. In his "book about wisdom," Bouelles discusses various sorts of human behavior which, as we see in **Figure 94,** he arranges as graduated states of consciousness. The steps leading to virtue, like the steps in Lull's *scala* are the same as the lower links in the conventional chain of being. At the far left comprising the lowest step is the "mineral" state, with "a stone" as its type. An item in the mineral state has only one quality: "It exists." The next step is the "vegetable" state, with "a tree" as its type. An item in the vegetable state, being one step up from the mineral state, has two qualities: "It exists," but also "it lives." The following step is the "sensible" state — that is, capable of sensation — and it has "a horse" as its type. An item in the sensible state has three qualities: "It exists" and "it lives," but also "it feels." Finally, at the top is the "rational" state — that is, capable of reason — and it has "a man" as its type. Man, as the summation of this scale, embraces the three qualities of the lower states of being, but adds the uniquely human quality that makes him lord of creation: man not only "exists," "lives," and "feels," but most importantly, "he understands."

The ascension of this scale leads to successive states that bring man ever closer to godliness; conversely, however, a descent leads to successive states that are increasingly dehumanized. The rake's progress to annihilation is detailed in the other half of this diagram on the right. In continuation at the top of the scale, corresponding to the rational state, "a

Fig. 94. *The steps up and down the levels of being according to Bouelles.*

scholar" studies at his reading desk and exhibits the essence of virtue. In this state of "manliness" (*virtus* < *vir*, man), he "understands," as well as "feels," "lives," and "exists." One step down, corresponding to the sensible state, "a sensual man" gazes with vanity into a mirror and exhibits the vice of "prodigal dissipation." Like an animal, he "feels" and "lives" and "exists," but without understanding. One step farther down, corresponding to the vegetable state, "a sensuous man" sits at a laden table and gorges his body with food and drink, exhibiting the vice of "gluttony." Like a plant, he "lives" and "exists," but does not feel or understand. Finally, at the bottom of this descent, corresponding to the mineral state, "a clod" sits hunched over with his body contracted into an inac-

tive lump, and he exhibits the vice of "indolence." He barely "exists," but shares no other qualities to alleviate his inert state.

Figures 93 and 94 use the terminology of the great chain, and obviously they display a sequential arrangement of categories that are ranked in a spatial design. But they project the image of steps in a stairway, rather than links in a chain. The divergence from the traditional chain of being, moreover, goes even further than that. Bouelles and Lull are drawing upon a quite different set of conventions. They are working in the mystical tradition, where the stages of mystic awareness provide the controlling image. Not even remotely do these authors recall the classical tradition of the golden chain or the Scholastic synthesis of Greek philosophy and Christian doctrine. For

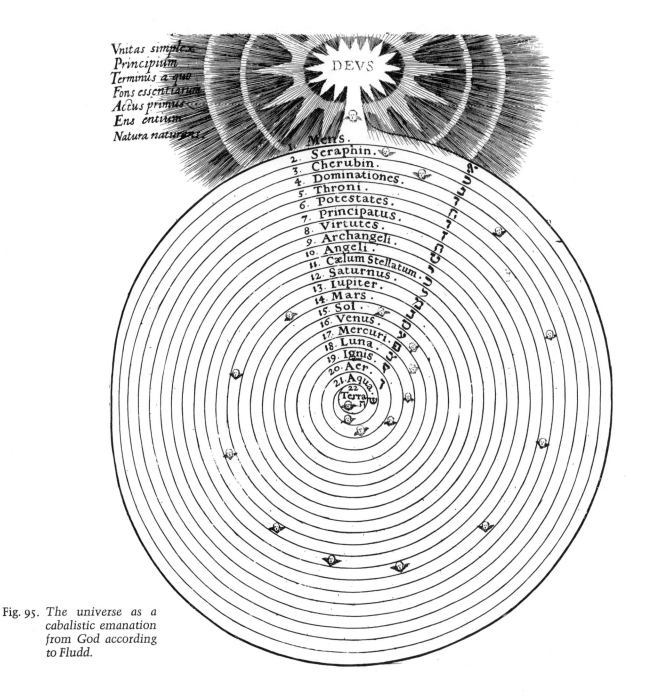

Vnitas simplex
Principium
Terminus a quo
Fons essentiarum
Actus primus
Ens entium
Natura naturans

DEVS

Mens.
2. Seraphin.
3. Cherubin.
4. Dominationes.
5. Throni.
6. Potestates.
7. Principatus.
8. Virtutes.
9. Archangeli.
10. Angeli.
11. Cælum Stellatum.
12. Saturnus.
13. Iupiter.
14. Mars.
15. Sol.
16. Venus.
17. Mercuri.
18. Luna.
19. Ignis.
20. Aer.
21. Aqua.
22. Terra.

Fig. 95. *The universe as a cabalistic emanation from God according to Fludd.*

all their devotional fervor, they have come to their religion in an apocryphal way, not through ministration of the Church.

The renaissance abounds in diagrams of the universe that are rigorously theological, however, and authors of Christian persuasion were ingenious in adapting cosmographical lore to their religious purposes. One of the most ingenious, as we have seen in several previous plates, was Robert Fludd, who perhaps more than any other in the early seventeenth century carried the concept of cosmos to its logical extreme. While Bacon was seeking to control nature by learning its secrets through the tedious and piecemeal process of observation,

164

Fludd with wondrous virtuosity applied the principles of orthodox cosmology to reveal a fully formulated plan conceived and maintained by a beneficent deity. Each question raised by the physical sciences could be answered by reference to this master-scheme. Through careful reasoning and prodigious learning, Fludd sought to provide a comprehensive description of the universe and to fit the growing number of details into his vast design. He was the last practicing scientist to produce a work presumptuously encyclopedic. The world has chosen to follow Bacon, however, so that Fludd now appears to have been a muddle-headed eccentric.

For Fludd, as for most of his contemporaries, religion and cosmology were but different views of the same subject. Theology and astronomy had the same source, and the scientist perforce went back to creation to discover those first principles that govern our universe. **Figure 95** is Fludd's rendition of that crucial event, when God's word became physical fact. In the diagram, we see our universe complete, a continuous extension of the Supreme Being. God, the numinous entity at the top, generates a spiral of created beings, stretching from the pure "mind" of His own presence to the ultimate baseness of "earth." Through the agency of assisting intelligences, He produces and governs the insubstantial realm of *mens* (#1), the nine orders of angels (#2-10), the sphere of fixed stars and the seven celestial spheres (#11-18), and the spheres of the four elements (#19-22). These are the familiar categories of creation. Within each sphere, there is a letter of the Hebrew alphabet to suggest both the continuity and the completeness of this scheme, and to associate it with the cabala, that other authoritative account of the hexaemeron and related matters. There are exactly twenty-two categories because there are twenty-two letters in the Hebrew alphabet. At the upper left appears a list of several epithets for the deity: "the indivisible unity," "the principle," "the starting-point," "the fount of essences," "the first cause," "the being of be-

ings," "nature in action." In sum, this diagram shows how the universe emanates from God, and yet remains continuously within His confines. The physical is a product of the spiritual, different and yet the same. That is the paradox of *natura naturans,* a dynamic process within a static perfection.

The pythagorean tetrad was early and easily adapted for Christian homiletics, usually to praise the deity by expounding the wonder of his manifold powers. **Figure 96** is typical of the theological tetrad as it continued out of the middle ages. The woodcut comes from the text of Bartholomaeus Anglicus' *De proprietatibus rerum* translated into English by John Trevisa and printed by Wynken de Worde. In the diagram God holds the central position, en-

Fig. 96. *God enthroned within a tetrad of the Evangelists.*

165

throned in majesty within three concentric circles. These three circles reflect the trinal nature of God, and perhaps, though not explicitly, represent the three worlds that He created (see figure 52). In the corners of the diagram, circular vignettes display the four Evangelists, who were regularly distributed around the sides of the pythagorean tetrad in medieval versions of that cosmic scheme.[195] By implication, this diagram is a tetrad with all of the correspondences in operation, and with God occupying the one point of stasis, that point of exact balance in the center where all components are present and equal. The blackness that fills the background of this woodcut suggests that what we see is not really visible at all. It is a concept, intelligible to the mind, but not a sense-perceptible datum.

Pico in his essay *De ente et uno* makes explicit the identification of the deity and the pythagorean tetrad. "God is the fullest being," Pico asserts, and "this is that τετρακτύς, that

Fig. 97. *The theological tetrad according to Clavius after Finé.*

is, quaternity, by which Pythagoras swore and which he called the principle of ever-flowing nature."[196] A theological tetrad displayed in the scientific manner of the renaissance appears in **Figure 97**. It comes from the authoritative and extensive commentary on Sacrobosco prepared by Christopher Clavius, which was the most widely used advanced textbook of astronomy in Europe for the last quarter of the sixteenth century. Father Clavius' *Commentarius* seems first to have been printed about 1570, early in the career of this illustrious mathematician who was called the Euclid of his age. Figure 97 appears in the second edition, published at Rome in 1581. With no pretense at disguise, Father Clavius has taken it directly from the work of Oronce Finé (see figure 64), making no changes except to insert the initials I H S in the center medallion. Christ is made the focus of this intricate system of forces and counterforces, the epitome of this infinitely complex cosmos.

The seriousness with which the renaissance scientist took the theological tetrad is well exemplified by Tycho Brahe, the leading astronomer of his day. On August 8, 1576, Tycho laid the foundation stone for his famed observatory on the island of Hveen, significantly called Uraniborg because it housed a community devoted to study of the heavens. Tycho lived in Uraniborg for over twenty years and did the bulk of his important work there. The premises were extensive, as **Figure 98** reveals, comprising a large central building, numerous outbuildings, and carefully laid-out walls, gates, roads, paths, gardens, and orchards. Also as the plan reveals, Uraniborg was conspicuously patterned after the cosmic design of the tetrad.

Figure 98 comes from Tycho's *Astronomiae instauratae mechanica* published in 1598, just after Tycho's departure from Hveen and but a few years before his death. The volume has a retrospective quality, serving as a record of what Tycho had accomplished. When Tycho left Uraniborg, he brought along his printing

Fig. 98. *Tycho's observatory at Uraniborg.*

press; and he published this handsomely illustrated folio at Wandsbeck in an effort to elicit support from wealthy patrons after his loss of support from the king of Denmark. This "mechanics of renewed astronomy" contains drawings of many instruments that Tycho had devised and provides our best insight into the daily business of making observations before the advent of the telescope. Tycho reports his achievement with a justifiable sense of self-importance.

With obvious pride, Tycho sets forth in figure 98 a detailed drawing of his astronomer's utopia and punctiliously labels its several components. He gives the engraving an imposing title: "A plan for the entire layout of my headquarters, called Uraniborg." In this plan, A is the main building in the center of the premises, containing the principal residence for Tycho and his pupils, several observatories, and the library. It is oriented exactly north-south, as the caption explains, so that its four corners point to the four cardinal directions of the compass. B at the southern corner is the printing office, a complete publishing operation since dissemination of methodology and of observational data was a major objective of the enterprise. C at the northern corner houses the administrative offices, quarters for domestic servants, and the dungeon for punishing offenders. D is the west gate and E the east gate, while F, according to the caption, indicates "the four roads that lead to the four corners of the world." G is an area of formal gardens, which together form a square surrounding the circular enclosure for the main building. H is an even more extensive area of orchards. The entire establishment is enclosed by four walls forming a square; and midway along each wall a semicircular interruption provides space for a pergola, marked I. To give some notion of distance and size, the length of the road from D to E was about 350 feet, the diameter of the semicircular bend in each wall about 73 feet, and the width of the main building from north to south about 100 feet.

What a marvelous construction! How meticulously planned! All is symmetry, a formal interplay of squares and circles. And how evident the intention of its engineer. Tycho's observatory was the center of a tetrad that reproduces the cosmic tetrad. Thereby Tycho was made the analogue of God on earth, but not in the spirit of impiety. This arrangement, quite simply, placed him in the position of generic man and oriented him toward the deity. It fulfilled the promise of the hexaemeron. This is the optimum condition for the resolute astronomer who views the stars as the handiwork of a heavenly maker.

Another thought that probably crossed Tycho's mind was the topos of the enclosed garden, which similarly places man in a propitious relationship to his universe. The prototype for the *hortus conclusus* is Eden itself, which regularly in medieval depictions of it appears as a walled enclosure with a fountain at the center where two paths which traverse its diameter intersect. Beside this fountain at the intersection grows the tree of knowledge that brought about man's fall, but which fortunately and paradoxically also brought about his salvation. The walls of the enclosed garden may be circular or square, but always Adam and Eve, our first parents, occupy the central position. Their story is prototypical, and therefore applicable to each of us. The topos implies this universality.

Figure 99 is a late example of this motif, but nonetheless typical. It appears as frontispiece before Henry Hawkins' *Partheneia sacra. Or the mysterious and delicious garden of the sacred Parthenes*, a curious volume that displays the attributes of the Holy Virgin by means of "symbols." Henry Hawkins was an English Jesuit who had suffered imprisonment in London for his missionary activities on behalf of the Society of Jesus and who spent the last twenty-five years of his life in England as an illegally returned exile. Therefore not surprisingly he published his pious tribute to the "Partheneia sacra" in Rouen.

Fig. 99. *The enclosed sacred garden of Henry Hawkins.*

In figure 99 we see a circular enclosure surrounded by a high wall with a single gate. Inside there is a formal garden which is organized into a symmetrical pattern by two paths that cross its diameter and intersect in the middle. At that central point, the traditional fountain pours forth its symbolic waters—in fact, Hawkins tells us, by an underground system of pipes it waters the entire plot. Diverse flora grow in this garden: most prominently, a date palm and an olive tree; and various birds populate it: a phoenix and a swan without the walls, and a hen within. Somewhat incongruously, Philomela perches amidst the topmost branches of the olive tree. These creatures suggest the fecundity of the garden, though hardly its purported completeness. Moreover, a few large man-made structures mar the symmetry of this paradise. Nevertheless, overhead a sun and moon shine conjointly, a bright star and

169

Fig. 100. *Jerusalem as a dodecahedron of correspondences centering on Jesus.*

several smaller stars give evidence of God's abode in heaven, and a rainbow asserts eternal providence.

Henry Peacham in his *Minerva britanna* offers an emblem of this topos, and the first line of the verses provides a concise gloss for figure 99: "A garden thinke this spatious world to be" (page 183). Of course, this motif is as ancient as the fourth day of creation in Genesis, and it has always been a favorite with poets. Chaucer uses it to good effect in *The Parlement of Foules*, and Spenser gives it even

more pointed meaning in the episode of Arlo Hill, the high point of the *Cantos of Mutabilitie* (VII.vii. 3-4). For Coleridge, constructing such an enclosed garden became the all-consuming self-gratifying act of his generic man, Kubla Khan. The *hortus conclusus*, often exemplified by the Garden of the Hesperides, appears also in alchemical literature,[197] symbolizing the mental space set apart by the adept for the perfection of his opus.

A more severely formal example of the the-

170

ological tetrad appears in **Figure 100**, where the position of generic man created in the image of deity is appositely occupied by "King Jesus." This tetrad with its extensive amplifications from the cabala comes from Charles de Bouelles' *Liber de duodecim numeris*, which was published in the large folio works of this most interesting of early French humanists in 1510 at Paris. Bouelles' *schema* was still current 150 years later when Athanasius Kircher reproduced it as a foldout in his *Arithmologia sive de abditis numerorum mysteriis* printed in 1665 at Rome (facing page 290). The information contained in the scheme, of course, is quite similar to that contained in the table for the number 12 prepared by Agrippa (figure 74d).

From the text we know that figure 100 is an image of "the heavenly Jerusalem in a twelve-sided figure" (civitas hierusalem in dodecade; fol. 169ᵛ). South is at the top, north at the bottom, east on the left, and west on the right, in accordance with contemporary conventions of cartography. The central square contains the four syllables of "Hie-ru-sa-lem" in its corners, and symbolically provides a habitation for the smaller square representing "Jhesus Rex" placed askew within it. Enclosing the square of Jerusalem is an architectural construction that depicts the walls of the city and contains twelve gates distributed three to a side. Within these gates are names of the twelve tribes of Israel. The other sets of twelve items range outward from this central configuration. Reading outward along the left edge of the southern quadrant at the top, we have the nine orders of angels plus three other holy categories, beginning with Seraphim and concluding with Ministers. Along the right edge of the southern quadrant at the top, we have eight celestial spheres plus four elemental spheres, beginning with the sphere of fixed stars and concluding with earth. Along the top edge of the western quadrant on the right, we have the twelve virtues, beginning with fortitude and concluding with friendship. Along the bottom edge of the western quadrant on the right, we have the

twelve prophets, beginning with Hosea and concluding with Malachi. Along the right edge of the northern quadrant at the bottom, we have the twelve apostles, beginning with Peter and concluding with Matthias. Along the left edge of the northern quadrant at the bottom, we have the twelve precious stones, beginning with amethyst and concluding with jasper. Along the bottom edge of the eastern quadrant on the left, we have the twelve major events in biblical history, beginning with creation and concluding with regeneration. Along the top edge of the eastern quadrant on the left, we have the twelve forerunners of the Messiah, beginning with Adam and concluding with Christ. In all, there are ten sets of items (counting the tribes of Israel and the name "Hie-ru-sa-lem"); and each of these sets is arranged in a tetrad. The result is a neat configuration that exemplifies the divine number 10, the cosmic number 12, and the all-inclusive number 4. For someone with a pythagorean turn of mind, those are the appropriate numbers to represent the form of *civitas dei*.

Figure 100 depends upon the numbers 4 and 10 and 12 for its structure. Just as readily, however, the creating godhead informs the universe with the number 3, thereby displaying His trinal nature. As Pico says, "God is unity so distinguished in three aspects that He does not lose the simplicity of unity. There are many signs of the Holy Trinity in the creation."[198] **Figure 101** comes from Father Kircher's *Arithmologia*, and demonstrates the mystery of three-in-one, a mathematical paradox that extends throughout the many categories of creation. The omnipresence of this paradox makes multeity and unity interchangeable.

As the caption of figure 101 announces, "The Holy Trinity is impressed upon all things."[199] In the table itself, each category is identified in the left column, and its three parts are then placed horizontally in sequence on the same line beside it. For example, the top category is "the trinity in the archetypal deity," which is displayed, of course, by

Trinitas in Deo Archetipa.	Pater.	Filius.	Spiritus Sanctus.
In Anima.	Intellectus.	Memoria.	Voluntas.
In gradibus animæ.	Vegetatiua.	Sensitiua.	Rationalis.
In Intellectibus.	Diuinus.	Angelicus.	Humanus.
In Sapientia.	Diuina.	Angelica.	Humana.
In Intellectualibus.	Mens.	Intellectus.	Ratio.
In Ratiocinio.	Maior extremitas. Maior propositio.	Minor.	Conclusio.
In Eruditione.	Conceptus.	Vox.	Scriptura.
In Mundo.	Intellectualis.	Cœlestis.	Elementaris.

In Sole.	Lux.	Radius.	Calor.
In Luna.	Coniunctio.	Medium.	Oppositio.
In Circulo.	Centrum.	Diameter.	Circumferentia.
In Magnitudine.	Longitudo. Linea.	Latitudo. Superficies.	Profunditas. Corpus.
In numeris.	Linearis.	Planus.	Solidus.
In hominum positione.	Iacere.	Stare & ambulare.	Sedere.
In plantis.	Arbor.	Frutex.	Herba.
In nube.	Pluuia.	Nix.	Grando.
In arbore.	Folium. radix.	Flos. truncus.	Fructus. Rami.

Fig. 101. *A table demonstrating how the Holy Trinity is manifest in every category of creation.*

"Father," "Son," and "Holy Ghost." The next category is the trinity "in the soul," which is displayed by "the understanding," "the memory," and "the will." The third category is the trinity "in the ranks of the soul," which is displayed by "the vegetative," "the sensitive," and "the rational." And so on, through no less than eighteen categories, until we reach the trinity "in the tree," which is displayed by "leaf and root," "flower and trunk," and "fruit and branch." When Yeats inquires of his chestnut tree, "Great-rooted blossomer, / Are you the leaf, the blossom or the bole," he is calling upon this tradition of seeing the three-in-one pattern in every creature.[200] Three parts, one whole. Part is indistinguishable from whole. And part is indistinguishable from part, be-

cause each inheres in the same whole. Each is simply a different facet of the same underlying unity.

Just as Yeats gave mythic dimension to the Christian paradox of three-in-one, so also many renaissance thinkers conflated the Judeo-Christian tradition with classical mythology. The most ardent of these syncretists were, not surprisingly, the disciples of Ficino's platonic academy in Florence. Among these groups, which flourished into the eighteenth century, the terms of Greek and Roman mythology were used to express orthodox concepts. This tendency is neatly exemplified by use of the term "Jove" to designate the Judeo-Christian deity. Despite their devotion to classical lore, however, the syncretists were much more pious than pagan.

It was especially easy to translate the geocentric universe into mythological terms because the planets were named after gods in the

172

Fig. 102. *The geocentric universe populated by creatures from mythology according to Natalis Comes.*

classical pantheon. Mercury, Venus, Mars, Jupiter, and Saturn were, nominally at least, already mythologized, while the Sun was identified with Apollo and the Moon with Diana. And it was simple to complete the process with the four elements and the other celestial spheres.[201] The result is **Figure 102**, which folds out as frontispiece for the late but important edition of Natalis Comes' *Mythologiae* published by Peter-Paul Tozzi at Padua in 1616.[202] In the spirit of this popular handbook of ancient myth, classical deities preside over the numerous components of the Ptolemaic universe. In the text, the mythographer explains how the gods are disposed:

> Among the ancient gods, some were thought to be celestial, others terrestrial, and yet others aquatic. Of the aquatic gods, some were given charge of the seas, some of rivers, and others of springs. Of the terrestrial gods, some presided over mountains, some over forests, others over meadows, and yet others over farms; and these were thought to live for the most part in flat areas. The celestial gods controlled human affairs. Some were advisers, while others were responsible for changes in the weather and for various regions of the sky. Still others were thought to inhabit the infernal world and to supervise the punishment of the wicked.[203]

Figure 102 follows this disposition of the gods with a large degree of faithfulness. At the bottom it reveals the gods of the underworld, with Cerberus prominently at its entrance and with flames providing adequate torment for the sinners. Immediately above this lowest region, there is a region filled with aquatic gods depicted as sea-centaurs, some of whom blow upon conch shells. Next there is a region populated by various terrestrial gods and a river-god with his large jug. The elementary world is bounded by a winged Iris, who spreads out a rainbow. The lowest of the celestial spheres is that of the Moon, divided into three ranks of nondescript deities, and followed by a sphere for each of the other six planets. The sphere of

Saturn at the top holds not only the planet itself, but also the twelve signs of the zodiac. Outside the planetary spheres, presumably in a pagan empyreum, the twelve major gods of the Roman pantheon float on clouds. In the center above the others reign the king and queen of heaven: Jupiter riding an eagle and Juno sitting upon peacocks. In addition, from the left there are Neptune with a dolphin and a triton, Mercury with his winged hat and caduceus, Minerva with her shield and spear, a naked Venus with the apple that started the Trojan War, Vesta with her torch, a fully dressed Ceres with a staff and a bowl of grain, Vulcan with his implements from the forge, Mars in his armor and helmet, a radiant Apollo with his lyre, and Diana with a crescent tiara and her hind.

The impetus to mythologize the universe carried over to the pythagorean tetrad, with **Figure 103** as the product. In situ, it serves as title page for the magnificently printed translation of Ovid's *Metamorphoses* prepared by George Sandys and published by John Lichfield in 1632 at Oxford. Each of the fifteen books has an elaborate frontispiece which, like this title page, was designed by Francis Klein and engraved by Salamon Savery.

The four corners of figure 103 are dominated by four classical deities, each of whom is identified with one of the elements: Jove in the upper left corner, holding a thunderbolt and attended by a salamander, is identified with fire; Juno in the upper right corner, holding a regal scepter as queen of heaven and attended by a peacock, is identified with air (her Greek name, Ἥρα, is an anagram for ἀήρ); Ceres in the lower left corner, holding a cornucopia and attended by a cow, is identified with earth; and Neptune in the lower right corner, holding a triton and riding a dolphin, is identified with water. To give point to this arrangement, an inscription is distributed beneath the four deities which, when joined together, states: "From these, all things originate" (Ex his oriuntur cuncta).

Fig. 103. *The title page of Sandys's translation of Ovid's Metamorphoses.*

As additional mythological cosmology, an inscription beneath the drapery which displays the title states: "They are informed by Love and Wisdom." And these personified abstractions are similarly depicted as goddesses: on the left, Love appears as a semi-nude female very much like Venus, carrying an emblem of the burning heart and attended by Cupid; while on the right, Wisdom appears as a female caparisoned in warlike garb very much like Minerva, carrying a spear and shield and wearing a plumed helmet. On the page facing this engraving, a poem gives "the minde of the frontispeece," beginning:

Fire, Aire, Earth, Water, all the Opposites
That strove in *Chaos,* powrefull Love
    unites;
And from their Discord drew this Har-
    monie,
Which smiles in *Nature.*

To emphasize the harmony of this arrangement, Apollo with his lyre and laurel wreath sits astride the architrave that supports the drapery displaying the title, and an inscription states: "He taught these things." Above this figure of Apollo as god of music, another figure of Apollo drives the sun-chariot and disappears with his four horses into the clouds. An inscription beneath this scene states: "Virtue is in the heavens." In the opposite position at the bottom of figure 103 an octagonal vignette reproduces a scene from the *Odyssey,* the scene that more than any other touched the moral sensibility of the renaissance. As Circe transforms Odysseus' men into swine, the caption around the vignette states: "She dashes to the ground a portion of the divine spirit" — meaning, of course, that the sensuality represented by Circe reduces man on the scale of being from participation in the divine realm to bestiality. As usual in the syncretic process, this title page is a welter of interconnected information. It offers a foretaste of the lavish banquet of annotation and illustration that Sandys provides for each episode in Ovid's compendium of exotic tales.

One of the most popular myths with cosmological implications told how the demigod Atlas held up the heavens on his shoulders. It was typical of the renaissance to interpret myth euhemeristically, and to combine this rationalization of myth with an insatiable curiosity about the inventors of things. From early times, Atlas was readily rendered a figure of this sort. Polydore Vergil in his *De inventoribus rerum* cites a Roman authority for this information: "Plinie wryteth that Atlas was finder of it [astronomy], and therfore the Poetes fein that he beareth Heaven on his backe."[204] At the end of the sixteenth century, Thomas Blundeville in his technically proficient *Exercises* broaches the topic, "Who were first inventors of these [cosmographical] Sciences," and he endows the tradition of Atlas with precise detail:

> Some say that Atlas was the first inventor, whom the Poets faine to bear up the heavens with his shoulders, having his head placed in the North Pole, and his feete in the South Pole, and his right hand bearing the East part, and his left hande the West part of the world. (fol. 134ᵛ)

Even later in the seventeenth century, Vincent Wing fleshes out this tradition by citing Diodorus Siculus[205] and St. Augustine[206] when he gives a sketch of the origins of astronomy in the preface to his *Astronomia instaurata* (London, 1656).

The myth of Atlas was ready-made for visual presentation, and when we look at **Figure 104,** we know where Blundeville got his information. In this illustration from the first of many editions of Gregor Reisch's *Margarita philosophica,* we see Atlas with his head indeed at the North Pole and his feet at the South Pole. Furthermore, his right hand reaches toward the east, and his left hand toward the west. What we have, evidently, is a full-page woodcut of Atlas spread out across a geocentric world-system. From the center, the seven planetary spheres are labeled (in the genitive case of each planet). Next comes the

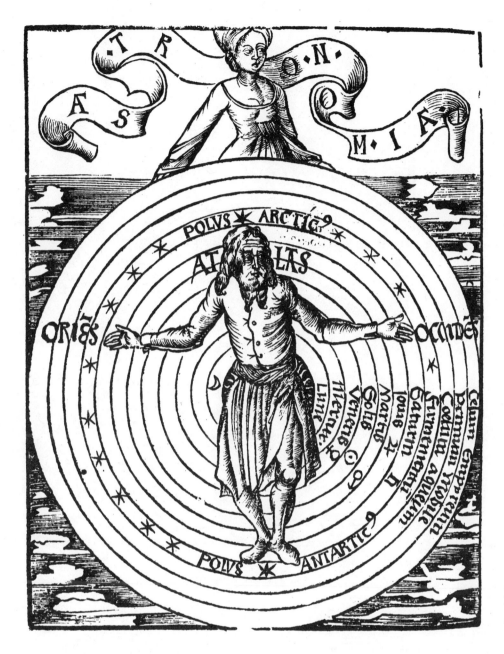

Fig. 104. *Atlas bearing the heavens on his shoulders from Reisch.*

firmamentum, adorned with the fixed stars that make up the constellations representing the signs of the zodiac. After that comes the *coelum aqueum*, a version of the cristalline sphere which recognizes its liquid quality and associates it with "the water above the heavens" that figures prominently in biblical cosmology and that had given medieval commentators so much difficulty. Outermost comes the *primum mobile*, followed by the *coelum empyreum* (which should again be in-finite, but which is confined by a sphere because the woodcut is necessarily limited). At the top presiding over this arrangement is a female figure of "Astronomy."

Not only Blundeville, but also Cuningham was aware of figure 104. Perhaps the handsomest illustration for his *Cosmographical glasse* is an adaptation of Reisch's woodcut (**Figure 105**), designed by the printer John Day, as the initials "I D" in the lower right corner indi-

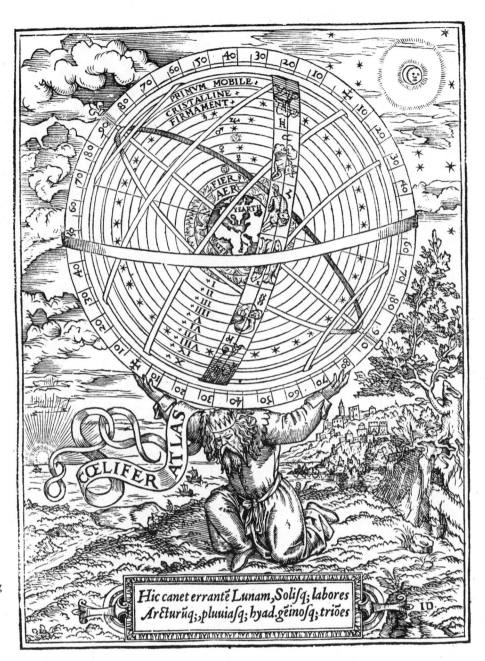

Fig. 105. *Atlas bearing the heavens on his shoulders from Cuningham.*

Within the woodcut:

PRIMVM MOBILE
CRISTALLINE
FIRMAMENT
FIER
AER
EARTH

COELIFER ATLAS

Hic canet errantē Lunam, Solisq; labores
Arcturūq;, pluuiasq; hyad.gēinosq; triōes

ID.

cate. The full-page woodcut is labeled "Coeli-fer Atlas," and the old demigod, crowned and attired like an ancient king, kneels beneath the weight of a fully detailed armillary sphere (see figures 31-33). In the center, a globe represents our planet and comprises the elements earth and water. The continents of Europe, Africa, and Asia are mapped upon its surface. Surrounding it are two more elemental spheres, one for air and another for fire. Sur-

rounding the elementary region are the seven planetary spheres, the "firmament" of fixed stars, the "cristalline" sphere, and the primum mobile, making up the requisite number of 10. Encompassing our finite universe are the circles that define the five climatic zones, including the Arctic and Antarctic Circles, the Tropics of Cancer and of Capricorn, and the Equator (see figure 34). The zodiac is also delineated, running diagonally from the Tropic

178

of Capricorn at the bottom to the Tropic of Cancer at the top. Six of its signs are visible, those from the winter solstice to the summer solstice. One colure is shown, and also the horizon (running horizontally, of course). A frame enclosing the system is marked off in tens of degrees, running from the equator to each pole. In the upper right corner, a sun-moon shines, representing dawn and therefore east; while in the lower left corner a setting sun heralds night and represents west. Beneath Atlas, a tablet bears two well-known lines from Vergil which occur in a passage near the end of Book I in the *Aeneid* when Dido entertains Aeneas at a feast. The queen's bard interprets a series of cosmological themes:

> Long-haired Iopas, once taught by mighty Atlas, makes the hall ring with his golden lyre. He sings of the wandering moon and the sun's toils; whence sprang human kind and the brutes, whence rain and fire; of Arcturus, the rainy Hyades and the twin Bears; why wintry suns make such haste to dip themselves in Ocean, or what delay stays the slowly passing nights. (I.740-46)

With Vergil and the mythological tradition as a context, figure 105 presents the gist of Ptolemaic astronomy, as Cuningham intended:

> Behold the Type of the world, conteinyng in it, as well the heavenly Region, with suche Spheres, & Circles, as have bene in sundry partes before set forth in this treatise: as also th'Elementarie region, comprehendyng the Fier, Aëre, Water, & Earth: in suche order & forme, as is consonant & agreyng both with Reason, Practise, and Authoritie of most approved authors. (page 51)

In this image of Atlas holding up the heavens, we have indeed a cosmographical glass. With Cuningham as our tutor, we "behold the Type of the world."

Another mythological topos that remained vigorous was the symphony of the Muses. Its *locus classicus* is Hesiod's *Theogony* (lines 53-103), though from that early source it passed into common literary usage and even touched the Christian tradition for angelic choirs. As we have seen in Figure 81, each Muse was assigned to a particular celestial sphere, and there she played her distinctive note. Furthermore, under the direction of Apollo, who by his presence significantly raised the sacred number 9 to the divine number 10, the diverse notes of the Muses joined in perfect consonance. Thereby once again the paradox of *concordia discors* was exemplified. Individuality was submerged in harmony, but without loss of identity. Unity arose from multeity without destroying its component parts. **Figure 106** is a fairly late version of this motif, used in six places as a headpiece appropriately ornamenting Joseph Blancanus' *Sphaera mundi, seu cosmographica*, printed at Bologna in 1620. Each Muse has a distinctive instrument on which to sound her note, while Apollo plays upon his viola in their midst.

Closely linked with mythological diagrams of the universe are allegorical depictions of it. In any cosmology that places ultimate reality

Fig. 106. *The symphony of the Muses under direction by Apollo.*

at some level above sense perception, the objects of physical nature become counters that correspond to the unchanging essences in the absolute world. The objects of physical nature become symbols or images or types of the concepts they embody. In the cabalistic tradition as it flourished in the renaissance, physical objects become hieroglyphs with arcane meanings — a tradition that culminated in Jakob Boehme's *De signatura rerum* (1622) and Thomas Browne's *Garden of Cyrus* (1658). More frequently, however, and more popularly, this propensity to abstract the universe was expressed as an allegory of human life. One typical man's experience, usually described as a journey, is seen as a prototype for all human life, and thence as a scheme for the universe as we know it.[207] This is an old motif in literature, with Guillaume de Deguilleville's *Le pèlerinage de la vie humaine* (1330) and Stephen Hawes' *Pastime of Pleasure* (1509) as prominent examples.

One of the earliest examples of the genre in Western culture is the Πίναξ or *Tabula* of Cebes, a disciple of Philolaus the pythagorean and of Socrates, and a speaker in the *Phaedo*. The text of the *Tabula* that we now have appears to be spuriously attributed to Cebes, and probably is a neoplatonic fabrication of the first century A. D. It purports to be an explication of a large picture on the wall of a temple dedicated to Χρόνος, a patriarch in the Greek theogony who was later identified with Saturn and whose name means "time."

Cebes was a favorite author of the renaissance. His *Tabula* was first printed in a Latin translation by Ludovicus Odaxius at Bologna in 1497, and went through innumerable editions after that, often as a complement to Epictetus' moral manual, the *Enchiridion*. It was translated into most vernaculars — into English by 1528 and into French as early as 1529 — and echoes of it can be heard in nearly every allegorical narrative of the renaissance. Its pervasiveness is understandable. The story of the *Tabula* is simple, and its method direct. A pilgrim traveling along the highway visits a

Fig. 107. *The pilgrim first seeing the tablet of Cebes.*

temple of Saturn, and there he sees a picture of the many way stations along the path of life. Within this minimal narrative frame, the picture is then described in great detail by an old man who steps forward to moralize its meaning.

Visual renditions of the *Tabula* to accompany the text abound in the renaissance — the earliest being a woodcut title page of 1507.[208]

Fig. 108a. *A key to the tablet of Cebes.*

1 THE Gate of the Inclofure of Humane Life.	16 Falſe Opinion.
	17 Falſe Doĉtrine.
2 Genius.	18 Poets, Orators, Geometritians, &c.
3 Impoſture.	
4 Opinions, Appetites and Pleaſures.	19 Incontinence, Luxury, and Opinion.
5 Fortune.	20 The way to true Doĉtrine.
6 The Inconſiderate.	
7 Incontinence, Luxury, Rapine, and Flattery.	21 Continence and Patience.
8 Laborioufneſs.	22 True Doĉtrine.
9 Sadneſs.	23 Truth and Perſuaſion.
10 Miſery.	
11 Mourning.	24 Science and the Vertues.
12 Rage.	25 Felicity.
13 The Houſe of Misfortune.	26 The firſt pleaſure of the Wiſe Man.
14 Repentance.	27 The Cowardly, who have loſt courage.
15 True Opinion.	

Fig. 108b. *The tablet of Cebes according to John Davies.*

A particularly attractive printing is a French translation by Gilles Corrozet published at Paris in 1543, which contains eleven small woodcuts distributed through the text to serialize the various stages of the explication. **Figure 107** acts as frontispiece for the volume and bears a caption, "The Pilgrim visiting the temple of Saturn, and about the picture that he sees there." The woodcut does not contain much detail because of its smallness, but it shows the Pilgrim and a servant supplicating the old man to explain the curious painting that hangs from the ceiling of the temple. In the painting itself, there are three concentric walled areas, and these will determine the course of the Pilgrim as he seeks his final destination.

N. J. Visscher engraved a much more elaborate visual presentation of Cebes' *Tabula* as a frontispiece for the pretentious edition prepared by Johann Elichmann and printed at Leyden in 1640. By then the iconographic movement was at its height, and the expectation of visual as well as verbal statement was rampant. This exemplum of the manneristic style is too large to reproduce here; much of the extravagant detail would be lost. **Figure 108b**, however, is a derivative of it.

Figure 108b serves as the sole illustration for an English version of Epictetus and Cebes prepared by John Davies from the French of Gilles Boileau and published at London in 1670. Davies earned a meager livelihood by translating exotic works for the booksellers, and in this volume he gives Cebes' *Tabula* a fashionable title: *The embleme of humane life.* This engraving too is a large (10 inches wide by 13 inches high) foldout, a goodly ornament to the printed text, and it exhibits in detail every episode of the Pilgrim's progress from "The Gate of the Inclosure" in the center foreground to "Felicity" at the summit of the ascent. The engraver has closely followed the text. He has numbered the episodes from 1 to 25, and provides a key (**Figure 108a**). Evidently, Cebes' *Tabula* is a temporal and spatial diagram of the universe expressed as the journey of a single man's life. It well demonstrates the fullness of the mythological tradition in cosmology — how it provided an image of our world in all its detail and completeness, and how it lay behind the literary technique of allegory.

The proclivity of the renaissance to syncretize is nowhere more openly or succinctly exposed than in its conflation of cosmology, mythology, religion, and the occult to exhibit the mystical experience. The mystic in his desire for oneness with the One sought cohesion and continuity in the universe, and devised syncretism as his methodology. It is an inductive method like its "scientific" counterpart, though it draws its data from the insubstantial world of learning rather than the corporeal world of physical nature. In any case, the basis of syncretism is its inclusiveness: all knowledge from every discipline must be comprehended in the ultimate synthesis. Such a conflation is evident in **Figure 109**, taken from the *Cabala, Spiegel der Kunst und Natur: in Alchymia* (Augsburg, 1616) of Steffan Michelspacher.[209]

Michelspacher was a physician living in the Tyrol early in the seventeenth century. Plate 109 is the third of four foldouts in his curious little volume, which uses the visual medium of picture more than the medium of words to make its statement about the arcane relationship of art and nature. Michelspacher reduced alchemical lore to four large *picturae* or *specula.* The first is a general picture, "Spiegel der Kunst und Natur." The second is introductory, "Anfang: Exaltation." The third is climactory, "Mittel: Conjunction." The fourth is conclusory, "Endt: Multiplication."

Figure 109, then, depicts the climactic event of conjunction. As in figure 108, its overall design depends upon a journey undertaken by a single man. The ignorant of our world, like the blindfolded man on the right, do not know where to turn and are lost. The adept, however, like the rabbits in the foreground, follows his natural instinct and seeks to ascend

IGNIS.

AERIS.

AQVÆ.

TERRÆ.

TINCTVR.
COAGVLATION.
DISTILLATION.
PVTREFACTION.
SOLVTION.
SVBLIMATION.
CALTINATION.

PC Sculp

Fig. 109. *An ascent defining the phase "conjunction" in the alchemical opus.*

the mystical route to knowledge. Before him lies an architectural structure approached by several steps that he must climb in his search for truth. That this stairway represents a cosmic scheme is indicated by the zodiac that circles overhead and by the four elements designated in the corners. The zodiac and the elemental tetrad testify to the perfection of the scheme, and the task of the neophyte may be seen as an effort to arrange his microcosm in accordance with the macrocosm.

In this microcosmic-macrocosmic analogy, the occult sciences of alchemy and the cabala predominate, as the title of the text advertises, and the seven stages of the opus rise immediately before the neophyte. They provide the steps leading up to the cupola that surmounts the ascent. Seated within its lavish interior are a king holding a scepter and a queen holding a spray of lilies, a marriage symbolizing the conjunction that precurses the completed work. Emblazoned on the roof of the cupola are a sun and a moon, whose conjunction, like the alchemical hermaphrodite (see figure 114), likewise precurses the completed opus. Moreover, astride the peak of the cupola is a phoenix, yet another symbol of the philosophers' stone. The phoenix, though a bird of mythology, is a symbol also of the resurrection, and here works to keep this diagram within a Christian context.

This structure of stairs and cupola is encased within a mountain to suggest its esoteric state, while the mountain in turn is graded in tiers to reflect the gradations of the ascent. Each tier of the mountain is populated by two allegorical figures representing the planets, which when added to the figure at the summit comprise a total of seven. The figure on the lower right with a scythe in one hand and infant in the other is Saturn in his role as Father Time. The figure opposite him on the lower left is Venus, holding a burning heart in one hand and a facial mask in the other to suggest the duplicity of her fair seeming. Above Venus stands Mars, dressed in heavy armor and brandishing a sword. Across from Mars on the same tier is Jupiter with a thunderbolt in his

right hand and a royal scepter in the other. Above Jupiter is the Moon, wearing her crescent tiara and holding both hunting horn and spear to indicate her mythological identity as Diana. Across from the Moon on the same tier stands the Sun, wearing a crown and holding a scepter to show his supremacy in the heavens (but not overtly identified in his mythological role as Apollo). The very top of this mountain is occupied by a fenced-in fountain pouring forth its waters from two spouts, and surmounted by a statue of Mercury, the *summum bonum* of Paracelsans. Mercury wears his winged sandals and winged hat, in his right hand he carries the caduceus, and in his left a six-pointed star, perhaps the seal of King Solomon. To us, this diagram holds a passing interest as a quaint puzzle; to most men of the renaissance, however, it proferred a belief that was at least serious, and more likely sacred.

The perfection achieved by alchemy in figure 109 is stated more concisely in **Figure 110**, which depends upon the symbolic significance of simple geometric forms. The diagram appears on the title page of a medical treatise by

Fig. 110. *The squared circle of alchemical medicine.*

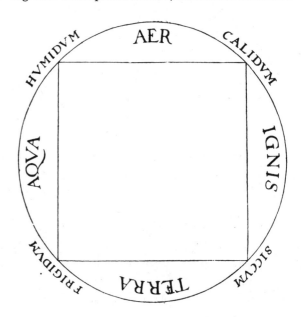

Count Michael Maier, private physician to the Emperor Rudolph II in Prague and one of the purported founders of Rosicrucianism. The title of the treatise is *De circulo physico, quadrato: Hoc est, auro* (Oppenheim, 1616), and figure 110 is a schematic statement of how the natural circle may be squared, and thereupon made golden.[210] The circle, of course, represents divine perfection; but its infinity and eternity are rendered finite and timely — that is, made operative in our physical world — by transformation into the square of an elemental tetrad. That was the perennial aim of those natural philosophers who through the ages sought to square the circle.

In figure 110 through the potency of occult science the circle is rendered physical in the form of a square whose sides correspond to the four elements. The square is inscribed within the circle, and where its corners touch the circle, we find the four basic qualities. This positioning of the basic qualities suggests that they are ambivalent, existing in both the conceptual realm (the circle) as essences, and also the physical realm (the square) as actualities. And through their agency, the unified perfection of the circle is reduced into the palpable diversity of four elements. The basic qualities are the entrepreneurs in this operation of reducing the infinite to the finite.

The process is reversible, as we might expect, so also the square can be circularized. Figure 110, in fact, is an abstraction of the pythagorean tetrad (see pages 102-10, above). The perfect balance between the elements produces a stable unity that is emblematized in the circle. The physical is consequently rendered timeless. In alchemical terms, this perfection of the physical was the aim of the opus and was designated the philosophers' stone. Hence the squared circle is "golden." And in terms of the medical science that governs the intention of this text, good health derives from the balance of the four bodily humours that correspond to the four elements. Then the microcosm reproduces the equilibrium of the macrocosm. It is likely that the interplay be-

Si de quattuor unum Occidas, subitò mortuus omnis erit.

EPIGRAMMA XIX.

Bis duo stant fratres longo ordine, pondera terrae
Quorum unus dextrâ sustinet, alter aqua:
Aëris atque ignis reliquis est portio, si vis
Ut pereant, unum tu modò morte premas:
Et consanguineo tollentur funere cuncti,
Natura quia eos mutua vincla ligant.

Fig. 111. *The mutual dependence of the four elements in an alchemical setting.*

tween square and circle seen so often in church architecture, like the interplay between equilateral triangle and circle, reflects the same cosmic significance.

The interdependence of the four elements in any stable configuration, such as our universe or the body of man, is confirmed in **Figure 111**. It comes from another text by

Maier, a handsome emblem book entitled *Atalanta fugiens* (Oppenheim, 1618). The title, "Atalanta fleeing," expresses the elusiveness of the philosophers' stone. The volume contains fifty engravings by the remarkable Johannes Theodorus de Bry, and so greatly impressed Sir Isaac Newton that he left an extended précis of it. All of the emblems deal with alchemical topics, though in terms of classical mythology, so that a new discipline, mythological alchemy, was established. But Maier not only mingled alchemy with mythology; he also provided a musical setting for each of his emblems, to show that the processes of alchemy are harmonious.[211]

To return to figure 111, the four elements are personified as four brothers under threat of attack. At the top the emblem carries a summary statement of its meaning: "If you kill one of the four, immediately all will be dead." Beneath the engraving is a hexastich in elegiac couplets:

Fig. 112. *An alchemical diagram interrelating the zodiac, the elements, the planets, and seven "metals."*

Twice two brothers stand side-by-side in a row, one holding the essence of earth in his right hand, while another holds the essence of water. The remaining two hold air and fire, respectively. If you wish to destroy them, you need kill only one. They will all sink to death because of their consanguinity, since the forces of nature bind them inextricably together.

Here is an emblematic, even dramatic, expression of what the pythagorean tetrad means. One for all, and all for one.

Another depiction of the squared circle in an occult milieu appears in **Figure 112**, which serves to illustrate an anonymous alchemical treatise entitled *Tractatus aureus de lapide philosophico*. This "golden tract on the philosophers' stone" was published in the important collection of alchemical treatises entitled *Musaeum hermeticum*, printed at Frankfurt in 1625. In this diagram, as in figure 110, the central motif is the geometrical configuration of a square inscribed within a circle. The square represents the elemental tetrad, with one element assigned to each of its four sides. The circle represents divine perfection and incorporates the twelve signs of the zodiac, thereby placing the figure in a cosmic context. The cosmological significance is further enhanced by the medallion in the center with seven points, like a cartographer's compass. At each point of this compass an astronomical symbol identifies one of the seven planets. Moreover, between the points of this compass are seven other symbols which represent the seven so-called "metals" employed in the alchemical opus. Proceeding clockwise from the one o'clock position at the top, they may be identified as vitriol, sal ammoniac, alum, saltpeter, common salt, sulphur, and antimony. This scheme, which assimilates the occult lore of both alchemy and astrology, is justifiably labeled "the miracle of nature."

The alchemical tetrad in its full bloom ap-

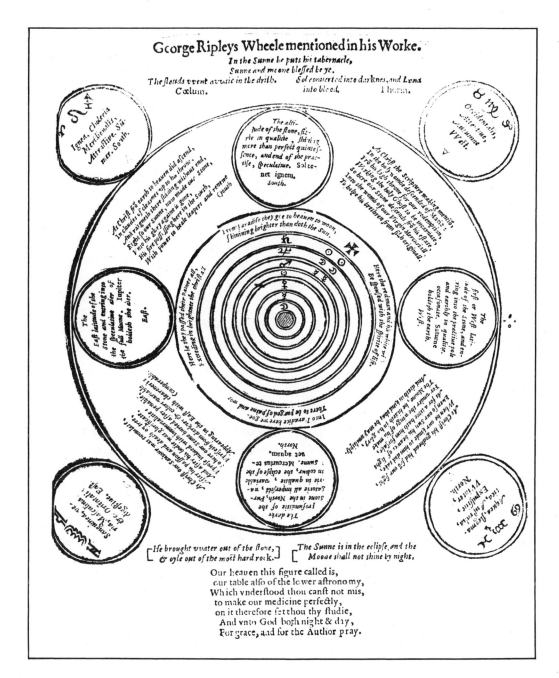

Fig. 113. *An alchemical tetrad after George Ripley.*

pears in **Figure 113**. This diagram is taken from an Elizabethan edition of *The compound of alchymy* by George Ripley, a canon of the Augustinian Priory at Bridlington in Yorkshire and one of the first Englishmen to draw upon the alchemical works attributed to Ramon Lull. *The compound of alchymy* was also known as "The Twelve Gates," and essentially it recounts a twelve-step recipe for preparing the philosophers' stone, versified in rime royal stanzas. When Ralph Rabbards prepared Ripley's enigmatic manuscript for publication in 1591, he included this elaborate diagram, which in loose fashion illustrates the *recapitulatio* of the text (K3-K4ᵛ).

187

Of primary interest to us in this busy scheme of wheels within wheels are the concentric circles representing the planetary spheres, and the four small circles in each corner which together comprise a pythagorean tetrad (see figures 65-68). In the upper left corner we have elemental fire, which is correspondent to the choleric humour, south, summer, and Aries, Leo, and Sagittarius among the zodiacal signs. In the upper right corner, we have elemental earth, which is correspondent to the melancholy humour (though not so stated), west, autumn, and Taurus, Virgo, and Capricornus among the zodiacal signs. In the lower right corner, we have elemental water, the phlegmatic humour, north, winter, and Cancer, Scor-

pio, and Pisces among the zodiacal signs. And in the lower left corner, we have elemental air, the sanguine humour, east, spring, and Gemini, Aquarius, and Libra among the zodiacal signs. In the next century when Elias Ashmole put together his alchemical omnibus, the *Theatrum chemicum britannicum* (London, 1652), John Goddard engraved an even more detailed alchemical tetrad in the manner of figure 113, which is labeled "The Figure conteyning all the secrets of the Treatise both great & small" (foldout after page 116).

Another topos in alchemy that appears prominently in the literature is the hermaphrodite. This composite man-woman, often a king-queen,[212] symbolizes a critical stage in the opus known as *conjunctio* and precedes the self-sufficient perfection of the completed work. **Figure 114** is a particularly interesting example because it explicitly places the alchemical hermaphrodite within the context of the tetrad as well as the zodiac. The microcosm is clearly related to the macrocosm, both the heavenly zodiac and the earthly tetrad.

This diagram is divided vertically into two parts, a female half on the left and a male half on the right. The male holds a flask with its neck up, out of which ascends a black dove, symbolizing one of the opposites to be reconciled in the alchemical process. The female, in exact counterpart, holds a flask with its neck down, out of which descends a white dove. A continuous pneuma that circles around between them indicates the necessary union of these two spirits. Distillation was often described as a twofold process with spirits, represented by birds in flight, that "ascended" and "descended." The ascension was technically known as "sublimation," while the descension was known as "condensation," and both were designated as necessary stages in the opus.

The motif of reconciling opposites is carried on in the two sets of heating apparatus immediately behind the figure. In each a flask has been "hermetically" sealed to make a "vase of

Fig. 114. *The alchemical hermaphrodite.*

Hermes" or "philosophers' egg," and this has been inserted neck-down into an athanor, which is heated over a fire. The Hermetic vase at the male's foot is marked with the symbol for mercury, and the athanor is labeled *Harpo*[s?]. The Hermetic vase at the female's foot is marked with the symbol for sulphur, and the athanor is labeled *Zarintho*[s?].[213] In alchemical theory, mercury possessed the qualities of cold and moist, correspondent to water, while sulphur possessed the qualities of hot and dry, correspondent to fire; and the opus was often delineated as the fusion of these two opposites into a tetradic pattern which included all four basic qualities.

Figure 114, in fact, is further articulated into four parts comprising a tetrad. The upper right quarter contains the sanguine humour, which is correspondent to air, and the signs Aries, Taurus, and Gemini. The lower right quarter contains the choleric humour, which is correspondent to fire, and the signs Cancer, Leo, and Virgo. The lower left quarter contains the melancholic humour, which is correspondent to earth, and the signs Libra, Scorpio, and Sagittarius. And the upper left quarter contains the phlegmatic humour, which is correspondent to water, and the signs Capricornus, Aquarius, and Pisces. Note, however, that the signs of the zodiac are not distributed in a tetrad pattern—as, for example, in figure 113; but rather they follow one another sequentially clockwise in the order that the sun goes through them in his annual journey. Nevertheless, figure 114 makes the same comprehensive statement as the previous four plates, though its dominant feature is the hermaphrodite. It comes from a famous alchemical text, the *Quinta essentia, das ist die höchste subtilitet krafft* by Leonard Thurneisser zum Thurn, first printed at Münster in 1570. Thurneisser was a world traveler, noted physician, and notorious Paracelsan. For him, of course, "the most subtle art" was alchemy.

Figure 115 presents a fascinating metamorphosis of the alchemical hermaphrodite. This engraving also comes from Michael Maier's *Atalanta fugiens,* and it shows the adept as a geometer drawing upon a wall with a giant pair of compasses. At his feet lie a quadrant and a cross-staff, instruments for making observations of the heavenly bodies, and behind him in a corner lies a white tablet inscribed with various geometrical figures, including a six-pointed star (Solomon's seal) within a circle. The caption above the engraving explains: "Make a circle from a man and a woman. From this circle, derive a square, and then a triangle. In turn, make this a circle, and you will possess the philosophers' stone." The adept with his compass is indeed completing such a figure. The male and female are conjoined within a circle, which is next squared, then enclosed within a triangle, and finally the whole is circumscribed by another circle. Beneath the engraving, as in figure 111, there is a hexastich:

> Female and male are made one circle by you, from which arises a quadrangular form having equal sides. You extend this into a triangle, which in turn transforms its parts back into a round sphere. Then the philosophers' stone will be generated. If a thing so obvious does not come readily to your mind, grasp the principles of geometry, and you will know everything.

By this geometrical operation the hermaphrodite is transformed into the squared circle of figure 110. But further than that, it transmutes into the sort of cosmic figure that Robert Fludd projected as the archetypal idea for our universe in the mind of God (see figure 52). In such an interplay of circles and squares and triangles, man is indisputably created in the image of deity. And by participating in heterosexual love, he reiterates the harmony and symmetry—the fair proportion—of the cosmic scheme.

Figure 115 concludes a sequence of diagrams that begins with figure 52, Fludd's geometrical depiction of God as both circle and triangle. Each of these diagrams presumes a

Fig. 115. *The alchemical hermaphrodite as a geometrical configuration.*

Fac ex mare & fœmina circulum, inde quadrangulum, hinc trian-
gulum, fac circulum & habebis lap. Philofophorum.

EPIGRAMMA XXI.

Fœmina másque unus fiant tibi circulus, ex quo
    Surgat, habens æquum forma quadrata latus.
Hinc Trigonum ducas, omni qui parte rotundam
    In ſphæram redeat: Tum LAPIS ortus erit.
Si res tanta tuæ non mox venit obvia menti,
    Dogma Geometræ ſi capis, omne ſcies,

platonic cosmology, wherein ultimate reality lies among ideas (or insubstantial forms) in a permanent realm of absolute being. In contrast, the objects we perceive with our senses in this changing world around us are not real because of their transitoriness. They are merely projections of those true essences, often badly weakened and distorted and perverted; and these objects are always becoming something else, never sustaining a fixed identity. According to the platonists, we expend our allotted time in a world that is continually *becoming*, but never has *being* as an absolute state.

Nevertheless, this constant change can itself be a source of hope. Perhaps it conceals a

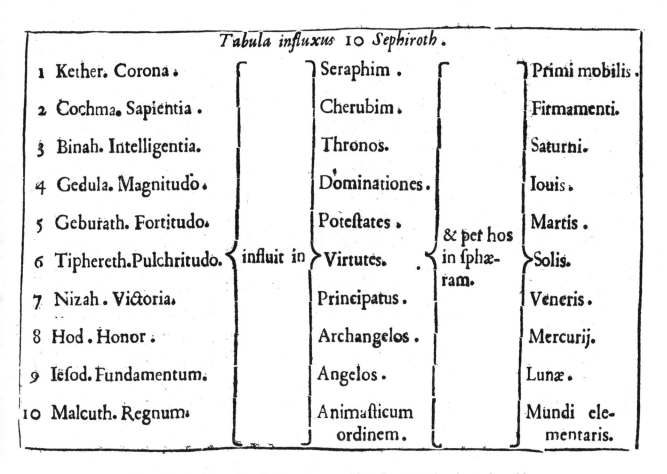

1 Kether. Corona.		Seraphim.	Primi mobilis.
2 Cochma. Sapientia.		Cherubim.	Firmamenti.
3 Binah. Intelligentia.		Thronos.	Saturni.
4 Gedula. Magnitudo.		Dominationes.	Iouis.
5 Geburath. Fortitudo.		Potestates.	Martis.
6 Tiphereth.Pulchritudo.	influit in	Virtutes.	& per hos in sphæram.
7 Nizah. Victoria.		Principatus.	Veneris.
8 Hod. Honor.		Archangelos.	Mercurij.
9 Iesod. Fundamentum.		Angelos.	Lunæ.
10 Malcuth. Regnum.		Animasticum ordinem.	Mundi elementaris.

Tabula influxus 10 *Sephiroth.*

Solis.

Fig. 116. *A table indicating how the ten sefirot flow into the physical world according to Kircher.*

pattern, a cosmic scheme, a sacred plan, and the constant change is the efficient means whereby the divine will is realized. Perhaps the objects of this world are arranged hierarchically and aspire to the perfection of the ideas from which they receive their forms, so that by change the lower transmute toward the higher. There is even the optimistic hope that man, placed midway on the *scala intellectualis,* will ascend to consort with superior creatures, with saints and angels, rather than descending to grovel with beasts, and he will fulfill the claim of Genesis that he is created in the image of deity. For instruction about the human condition, what text is more illuminating than the book of nature, especially those chapters that deal with the science of astronomy? In that cosmographical glass, as in a magic mirror, man can see heaven and earth and all that is therein.

The inclusiveness of this euphoric dream is demonstrated by **Figure 116**—not striking in its visual impact, but overwhelmingly convincing to the mind of a believer. It comes from Father Kircher's *Arithmologia,* and marks the high point of renaissance syncretism. Its simplicity is the clearest evidence of its verity. As the caption at the top asserts, this is a "table of the influence of the ten sefirot"—that is, the ten divine emanations of the cabala. It represents the ten successive stages as the divine numen spreads itself throughout creation. The column at the left, numbered from 1 to 10, gives the name of each sefirah in Hebrew and its equivalent virtue in Latin. These ten virtues then "flow into" the nine orders of angels plus the "order of souls" that make up the middle column. And "through these" Christian angels, in turn, the sefirot flow "into the [physical] spheres" that make up the column on the right — that is, from the top, the primum mobile, the sphere of fixed stars, the seven planetary spheres, and the elementary region.

The table should be read horizontally, so that, for example, the chief virtue (Corona), Kether, flows into the Seraphim, and through them into the primum mobile. The virtue of wisdom, Cochma, flows into the Cherubim, and through them into the sphere of fixed stars. The virtue of knowledge, Binah, flows into the Thrones, and through them into the sphere of Saturn, and so forth. But in effect, we have another table of correspondences, similar to figures 74-76, since each of the three columns displays a hierarchy within its own system of categories. Father Kircher has interrelated three distinct disciplines — the cabala, Christianity, and cosmology — and therefore is broadly syncretic.

Despite its inclusiveness, however, and despite its intent to explain our phenomenal world, figure 116 does not make its appeal to the senses. This scheme of Father Kircher is not a visual experience, but rather a concept. And when we interpret the art of this period, we must remember the thrust of such statements. For all the iconography of the seventeenth century, the statement that spoke with the greatest impact addressed itself to the mind, even though it may begin with sense impression. Without question, the art object in this esthetics — be it painting, statue, madrigal, or poem — was directed to the senses. But the sense impression, the visual or aural experience, the palpable image — this was but the starting point for understanding. The percipient left from there, and placed the sense-perceptible world behind him. Since ultimate knowledge lay in the suprasensible realm — in Plato's world of being, in the Judeo-Christian heaven, in the alchemists' *cupola aurea* or the cabalists' *domus sapientiae* — we must ascend from the physical to the conceptual. There reside truth and goodness and beauty, the only

absolute values, and consequently the only values worthy of the artist's imitation.

Within a decade of Father Kircher's elegantly simple *schema* relating the physical to the conceptual, Sir Edward Sherburne published his translation of Manilius' *The sphere* (London, 1675), enhanced by the several diagrams of world-systems engraved by Wenceslaus Hollar (see figure 50). As an additional illustration in Sherburne's volume, Hollar prepared also **Figure 117**, "a world-system of the ancients" — specifically, the cosmology associated with the atomists, Democritus and his followers. The atomists were anathema to Christians because they had denied the doctrine of divine governance and taught instead that chance, often the Goddess Fortuna, ruled the world. Such heresy must be refuted, and so Du Bartas frumpishly objected, "All was made; not by the hand of *Fortune* / (As fond *Democritus* did yerst importune)."[214] What led the atomists to their conclusion that chance prevails was their theory of an infinite universe in which objects are formed as atoms fortuitously come together, and just as fortuitously disintegrate. Even the human body is such a congeries of atoms, and the human soul (if there be such a thing) disintegrates with the body at death. So much for providence and immortality — indeed, so much for deity.

The atomistic cosmology, comprising three concentric circles, appears in figure 117. The innermost circle is the repository of creation, "the location of earth and the planets." Encircling it is "the starry heaven," confined within limits, but nevertheless massively thick. Most interestingly, though, the whole system is contained within an area labeled "the infinite Chaos, which is composed of atoms." Sherburne provides an explanation of this diagram, which is well worth quoting in full:

The Antient Philosophers, especially those of *Democritus* his School, and most of the

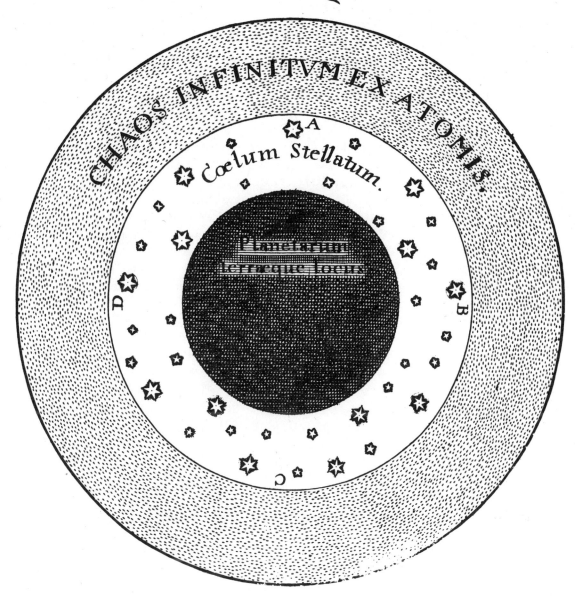

CHAOS INFINITVM EX ATOMIS.

Coelum Stellatum.

Planetarum terræque locus.

Fig. 117. *The atomistic world-system of Democritus.*

Mathematicians of those Times, asserted the *Universe* to be *Infinite,* and to be divided into two chief Portions; whereof the One they held to be the World, or rather Worlds, finite as to Bulk and Dimension, but infinite as to Number. The other Part or Portion, they extended beyond the Worlds, which they fancied to be a *Congeries* of infinite Atoms. Out of which not only the Worlds already made received their Sustenance, but new Ones also were produced. And therefore the Cosmical System according to them was, or may be imagined to be as followeth. First the Place of the Planets and the Earth; then the Starry Firmament marked A, B, C, D, embracing within its Circumference the Planetary and Elementary System; beyond which, a certain infinite *Chaos* of Atoms, in which this World of ours is supposed to float, and of which it was composed, and into which in time it is to be resolved. (page 213)

193

The respected astronomer Pierre Gassendi had recently revived the atomic theory of matter in his *De vita et moribus Epicuri libri octo* (Lyons, 1647). With such authority from the ancients, the moderns were soon to launch their own description of the universe as an infinite system.

By the end of Father Kircher's career, then, despite his prodigious effort to compile and substantiate and preserve the tradition based upon the old cosmology, a new cosmology was pushing forward. Descartes almost a half century before had devised a new mathematics, an algebraic geometry that allowed the analysis of variable magnitudes. Newton was applying this mathematics in radical ways, and not the least important of his results was a new astronomy that explained celestial mechanics in terms of physical bodies in motion controlled by attractive forces quite apart from any deity. Boyle, echoing the Greek atomists, had already presented a "corpuscular theory" of matter, rejecting all notion of occult powers in chemistry and proposing instead a mechanistic basis for processes that he demonstrated in his laboratory. Locke was on hand to describe a new psychology based upon individual perception, thereby providing an epistemology for empirical science. Milton in the guise of humanism explored how these developments conditioned man's view of man, arriving at a new theology that justified iconoclastic attitudes by depicting the imperatives of free will. And the ancients of Greece and Rome were exhumed as supporting authorities for what the moderns were doing. In the century between the death of William Cuningham and that of Father Kircher, a new earth, if not a new heaven, was born. The Royal Society was founded. America was colonized. The modern era began. The emerging theory of a universe with infinite space and limitless time destroyed the old concepts of natural order and divine providence and universal harmony. The cosmographical glass was shattered.

NOTES

¹See the license issued by the crown which Day printed at the end of *The cosmographical glasse.*

²Day adapted this motto from Oronce Finé, the distinguished regius professor of mathematics at the Collège de France who is several times cited by Cuningham (pp. 5, 14, 30, and 49). At the end of his *Protomathesis* (Paris, 1532), Finé published a brief statement that reaches the conclusion: *Virescit vulnere virtus* (Dd6ᵛ). The motto appears also on the title page of the *Protomathesis* in a position corresponding to that held by *Virescit vulnere veritas* on the title page of *The cosmographical glasse.*

³This iconography for the quadrivial disciplines derives directly from the title page of Oronce Finé, *De sphaera mundi . . . libri V* (Paris, 1542), published by Simon Colinaeus. Cf. also the title page of Finé's *Quadrans astrolabicus* (Paris, 1534), likewise published by Colinaeus, where the four figures appear in a more rudimentary form. Ultimately, perhaps, the iconography of Arithmetic, Music, Geometry, and Astronomy goes back to the title page of the first edition of Gregor Reisch's *Margarita philosophica* (Freiburg, 1503), which was probably cut by Michael Wohlgemut, the mentor of Albrecht Dürer. Finé produced the best edition of Reisch's text (Basle, 1523). For a verbal description of the four female figures in this tradition, see Guillaume Saluste du Bartas, *Devine weekes and workes,* tr. Joshua Sylvester (London, 1605), pp 472, 474, 478, 493. For a more expansive treatment of this topos in the plastic arts, see "Appendix A: Bibliographical Survey of the Seven Liberal Arts in Medieval and Renaissance Iconography," in William H. Stahl and Richard Johnson, *Martianus Capella and the Seven Liberal Arts* (Columbia Univ. Press, 1971), pp. 245-49.

⁴See Erwin Panofsky, "Father Time," in *Studies in Iconology* (Oxford Univ. Press, 1939), pp. 69-93.

⁵Carl G. Jung has popularized the basic principles of this discipline in his seminal work, *Psychology and Alchemy,* tr. R. F. C. Hull (New York, 1953).

⁶*The considerations of Drexelius upon eternitie,* tr. Ralph Winterton (Cambridge, 1636), p. 9. Cf. Plato's *Timaeus,* where the institution of measured time is a specific act performed by the creating deity:

Simultaneously with the construction of the Heaven He contrived the production of days and nights and months and years, which existed not before the Heaven came into being. And these are all portions of Time. (37E)

In this wise and for these reasons [so that living creatures could participate in time] were generated Night and Day, which are the revolution of the one and most intelligent circuit; and Month, every time that the Moon having completed her own orbit overtakes the Sun; and Year, as often as the Sun has completed his own orbit. (39C)

⁷*Speculum mundi* (Cambridge, 1635), pp. 361-62.

⁸Cuningham was familiar with all three of these works and mentions them specifically in *The cosmographical glasse* (p. 4). See also pp. 14 and 55 for reference to *The pathway to knowledg* and p. 51 for reference to *The castle of knowledge.*

⁹<L. *fatum,* past participle of *fari,* "to utter."

¹⁰This iconology for Destiny and Fortune goes back to the frontispiece for Charles de Bouelles' *Liber de sapiente,* in his *Liber de intellectu,* et al. (Paris, 1510), fol. 116ᵛ. A passage in Recorde's text explains the significance of the cube and the sphere: when the Master comments, "Manye aunciente Philosophers by the forme of a Cube dydde secretely signifie constancy and stablenes: and contrarye waies by the forme of a globe they expressed changable alteration, and continuall moving," the Scholar replies, "That I may perceave by the placing of Fortune on a rouling globe, in token of hir inconstancy & voluble changinge" (p. 113).

¹¹In the sixteenth century especially influential was the text of Sacrobosco edited with commentary by Jacques LeFèvre d'Etaples and first published at Paris in 1495, and the text of Proclus translated into Latin by Thomas Linacre and first published at Venice in 1499 (in an Aldine anthology known as *Scriptores astronomici veteres).*

¹²First edition: Landshut, 1524; revised by Gemma Frisius in 1529, translated into Spanish, French, and Dutch, and kept continuously in print throughout the sixteenth century.

¹³First published in Finé's *Protomathesis* (Paris, 1532). First separate edition: Paris, 1542; several editions in Latin and French during the 1550s.

¹⁴First edition: London, 1594; another augmented edition in 1597, and five more editions by 1636.

¹⁵First edition: London, 1659; six more editions by 1699.

¹⁶*Exercises* (London, 1594), fol. 134.

¹⁷*Cosmographicus liber,* ed. Gemma Frisius (Antwerp, 1533), fol. 2-3ᵛ.

¹⁸*De Incertitudine et vanitate scientiarum et artium* (Antwerp, 1530), published in English as *Of the vanitie and uncertaintie of artes and sciences,* tr. James Sanford (London, 1569), fol. 37ᵛ-38, 41ᵛ, 44ᵛ-45.

¹⁹*Cosmographical glasse,* pp. 5-8.

²⁰"Mathematicall praeface," in Euclid, *The elements,* tr. Henry Billingsley (London, 1570), a3ᵛ-b3.

²¹*Exercises,* fol. 134.

²²"Opinions of Philosophers" [II.i], in *The morals,* tr. Philemon Holland (London, 1603), p. 818.

²³Cf. Pliny, *Historia naturalis,* II.iv; Recorde, *Castle of knowledge,* p. 4; and Pierre de la Primaudaye, *The French academie,* tr. Thomas Bowes (London, 1586), *4ᵛ and p. 179.

²⁴Du Bartas professes the belief in his own inimitable style:

. . . before th'All-working Word alone

Notes

Made Nothing be Alls wombe and *Embryon*,
Th'eternall Plot, th'*Idea* fore-conceaved,
The wondrous Forme of all that Forme received,
Did in the Work-mans spirit devinely lye,
And, yer it was, the World was wondrously:
Th'Eternall *Trine-One*, spreading even the Tent
Of th'All-enlightening glorious Firmament.
(Devine weekes, tr. Sylvester [1605], p. 483)

This passage shows Christian coloration in the epithets that Du Bartas uses for the creating godhead: "th'All-working Word" and "th'Eternall *Trine-One*." The cosmogony of Plato's *Timaeus* was readily Christianized, and had been so transformed by the Church Fathers. La Primaudaye takes the suggestions in Du Bartas and works them out in detail:

God almightie, the unit from which all number proceedeth, and whereto all multitude referreth it selfe, did increase himselfe in himselfe, before he communicated his unitie with creatures, engendring one eternitie, and by an *alone unique action never disturbed*, his linage full of understanding, the very image of the father, his worde, the perfect patterne of the worlde, and his love and power the holie Ghost, which allieth the understanding with the thought, three persons in one essence and substance. *(The third volume of the French academie*, tr. R. Dolman [London, 1601], pp. 5-6)

According to La Primaudaye's analysis, the *"Trine-One"* of Du Bartas is differentiated into God the Father, Who acts as the final cause, and God the Son, Who in the form of the λόγος acts as the efficient cause, and the Holy Ghost, Who acts as a sustaining force recognized as *caritas* or *providentia*.

25A key passage is the *Physica*, 184a10-b9. For Aristotle's critique of Plato's theory of matter, see *Physica*, 187a17-20, 191b35-192a34.

26"Mathematicall praeface," in Euclid, *Elements*, tr. Billingsley, b2.

27*Institutes of the Christian Religion* [I.v.1], tr. F. L. Battles (2 vols.; Philadelphia, 1960). Cf. also, "I make the worlde as a looking glasse, wherein we must beholde God" (*A commentarie of John Calvine, upon the first booke of Moses called Genesis*, tr. Thomas Tymme [London, 1578], p. 20).

28*Commentarie . . . upon . . . Genesis*, tr. Tymme, p. 18. For a general statement in this tradition, see the introductory comments of La Primaudaye to that section of his *French academie* that deals with the macrocosm (*Third volume of French academie*, tr. Dolman [1601], A7-A8^V).

29First edition: Venice, 1505.

30First edition: Paris, 1578.

31*Astronomia instaurata* (London, 1656), B1. For the phrase in Greek, see *Timaeus*, 28C; cf. p. 16, below.

32"The created world in its entirety is like a book; it is both a picture and a mirror for us. It is a faithful representation of our life and of our death, of our present state and of our destiny" (J.-P. Migne, *Patrologia Latina*, CCX.579).

33*Third volume of French academie*, tr. Dolman (1601), A2.

34*The second part of the French academie*, tr. Thomas Bowes (London, 1594), p. 12. Cf. Sir Thomas Browne, *Religio Medici* [I.xvi] et al., ed. L. C. Martin (Oxford, 1964), p. 15.

35*Castle of knowledge*, a4. Another typical example of renaissance *contemptus mundi*—in this instance, concluding in a list of social evils worthy of a malcontent—may be found in Du Bartas, *Devine weekes*, tr. Sylvester (1605), pp. 90-92.

36(London, 1585), A1^V. The reference to Plato is *Timaeus*, 47A, a famous passage where Plato says that eyes were given to men for the express purpose of scrutinizing the skies. Recorde also cites this passage (*Castle of knowledge*, a4).

37*Exercises*, fol. 167.

38*Astronomia instaurata*, B1^V-B2.

39"Mathematicall praeface," in Euclid, *Elements*, tr. Billingsley, b2^V. See also p. 18, below.

40*Exercises*, fol. 167-67^V.

41*Castle of knowledge*, a4-a4^V.

42*Devine weekes*, tr. Sylvester (1605), p. 3.

43(London, 1595), A2.

44*Metamorphosis*, tr. Sandys (Oxford, 1632), p. 19.

45Renaissance men tended to join one camp or the other according to where they placed ultimate reality, among the objects of physical nature or among the ideas in a world of absolute essence. La Primaudaye delineates the choice with utmost clarity:

Aristotle with all the troupe of those, who beleeve nothing but that which they can invent and comprise by naturall reasons and syllogismes taken from sensible things, which guide them to a certaine demonstration, not being able thereby to understand, how, and wherefore heaven & earth have beene created, affirme that they were never made, but that they have beene from eternitie. But *Plato* followed of a great number of the most cleere-sighted wisemen, hath confessed the generation of the world which he teacheth to be ordered, and disposed by compleat and perfect numbers. *(Third volume of French academie*, tr. Dolman [1601], p. 3)

La Primaudaye's bias is evidently platonic. He wishes to be among "the most cleere-sighted wisemen" who follow Plato in propounding a neat cosmos ordered by number. He rejects the argument of Aristotle that the world is uncreated and therefore indestructible. But even more interestingly, La Primaudaye rejects the methodology that he ascribes to aristotelians:"naturall reasons and syllogismes taken from sensible things, which guide them to a certaine demonstration." This is, of course, empiricism, using the "sensible things" of physical nature as its data—the methodology of the new science. We can see in this passage the first rift between religion and science, a rift that since the renaissance has widened into an ever more obvious schism.

46*Legum allegoria*, I.ii. Cf. La Primaudaye, *Third volume of French academie*, tr. Dolman (1601), pp. 54-57.

47Again, Milton tries resolutely to explain the paradox. In *Paradise Lost* Christ in an instant carries out God's command to create the world; but to make the process understandable to mortal minds, it is recounted as a durational narrative. Raphael instructs Adam about creation:

So spake th'Almighty, and to what he spake
His Word, the Filial Godhead, gave effect.
Immediate are the acts of God, more swift
Than time or motion, but to human ears
Cannot without process of speech be told,
So told as earthly notion can receive.
(VII.174-79)

The acts of God have no dimension in time. Christ performed His decree instantaneously. But the immediate is stretched out into a portion of time through the use of words in sequence, a narrative, so that human ears can comprehend it. In this fashion, Milton has it both ways: the act of creation was abrupt, but the account of it takes place in time.

48Recorde was aware of this literal meaning; see *Castle of knowledge*, p. 8. See also Blundeville, *Exercises*, fol. 137.

49Following the example of cosmographers, such as Du Bartas, we should use the word "perfection" with its technical meaning:

God's none of these faint idle Artizens
Who, at the best abandon their designes,
Working by halfes, as rather a great deale,
To doo much quickly, then to doo it well:
But rather, as a workeman never wearie,
And all-sufficient, he his worke does carrie
To happie end; and to *perfection*,
With sober-speed brings what he hath begun.
(Devine weekes, tr. Sylvester [1605], p. 117)

Cf. also ibid., p. 231, for "perfected"—when an artist "hath perfected" his picture.

196

50It is worth quoting in translation the complete title of this Herculean feat of learning: "The universal work-of-the-Muses, or great art of the consonant and the dissonant compiled in ten books. By which is set forth in the greatest variety the universal doctrine and philosophy of sounds and the science of music, theoretical as well as practical; the wonderful powers and effects of the consonant and the dissonant in the world — in fact, the universal nature — are disclosed and demonstrated by the exhibition both new and foreign of various specimens of the particular usages in almost every faculty, but especially in philology,. mathematics, physics, mechanics, medicine, politics, metaphysics, and theology."

51The woodcut in figure 14 derives from an illustration of the same event in Schedel's *Liber chronicarum*, fol. 6ᵛ. The woodcut itself was used again as a frontispiece before the first edition of Sebastian Münster's *Cosmographia* (Basle, 1544), a6ᵛ. The first illustration of the creation of Eve in an English book appears in William Caxton's translation of Gossouin's *The mirrour of the world* (Westminster, 1481), fol. 8; cf. also Bartholomaeus Anglicus, *De proprietatibus rerum*, tr. John Trevisa (Westminster, 1495), c6.

52*Castle of knowledge*, p. 3. The passage that Recorde is translating reads as follows in Finé's Latin:

Mundum igitur appellamus, perfectam & absolutam omnium rerum congeriem, vel ornamentum: unde a graecis κόσμος dicitur. Divinum certe, & admirandum naturae naturantis opus. *(Protomathesis, O2ᵛ)*

53Cf. *Timaeus*, 29C, 29E, 30B, 31B, 32B . . . 90D, 92C, etc. Aristotle also uses the term τὸ πᾶν; see *De caelo*, 268a12, 21, etc.

54See *OED*, "all," B.3.

55Cf. Spenser, *Shepheardes Calender*, "May," line 54 and gloss; and Milton, "On the Morning of Christ's Nativity," line 89. For Christ = "all," see Donne, "The Litanie," lines 73-74.

56*Devine weekes*, tr. Sylvester (1605), p. 2.

57Donne builds one of his most serious and difficult poems, "A Nocturnall upon S. Lucies Day," upon this semantic tension between the cosmic meanings of "all" and "nothing" and "chaos." Cf. "A Valediction: of Weeping," lines 10-13.

58Published in Bouelles' *Liber de intellectu*.

59Cf. La Primaudaye's formulation: "Of nothing, nothing is created" *(Third volume of French academie*, tr. Dolman [1601], p. 12, repeated p. 14).

60La Primaudaye offers the usual differentiation between these two levels of existence:

When they [philosophers] speak generally of nature, they make two principall kinds: the one spirituall, intelligible, and the unchangeable beginning of motion and rest, or rather the vertue [i.e., potential], efficient [i.e., agent], and preserving cause of all things: the other, sinsible, mutable, and subject to generation and corruption, respecting all things that have life, and shall have end. *(French academie*, tr. Bowes [1586], pp. 171-72)

61In "An Hymne of Heavenly Beautie" Spenser provides a firm poetic statement of this notion:

. . . As every thing doth upward tend,
And further is from earth, so still more cleare
And faire it growes, till to his perfect end
Of purest beautie, it at last ascend:
Ayre more then water, fire much more then ayre,
And heaven then fire appeares more pure and fayre.
(lines 44-49)

62It might be useful to locate all symbols along such a scale stretching from total physicality to total conceptuality. Jacob Masenius, another studious Jesuit of the mid-seventeenth century, collected all the symbols he could find and published them in a compendium entitled *Speculum imaginum veritatis*

occultae exhibens symbola, emblemata, hieroglyphica, aenigmata, omni, tam materiae, quam formae varietate (Cologne, 1650). The title can be translated: "A mirror of the images of hidden truth, showing symbols, emblems, hieroglyphs, and enigmas in their full range, material as well as formal." Masenius' use of the terms "material" and "formal" suggests Fludd's diagram showing the interpenetrability of materiality and formality.

63*Cosmographical glasse*, p. 9, cf. Recorde, *Castle of knowledge*, pp. 3-4.

64*Exercises*, fol. 135ᵛ. Cf. La Primaudaye, *Third volume of French academie*, tr. Dolman (1601), p. 81.

65Cuningham found this diagram in Finé, *Protomathesis*, O2ᵛ. It also appears in the several later editions of Finé's *De sphaera mundi . . . libri V*, printed separately in 1542, 1551, and 1555, and in French translation in 1551 and 1552.

66*Castle of knowledge*, p. 6. Cf. Aristotle, *De caelo*, 302a16-19.

67*De caelo*, 268b11-270b31, 301a20-b16, 303b4-8, 310a16-b20, 311a15-312a12. Aristotle developed a passage in Plato's *Timaeus* which explains why there is accident and change in our world. According to Timaeus:

The whole of the living creature [i.e., the created world] was moved, but in such a random way that its progress was disorderly and irrational, since it partook of all the six motions: for it progressed forwards and backwards, and again to right and to left, and upwards and downwards, wandering every way in all the six directions. (43B)

For further analysis of the elements according to their heaviness and lightness, see *Timaeus*, 67A-E.

68*De caelo*, 270a23-35; cf. also ibid., 286a32-b9, 304b23-305a32. Du Bartas puts it all neatly into verse:

Treading the way that *Aristotle* went,
I doo deprive the Heav'ns of Element,
And mixture too; and thinke, th'omnipotence
Of God did make them of a Quint-Essence.
Sith of the Elements, two still erect
Their motion up; two ever downe direct:
But the Heav'ns course, nor wandring up nor downe,
Continually turnes onely roundly-round.
(Devine weekes, tr. Sylvester [1605], p. 65)

69*In sphaeram Joannis de Sacro Bosco, commentarius* (Lyons, 1594), pp. 33-37.

70"The fire, aire, water or earth which we daily feele or see, are not the Elements themselves, but things compounded of them" (Blundeville, *Exercises*, fol. 179).

71Blundeville provides a succinct account of these three regions of air:

This Element [air] is devided of the naturall Philosophers into three Regions, that is to say, the highest Region, the Middle Region, and the lowest Region, which highest Region being turned about by the fire, is thereby made the hotter, wherein all fierie impressions are bredde, as lightnings, firedrakes, blazing starres and such like.

The middle Region is extreme cold by contra opposition by reason that it is placed in the midst betwixt two hotte Regions, and therefore in this Region are bred all cold watry impressions, as frost, snow, ice, haile, and such like.

The lowest Region is hotte by the reflexe of the sunne, whose beames first striking the earth, doe rebound backe againe to that Region, wherein are bred cloudes, dewes, raynes, and such like moderate watry impressions. *(Exercises*, fol. 179ᵛ)

72Figure 23 is closely adapted from a similar diagram in the first edition of *Das buch der natur* (Augsburg, 1475), [c]10ᵛ.

73Cf. Ptolemy, *Almagest*, I.iii.

74*Castle of knowledge*, pp. 9-10.

Notes

75See *Timaeus*, 33B; cf. Aristotle, *De Caelo*, 286b10-287a5. See also Nicolaus Copernicus, *De revolutionibus orbium coelestium libri VI* [I.i] (Nuremberg, 1543), al.

76*Exercises*, fol. 135.

77Cf. also Recorde, *Castle of knowledge*, pp. 145-46; and Blundeville, *Exercises*, fol. 180ᵛ.

78The legend that Columbus was the first to prove the earth is round is a modern fabrication to enhance the reputation of a culture hero. I can think of no one of consequence in the 1490s who might have disputed the matter with him. The only authority to doubt the rotundity of the world was Lactantius (cf. *Divine Institutions*, III.xxiv).

79This diagram appears also in Blundeville, *Exercises*, fol. 136ᵛ.

80Cf. *De sphaera mundi*, in *Protomathesis*, O4ᵛ.

81Recorde in his role as *magister* admonishes his *discipulus*: "I thinke it best to tell you of no mo spheres, then are perceptible by sight, for so manye are we certaine of" (*Castle of knowledge*, p. 10).

82Pole = L. *polus* = Gr. πόλος, "axis." Joshua Sylvester gives a succinct definition of the term: "the imagined Hindges of the Heavens whereon the World is turned" (Du Bartas, *Devine Weekes*, tr. Sylvester [1605], p. 593).

83Ecliptic = L. *linea ecliptica* < Gr. ἐκλειπτικός (κύκλος), "circle of the eclipse." This is the path of the sun, so called because solar eclipses can occur only when the moon is on or very near this line. Again Sylvester defines the term with utmost brevity: "a great Circle in the middle of the Zodiak through which the Sunne, runneth his proper course in 365 dayes" (Du Bartas, *Devine weekes*, tr. Sylvester [1605], p. 584).

84Zodiac = Gr. ξωδιακός (κύκλος), "circle of animals." Blundeville is helpful with the derivation of this term:

It is named the Zodiaque either of this Greeke worde *zoe*, which is asmuch to say as life, because the sunne being mooved under this Circle, giveth life to the inferiour bodies, or else of this Greeke word *Zodion*, which is as much to say as a beast, because that 12. Images of stars, otherwise called the 12. signes, named by the name of certaine beasts, are formed in this Circle: and therefore the Latines doe call this Circle *Signifer* because it beareth the 12. signes. (*Exercises*, fol. 142ᵛ)

Blundeville is translating Sacrobosco; cf. Lynn Thorndike, *The "Sphere" of Sacrobosco and Its Commentators* (Univ. of Chicago Press, 1949), p. 124. for the term "signifer," see Pliny, *The historie of the world* [II.xx], tr. Philemon Holland (London, 1601), p. 14 (quoted p. 138, below).

85Colure < Gr. κόλουρος, "stump-tailed" (since half of the colure is below the horizon, we can see only the upper half of it). Recorde gives the necessary explanation:

The circles that go by the poles ar those, whiche some men call Colures: thei have the poles of the worlde in their circumference. And are named Colures in greek, that is trunked circles, because some partes of them come not into oure sighte, for the other circles by the turning of the world are all seene, but some parts of the Colures are not seene, that is, those partes whiche are in the Antartike circle, and remaine under our Horizonte. (*Castle of knowledge*, p. 33)

Cf. Cuningham, *Cosmographical glasse*, pp 35-36; and Blundeville, *Exercises*, fol. 148ᵛ.

86Tropic < Gr. τρόπος, the "turning" of the sun. Blundeville is again helpful with the etymology.

These two Circles are called Tropiques of this Greeke worde *Tropos*, which is as much to say as a conversion or turning, for when the Sunne arriveth to any of these two Circles, hee turneth backe againe eyther ascending or descending. (*Exercises*, fol. 154ᵛ)

Blundeville is still translating Sacrobosco; cf. Thorndike,

Sacrobosco, p. 127. See also Cuningham, *Cosmographical glasse*, p. 34.

87Henry Peacham explains the etymology of "Arctic": "It is so called from *Arctos*, the Bear or Charles's Wain, the Northern Star being in the tip of the tail of the said Bear" (*The Complete Gentleman* et al., ed. Virgil B. Heltzel [Cornell Univ. Press, 1962], p. 73).

88 Horizon = Gr. ὁρίζων, "the bounding circle"—i.e., the circle beyond which we cannot see, and therefore the great circle at the midriff of a sphere. Blundeville provides a definition and an etymology:

It [the horizon] is a great immooveable circle which devideth the upper Hemisphear, which is as much to say, as the upper half of the world which we see, from the nether Hemispheare which we see not. . . . Therefore this circle in Greeke is called *Horizon*, and in Latine *Finitor*, that is to say, that which determineth, limitteth or boundeth the sight. (*Exercises*, fol. 150)

Once more Blundeville is translating Sacrobosco; cf. Thorndike, *Sacrobosco*, pp. 126-27.

89As Cuningham notes, "The poles of the zodiacke, do muche differ from the poles of th'equinoctiall [i.e., the equator]" (*Cosmographical glasse*, p. 33).

90Meridian < L. *medius*, "middle" + *dies*, "day." Cuningham defines the term and implies an etymology:

The meridiane or middaie circle . . . is describid and drawn by the poles of the worlde, and the point directlye over oure heades called Zenit in whiche whan the Sonne entreth (whiche is twyse in a naturall day) it is mydday, or mydnight. (*Cosmographical glasse*, p. 21)

91The celestial globe is fully explicated by Recorde, *Castle of knowledge*, pp. 15-31; and instructions for making one are given, pp. 35-60. Cf. also Cuningham, *Cosmographical glasse*, pp. 14-40; and Du Bartas, *Devine weekes*, tr. Sylvester [1605], pp. 478-83. For the description of a famous pair of Elizabethan globes constructed by Emery Molyneux, see Robert Hues, *Tractatus de globis et eorum usu* (London, 1594).

92Zone = L. *zona* < Gr. ζώνη, "belt" or "girdle." Cf. Cuningham, *Cosmographical glasse*, p. 63.

93See Recorde, *Castle of knowledge*, pp. 62-65; Cuningham, *Cosmographical glasse*, pp. 63-67; and Blundeville, *Exercises*, fol. 154ᵛ-55, 191ᵛ-92.

94Pseudo-Plutarch, *De placitis philosophorum*, III.xiv.1.

95See Macrobius, *Commentary on the Dream of Scipio*, tr. William H. Stahl (Columbia Univ. Press, 1952), p. 202, n. 6.

96Tr. Stahl, pp. 201-02. Isidore of Seville gives a similar account of the five zones (*De natura rerum*, x.1-4).

97Solstice = L. *solstitium* < L. *sol*, "sun" + *status* (past participle of *sto*), "having stood in place." Dolman, translating La Primaudaye into English, uses the appealing neologism "sunstead" (*Third volume of French academie* [1601], p. 93).

98The point is made by Du Bartas, *Devine weekes*, tr. Sylvester [1605], pp. 137-38.

99*Castle of knowledge*, p. 15.

100. . . appetentiam quandam naturalem partibus inditam à divina providentia opificis universorum, ut in unitatem integritatemque suam sese conferant in formam globi coëuntes (*De revolutionibus orbium coelestium*, b3); translated by Charles Glenn Wallis (Chicago, 1952), p. 521.

101The title of the first chapter in Book I is "Quod mundus sit sphaericus" (a1).

102*De revolutionibus orbium coelestium*, c1-c1ᵛ; tr. Wallis, p. 526.

103In actual fact, some epicycles are still necessary to allow for circular rather than elliptical orbits for the planets, but their number is appreciably reduced. It was Kepler, of course, who early in the next century discovered that planetary orbits are ellipses, and thereby did away with the need for epicycles (see pp. 127-28, below).

104Tr. Wallis, pp. 527-28.

105The closest he comes is on the third day of the *Dialogo . . . sopra i due massimi sistemi del mondo* (see p. 53, below). Cf. *Dialogue on the Great World Systems*, tr. Thomas Salusbury, ed. Giorgio de Santillana (Univ. of Chicago Press, 1953), p. 333, n. 25; also ibid., p. 23, n. 16.

106Tr. Wallis, p. 508.

107*Melior Mundi speculator* (*Mysterium cosmographicum* [Tübingen, 1596], A1^V).

108*Dialogue*, tr. Salusbury, ed. Santillana, p. 5.

109*Castle of knowledge*, p. 165.

110See Dee's epistle prefixed to John Feild's *Ephemeris anni 1557. currentis juxta Copernici et Reinhaldi canones* (London, 1556).

111Digges had in mind the foreword to the *De revolutionibus orbium coelestium*, which we now know to have been inserted by a well-meaning but undistinguished theologian named Andreas Osiander in order to avert possible controversy.

112*De revolutionibus orbium coelestium*, I.vii-viii.

113Galileo, *Dialogue*, tr. Salusbury, ed. Santillana, pp. 336-39.

114Stellar parallax was first observed in 1838 by Friedrich Wilhelm Bessel.

115See Grant McColley, "Nicolas Reymers and the Fourth System of the World," *Popular Astronomy*, 46 (1938), 25-31.

116This statement has reference to the controversy over whether the planetary spheres are solid, or even material. In order to allow the orbit of Mars to intersect the orbit of the sun, Tycho was compelled to argue that the planetary spheres are "liquid," like air. Therefore in Tycho's system, as Burton says, the planets wander "without Orbs," and maintain their orderly courses only by virtue of divine providence. During Burton's century, Kepler and Newton were to define this virtue in mathematical terms as "gravity." For a contemporary version of this controversy, see the final paragraph of figure 50 (pp. 78-79, below).

117Philippe van Lansberge was a Flemish Protestant, an active clergyman as well as mathematician and cosmologist who strongly supported the Copernican hypothesis. His most important work in this respect is *Commentationes in motum terrae diurnum, et annuum, et in verum adspectabilis caeli typum* (Middelbourg, 1630).

118Burton, *The Anatomy of Melancholy*, ed. Floyd Dell and Paul Jordan-Smith (New York, 1929), p. 427.

119See Figures 45a-b.

120*De revolutionibus orbium coelestium* [I.x], b4^V.

121Gassendi later published a more concise and coherent history of astronomy as part of the preface to his *Tychonis Brahei . . . vita* et al. (Paris, 1654), ā4ēēl^V. He covers astronomy from its legendary beginnings to his own time. Joseph Moxon printed an English translation of this text as an appendix to *A tutor to astronomie and geographie* (London, 1659), with the title "A discourse of the antiquity, progress, and augmentation of astronomie" (pp. 1-40).

122Riccioli, *Almagestum novum* (2 vols.; Bologna, 1651), II.489.

123The first edition of this work—*Itinerarium exstaticum* (Rome, 1656) — has no plates.

124A serious contender for this accolade is the splendid series of double-page engravings that adorns Andreas Cellarius' *Harmonia macrocosmica* (Amsterdam, 1661).

125*Cosmographical glasse*, A2.

126*Third volume of French academie*, tr. Dolman (1601), p. 5.

127Ibid., p. 64. Cf. also Michael Drayton, *Endimion and Phoebe*, lines 885-900, 955-74.

128Byrhtferth, *Manual* (A.D. 1011), ed. and tr. S. J. Crawford (EETS, OS 177; London, 1929), p. 199.

129Heinrich Cornelius Agrippa, *Three books of occult philosophy*, tr. J[ohn] F[rench?] (London, 1651), pp. 1-2.

130I.e., less than a year old, and therefore young and vigorous.

131In the Ptolemaic astronomy, of course, the heavens rotate completely every twenty-four hours. "Still" in this line means "always."

132The complete Hebrew text was first printed at Mantua in 1561, with at least two later editions. A complete Latin version appears in Johann Pistorius, ed., *Artis cabalisticae . . . tomus I* (Basle, 1587).

133For another unusually interesting depiction of the sefirotic tree, see Fludd, *Utriusque cosmi . . . historia* (4 vols.; Oppenheim, 1617-19), IV.157.

134A Hebrew text of Recanati's commentary on the Torah was printed in 1523 at Venice. Pico della Mirandola knew the work in manuscript.

135Pico is careful to specify that he means "white" magic rather than "black," which depends upon the assistance of satanic spirits. The kind of magic that Pico intends is little more than reading the book of nature to discern her secrets; it "includes the most profound and hidden contemplation of things, and finally, the knowledge of all nature" (*On the Dignity of Man, On Being and the One, Heptaplus*, tr. Charles Glenn Wallis et al. [Indianapolis, 1965], p. 28). Pico's magic is the same as other men's science: knowledge of absolute being is its aim. For a full definition of magic in these terms, see Agrippa, *Occult philosophy*, tr. F[rench?], pp. 2-5, 567-70.

136As early as 1494 in Basle, Reuchlin published a treatise that looked outside the Church for authority in matters ecclesiastical. The *De verbo mirifico* popularizes Jewish beliefs, demonstrates that they underlie pythagoreanism and its derivatives in Greek philosophy, and furthermore argues that they have conditioned the sacred scriptures of every nation. Book III employs cabalistic linguistics to show specifically that the basic teachings of Christianity accord with the Hebraic tradition. As the capstone of his presentation, Reuchlin proposes that "the miracle-working word" is none other than the tetragrammaton, YHWH, augmented by an S, the determinant letter in the word *esh* ("fire"), to produce the pentagrammaton, YHSWH, which he takes to indicate Jesus. Therefore, Reuchlin exultantly proclaims, the *verbum mirificum* reveals that Jesus is God Himself, the unutterable tetragrammaton made effective as primordial light. To culminate his scholarly career, Reuchlin compiled a massive volume as an introduction to and apology for the cabala, which he entitled *De arte cabalistica libri tres* (Haguenau, 1517).

137*On Dignity of Man*, tr. Wallis, p. 32.

138Ibid., pp. 75-79.

139Six is the only perfect number smaller than 28 (1 + 2 + 3 = 6).

140For this explanation, see Athanasius Kircher, *Musurgia universalis* (2 vols.; Rome, 1650), II.448-49, where it is called "a specimen of mystical arithmetic."

141*Occult philosophy*, tr. F[rench?], p. 173. I have changed the punctuation in this passage for the sake of clarity. For a table giving the number equivalent to each of the Hebrew letters, see ibid., p. 232.

142Giovanni Pico della Mirandola, *De hominis dignitate* et al., ed. Eugenio Garin (Florence, 1942), p. 104. La Primaudaye echoes Pico, as he often does; see the quotation from La Primaudaye on p. 82, above. See also pp. 10 and 16-17, above.

143*Occult philosophy*, tr. F[rench?], p. 170.

144As a few scattered examples, see Macrobius, *In somnium Scipionis* (Paris, 1519, b3^V); Chalcidius, *Timaei Platonis traductio, & eiusdem argutissima explanatio* (Paris, 1520), fol. 18^V; and Francesco Giorgio, *De harmonia mundi totius cantica tria* (2nd ed.; Paris, 1545), fol. 85^V -88^V.

Notes

145Third volume of French academie, tr. Dolman (1601), p. 178.

146Ibid., p. 176.

147Ibid., pp. 176-77.

148Ibid., p. 179. Cf. Isidore of Seville, De natura rerum, xi.3.

149Batman upon Bartholome, his booke De proprietatibus rerum (London, 1582), fol. 118V.

150The earliest depiction of the expanded tetrad that I know occurs as a large mosaic in the floor of a synagogue dating from A.D. 520 at Beth Alpha in Palestine. It consists of a square circumscribing a circle which contains the twelve signs of the zodiac. In the corners of the square are the four seasons. In the center of the circle a sun god drives a chariot drawn by four horses. See Scientific American, 228 (January, 1973), cover. A similar motif was often used to decorate medieval cathedrals — for example one appears in the pavement of the cathedral in Aosta dating from the twelfth century. The earliest depiction of the expanded tetrad that I know in a manuscript (essentially figure 66) occurs in Isidore's De natura rerum, of which several manuscripts survive from the seventh century; see Isidore of Seville, Traité de la nature, ed. and tr. Jacques Fontaine (Bordeaux, 1960), pp. 15-18, 19-37, 216. Another important rendition of the tetrad, of special interest to students of English culture, appears in the early eleventh-century manuscript of Byrhtferth; see Byrhtferth, Manual, ed. Crawford, frontispiece, and pp. 11, 86-87, 92-93, and 200-05. The most extensive treatment of the expanded tetrad that I know in medieval literature occurs in a profusely illuminated twelfth-century manuscript entitled Tractatus de quaternario; see A Descriptive catalogue of the Manuscripts in the Library of Gonville and Caius College (2 vols.; Cambridge Univ. Press, 1907-08), no. 428.

151For a similar use of the tetrad as a wind-rose, see Peter Apian, Cosmographicus liber (Landshut, 1524), p. 53; and many later editions. A wind-rose figured also in the manuscript tradition of Isidore of Seville's De natura rerum; see Isidore, Traité de la nature, ed. Fontaine, p. 296.

152See Rosemond Tuve, Seasons and Months: Studies in a Tradition of Middle English Poetry (Paris, 1933), esp. pp. 122-70. For an adaptation of this tetrad for purposes of divination, see Christophe de Cattan, The geomancie, tr. Francis Sparry (London, 1591), p. 48.

153De proprietatibus rerum, tr. Trevisa (1495), y6V-y8V.

154See Tuve, Seasons and Months, esp. pp. 143-70.

155The editio princeps at Antwerp in 1531 contains Book I only.

156Agrippa's "scales" for the numbers were still viable at the beginning of last century; see Francis Barrett, The Magus, or Celestial Intelligencer (2 vols.; London, 1801), I.103-39.

157In addition to the text accompanying the scale of 10, Agrippa provides a further gloss in Occult philosophy, tr. F[rench?], pp. 367-70.

158Agrippa's table for the number 12 is repeated by Stephen Batman as an addition to his translation of Bartholomaeus Anglicus, Batman upon Bartholome, fol. 140V-41.

159This diagram has had an unusually long life and wide dissemination. It was recut for the Musaeum hermeticum, a collection of alchemical texts printed in 1625 at Frankfurt (Kkk4V), and reprinted with additions in 1678 again at Frankfurt. Presumably from there William Cooper picked it up and used it as a frontispiece for A philosophicall epitaph in hieroglyphical figures (London, 1673). When A. E. Waite translated the Hermetic Museum in 1893, he reproduced the figure on II.9; cf. also II.322. The diagram appears also in Jean Jacques Manget, Bibliotheca chemica curiosa (2 vols.; Geneva, 1702).

160The first two are in separate passages of Astronomia nova (Prague, 1609), while the last is in Harmonices mundi libri V (Linz, 1619).

161For a full account of the difficulty Kepler experienced with the orbit of Mars, see Max Caspar, Kepler, tr. C. Doris Hellman (New York, 1959), pp. 125-35; and Curtis Wilson, "How Did Kepler Discover His First Two Laws?" Scientific American, 226 (March, 1972), 93-106. Another extremely helpful discussion of Kepler's work is Gerald Holton, "Johannes Kepler's Universe: Its Physics and Metaphysics," American Journal of Physics, 24 (1956), 340-51.

162In the renaissance before Kepler, the renowned mathematicians Charles de Bouelles and Oronce Finé had already broached this topic: cf. Bouelles, Liber de mathematicis corporibus, in Liber de intellectu, fol. 185-92, 192V-96V; and Finé, Protomathesis, M6V-N2V. A full resumé of what the regular solids meant to the renaissance is provided by Henry Billingsley in his commentary for the massive edition of Euclid's Elements, fol. 319V-20. See also Kepler, Harmonice mundi, Book I, pp. 2-22; Book II, pp. 57-60; and Book V, pp. 180-87.

163I have translated all quotations in this paragraph from Harmonice mundi, Book II, pp. 58-59.

164I have translated this passage from Mysterium cosmographicum, p. 6.

165Kepler's Mysterium cosmographicum received serious consideration as a world-system in the seventeenth century. At the time of its publication, it was enthusiastically approved by Michael Maestlin, Kepler's former professor of astronomy at the university of Tübingen, and also respectfully received by astronomers as accomplished as Tycho and Galileo. And it continued to be discussed until Newton took over Kepler's work in his own system of celestial mechanics; cf. Riccioli, Almagestum novum, II.335-39; Kircher, Musurgia universalis, II.373-90; Cellarius, Harmonia macrocosmica, p. 79; and John Heydon, The harmony of the world (London, 1662), pp. 75-76.

166"Aphelion" and "perihelion" are technical terms in the Copernican system taken over from Greek astronomy. Copernicus, like every major astronomer before him, assumed that the planets describe perfect circles in their revolution. It had long been known from observation, however, that each planet does not remain always the same distance from the sun, but sometimes is closer and sometimes farther away. When the planet's orbit is farthest from the sun, the planet is at its "aphelion"; when closest to the sun, at its "perihelion." To take into account this variation in the planet's distance from the sun, and yet to preserve the principle of circular orbits — to save the appearances and the theory of circular motion in the celestial region — it was proposed that the center of the planet's orbit did not coincide with the center of the universe. That is, the planet circled around some point other than the sun. The orbit of the planet was then an "eccentric," and the distance between the sun and the center of the planet's orbit was known as its "eccentricity."

167For a technical discussion of what this phrase implies, see D. P. Walker, "Kepler's Celestial Music," Journal of the Warburg and Courtauld Institutes, 30 (1967), 228-50.

168See Pliny, Historia naturalis, II.xx; Plutarch, "A Commentary on the Creation of the Soul," in Moralia; Censorinus, De die natali, ii; Macrobius, Commentarius in somnium Scipionis, esp. II.i.1-25, iv.1-10.

169Marin Mersenne reproduced this diagram for his Traité de l'harmonie universelle (Paris, 1627), p. 443, though he disagreed with it and engaged Fludd in a long and bitter controversy. For a knowledgeable discussion of this diagram, see Peter J. Ammann, "The Musical Theory and Philosophy of Robert Fludd," Journal of the Warburg and Courtauld Institutes, 30 (1967), 200-05.

170Gr. διαπασῶν from διά, "through" + πασῶν (genitive plural of πᾶς), "all," meaning "the total extent of a continuum."

171For a version of the same diagram with an explanation in English, see Thomas Morley, A plaine and easie introduction to practicall musicke (London, 1597), ¶2.

172The same woodcut reappears in Gafori, *De harmonia musicorum instrumentorum opus* (Milan, 1518), fol. 74^V. For an important discussion of it, see James Haar, "The Frontispiece of Gafori's *Practica Musicae* (1496)," *Renaissance Quarterly*, 27 (1974), 7-22.

173*De nuptiis Philologiae et Mercurii*, I.27-29.

174"Nomina Musarum," line 10, in Ausonius, [*Works*], tr. Hugh G. Evelyn White (2 vols.; London, 1919-21), II.280. The next (and last) line of the poem reads: "Apollo, sitting in the midst of the Muses, enfolds all of their qualities" (in medio residens complectitur omnia Phoebus).

175*Historie of world* [II.xx], tr. Holland, p. 14.

176"A commentarie of the creation of the soule," in *The morals*, tr. Philemon Holland (London, 1603), p. 1046.

177For other versions of this diagram, see Censorinus, *Liber de die natali*, ed. Henricus Lindenbrogius (Hamburg, 1614), p. 62; and Thomas Stanley, *The history of philosophy* (2nd ed.; London, 1687), p. 539. For additional commentary from the renaissance, see Agrippa, *Occult philosophy*, tr. F[rench?], pp. 259-62.

178The period of the Great Year was more usually given as 36,000 years, as Henry Peacham avers:

> The ninth, or crystalline, heaven . . . accomplisheth his revolution in 36,000 years. And this revolution being finished, Plato was of opinion that the world should be in the same state as it was before. I should live and print such a book again and you read it in the same apparel and the same age you are now in. (*Complete Gentleman*, ed. Heltzel, p. 70)

Cf. Blundeville, *Exercises*, p. 168.

179Louis LeRoy, *Of the interchangeable course, or variety of things in the whole world*, tr. Robert Ashley (London, 1594), fol. 2.

180Agrippa, *Occult Philosophy*, tr. F[rench?], p. 263. Cf. also ibid., pp. 457-64.

181Ibid., pp. 263-64. Human geometry seems to be a perpetual concern in esthetics; see Erwin Panofsky, "The History of the Theory of Human Proportions as a Reflection of the History of Styles" in *Meaning in the Visual Arts* (Garden City, N.Y., 1957), esp. pp. 88-103.

182For two examples in English, see *The kalender of shepardes* (London, 1518?), H4^V [STC 22410]; and Leonard Digges, *A prognostication everlastinge of righte good effecte* (London, 1576), fol. 19. For an especially detailed discussion with a diagram, interesting also because of its late date, see Kircher, *Musurgia universalis*, II.401-04.

183In the *Historia naturalis* (XXXVII.clii), Pliny mentions the *catoptritis*, a stone found in Cappadochia, though not identifiable today. This stone had a brilliance that reflected images (provenit candore imaginem referens).

184*Musurgia universalis*, II.403.

185Cf. also Agrippa, *Occult philosophy*, tr. F[rench?], pp. 367-70.

186These are the ten unexpungeable names of God mentioned in the Talmud; and like the sefirot, they represent progressive manifestations of the unutterable YHWH. Cf. Agrippa, *Occult philosophy*, tr. F[rench?], pp. 370-73, 417-19.

187*Mettatron* is the spirit representing the deity's intention to become manifest through creation of a physical universe, and therefore is the first stage from the unknowable toward the palpable. He bears the epithet "the garment of Shaddai" (*Shaddai* is one of the ten names of God; note the second box from the right). Although Mettatron is pure spirit, he supervises creation, maintains the harmony of its several parts, and governs the angelic hosts.

188When I have mentioned this fact to colleagues, several have recalled a frequently reproduced engraving from Fludd's *Utriusque cosmi . . . historia*, wherein a female figure representing Nature is attached by a chain to the deity (I.4-5, foldout). This is not a depiction of the traditional chain of being, however; none of the categories which comprise that topos appears here. The title of Fludd's large foldout is "A mirror of unified nature and an image of art" (Integrae Naturae speculum Artisque imago). At its top, a divine hand reaches from a cloud labeled with the tetragrammaton, and hanging downward is a chain, which attaches to the right wrist of a female figure representing Nature. The domain of Nature is displayed by a series of concentric spheres very much like figure 12, upon which Nature is superimposed. Hanging downward in turn from Nature's left hand is another chain, which attaches to the left hand of an ape representing *homo imitans*. This figure of man the artisan in the act of imitating sits upon a globe depicting our planet earth, which is in the center of the diagram, and he is surrounded by a scheme of the numerous arts that Fludd expounds in his text—i.e., arithmetic, music, geometry, perspective, painting, fortification, mechanics, the making of sun dials, geography, astrology, and geomancy. But again, this is not a depiction of the chain of being. It is an esthetic statement, rather than cosmological: it demonstrates that man in the practice of his arts imitates nature, and that nature in turn is controlled by the deity.

189See Paolo Rossi, "The Legacy of Ramon Lull in Sixteenth-Century Thought," *Mediaeval and Renaissance Studies*, 5 (1961), 182-213.

190Et incipimus ab imperfecto ut ad perfectum ascendamus. Et rursus de perfecto descendamus ad imperfectum (fol. 2).

191Secunda vero est de duodecim vocabulis cum quibus intellectus ipse transit ad attingendum res & earum secreta (fol. 2).

192Cum his autem .xii. vocabulis ascendit & descendit intellectus per primam scalam: ut ea quae in ipsa continentur intelligat & cognoscat (fol. 2).

193Per quos ascendit intellectus de sensibili ad intelligibile et econtra de intelligibili ad sensibile descendit (fol. 2^V).

194*On Dignity of Man*, tr. Wallis, p. 5.

195For two examples, see Jung, *Psychology and Alchemy*, tr. Hull, pp. 125, 354.

196*On Dignity of Man*, tr. Wallis, p. 60. Perhaps the most magnificent example of the theological tetrad resides in the south transept of the cathedral at Lausanne, consecrated in 1275. There Christ holds the center of a large rose window, surrounded by the four seasons, the twelve months, the four elements, the twelve signs of the zodiac, the sun and the moon.

197It was the central motif, for example, in the celebrated fresco painted by Nicolas Flamel under the fourth arcade of the Charnier des Innocents in Paris. Flamel, though only a scrivener, amassed great wealth through successful completion of the alchemical opus. His fresco purportedly depicted the seven steps as he performed them, though in hopelessly arcane symbolism. Nonetheless, they remained a near-religious shrine for alchemists until the structure was destroyed in the eighteenth century. Flamel's accompanying treatise was translated into English and published in 1624 with the title *Nicholas Flammel, his exposition of the hieroglyphicall figures which he caused to bee painted upon an arch in St. Innocents church-yard, in Paris*.

198*On Dignity of Man*, tr. Wallis, p. 139.

199On this ancient doctrine, see pp. 84-86, above. Charles de Bouelles offered a table of trinities with forty-two entries (*Liber de sapiente*, in *Liber de intellectu*, fol. 136-36^V).

200Bouelles actually provides a woodcut demonstrating that "the tree is a unit" (arbor una est), in which the "leaf" (folium), and "flower" (flos), and "fruit" (fructus) are shown to be "conjoined in the trunk, though separated on the branches" (in stipite conjuncta, in ramis discreta); ibid., fol. 133^V.

201Agrippa provides "The Orphical Scale of the *Number twelve*," which is based upon "Twelve Deities": Pallas,

Notes

Venus, Phoebus, Mercury, Jupiter, Ceres, Vulcan, Mars, Diana, Vesta, Juno, and Neptune. Correspondents of these are then listed among "Twelve signs of the Zodiake," "Twelve moneths," "Twelve consecrated birds," "Twelve consecrated beasts," "Twelve consecrated trees," and "Twelve members of man['s body] distributed to the [zodiacal] signs" (*Occult philosophy*, tr. F[rench?], pp. 220-21). For iconography of the planets and the signs of the zodiac, see ibid., pp. 292-303.

202This diagram appears also in later editions of Vicenzo Cartari's *Imagini delli dei de gl'antichi*—e.g., the augmented edition printed at Venice in 1647 (foldout, facing p. 2).

203I have translated this passage from *Mythologiae* [I.vii] (Padua, 1616), p. 5.

204*An abridgement of the notable worke*, tr. Thomas Langley (London, 1570), d2.

205*Bibliotheca*, IV.xxvii.4-5.

206*De civitate Dei*, XVIII.viii.

207A handsome study that covers much ground is Samuel C. Chew, *The Pilgrimage of Life* (Yale Univ. Press, 1962).

208Reinhart Schleier has done an admirable study, *Tabula Cebetis* (Berlin, 1973), and has reproduced a large number of the woodcuts, engravings, and paintings that illustrate Cebes' text.

209Architectural structures of this sort abound in the occult literature of the seventeenth century. For examples, see E. A. Grillot de Givry, *Witchcraft, Magic, and Alchemy*, tr. J. Courtney Locke (London, 1931), esp. pp. 209, 348, 350, 355, and 360; and John Read, *Prelude to Chemistry* (London, 1936), p. 215, facing p. 216, facing p. 217, and p. 220.

210For a brief discussion of this treatise, see Walter Pagel, "William Harvey and the Purpose of Circulation," *Isis*, 42 (1951), 36-37.

211Maier's musical strategy is too ingenious to pass without at least a footnote. Maier calls the setting for each emblem a "fugue," and three voices follow one another through it in a rather mechanical fashion. The lead voice is *Atalanta fugiens* herself, representing the philosophers' stone, chased by *Hippomenes sequens* as in the myth, representing the alchemist in pursuit. The third voice is *pomum morans*, "the delaying apple" that distracted Atalanta so that Hippomenes might catch her. See also Read, *Prelude to Chemistry*, pp. 236-37, 246-54, 281-89.

212In the cabala also the coupling of male and female entities is prominent. The second sefirah, Wisdom, was considered masculine, and the third sefirah, Intelligence, was considered feminine. While these two emanations were opposites, they were joined together by the first sefirah, the Crown, thereby making them a king and a queen; and through procreation, they produced the succeeding seven sefirot. Evidently this cabalistic doctrine was assimilated into alchemy.

213I have been unable to interpret the terms *harpos* and *zarinthos*. Neither is listed in Martin Ruland, *A Lexicon of Alchemy*, tr. A. E. Waite (London, 1964).

214*Devine weekes*, tr. Sylvester (1605), p. 2.

INDEX

Index

Index

The Cosmographical Glass: Renaissance Diagrams of the Universe

From reviews of the original edition:

Heninger has used the fine resources of the Huntington Library to produce scholarship which begins in the small detail of a picture and ends in a view of the entire universe.

—*Milton Quarterly*, December 1977

Professor Heninger has produced not only a very beautiful and interesting book, but one which makes easily accessible to all readers much information concerning pre-modern astronomy and geography.

—*University of Toronto Quarterly*, July 1978

The material [Heninger] has collected ... is an invaluable archive, and Heninger is an excellent guide through it.

—*Renaissance Quarterly*, Winter 1979

This work contains the most complete set of cosmographical diagrams contained in books printed before 1700. With Heninger's detailed examinations of all 117 diagrams, he presents the intellectual historian with a remarkably clear picture of Renaissance culture through its imaginative speculations on the order of the universe.

—*The Sixteenth Century Journal*, 1978

Professor Heninger [has] given us a work delighting the eye, a store of images for our visual time.

—*Scientific American*, March 1979